DATE			

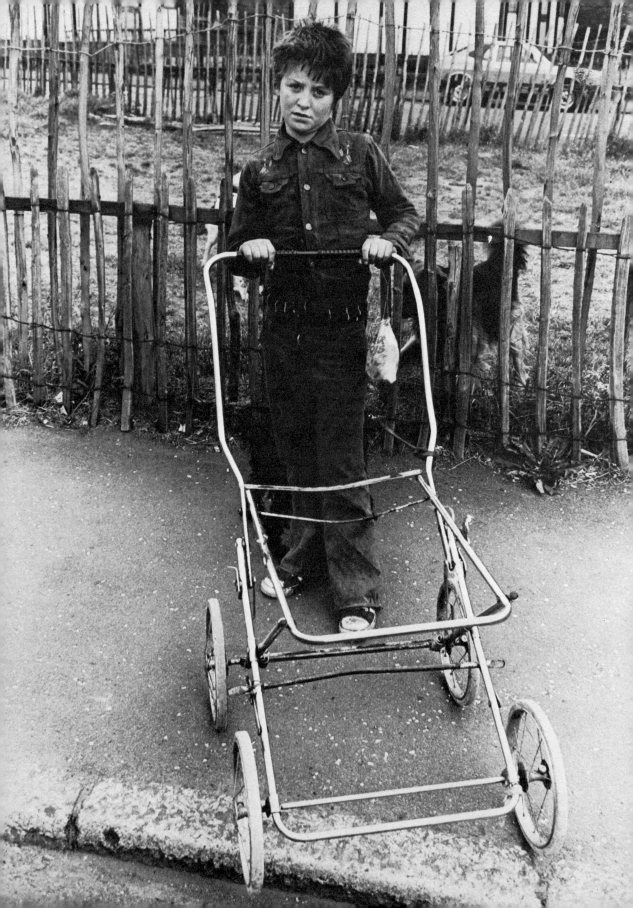

Colin
Ward

The Child
in the City

with photographs by Ann Golzen and others

Pantheon Books, New York

First American Edition

Copyright © 1978 by Colin Ward

All rights reserved under International and Pan-American Copyright
Conventions. Published in the United States by Pantheon Books, a division of
Random House, Inc., New York, and simultaneously in Canada by Random
House of Canada Limited, Toronto. Originally published in Great Britain by
The Architectural Press Ltd., London.

Library of Congress Cataloging in Publication Data

Ward, Colin.
   The Child in the City.

   Includes index.
   1. City children. I. Title.
HT206.W37   301.43′14′091732   77-88765

ISBN 0-394-49845-3
ISBN 0-394-73594-3 pbk.

Manufactured in Great Britain

ntents

Foreword

This book is an attempt to explore the relationship between children and their urban environment. It asks whether it is true, as very many people believe it to be true, that something has been lost in this relationship, and it speculates about the ways in which the link between city and child can be made more fruitful and enjoyable for both the child *and* the city.

But the title, and perhaps the very concept, are open to criticism because they imply that it is possible to speak in general terms about either children or cities. We need to be reminded, as Margaret Mead never fails to remind us, that "It's a good thing to think about the child as long as you remember that the child doesn't exist. Only children exist. Every time we lump them together we lose something." It is not just a matter of the enormous differences between individuals. Every child is in a different state of being or becoming. The legal definition of childhood varies from one place to another, and according to the kind of right or obligation we are discussing. In Britain a whole series of laws, or rather a random accumulation of laws, grants rights or imposes duties at different ages, which in very general terms define the status of childhood. This book is concerned broadly with people within the age-range of compulsory schooling in Britain: five to sixteen. But many would claim that, in terms of life-chances and formative experiences, the most crucial things have already happened to us by the time that as five-year-olds in Britain, or as seven-year-olds in many other countries, we first attend school. The most important thing of all is the accident of whose children we happen to be.

Similarly in most parts of the world it would be foolish to describe a fifteen-year-old as a child. We may adopt the word adolescent to describe those fellow-citizens who are between puberty and the age of full adult rights, an age which, without much debate or opposition, has been lowered from 21 to 18 in many countries in the last decade. But is adolescence simply a creation of society? Frank Musgrove, in a memorable phrase, claimed that "the adolescent was invented at the same time as the steam engine. The principal architect of the latter was James Watt in 1756, of the former Rousseau in 1762." Today not merely adolescence, but the self-evident condition of childhood is under question as a timeless and universal concept. The work of sociologically-minded historians like Philippe Ariès and Peter Laslett has made us realise how recent is our concern for childhood as such. "Children are a modern invention," remarks the playground pioneer Joe Benjamin. "They used to be part of the family."

The family is almost always a more crucial element in a child's destiny than the city, and in diagnosing the social ills of the city moralists point to the high incidence of "broken families" and lament the death of the "extended family", but the social historians point to the mortality statistics. A walk through any old graveyard supports the view that in breaking families the divorce court has simply taken over where the funeral undertaker left off, and explains a great deal about our ancestors' attitude to childhood. By selecting the evidence we can show that the child in past societies was accorded something of the dignity that accrues to someone with an economic role in this world, or we can exhibit the child as the victim of grotesque exploitation, or we can show that the history of childhood, as Lloyd Demause argues in the opening chapter of his book of that name, "is a nightmare from which we have only recently begun to awaken."

Mr Demause believes that the history of child-rearing can be seen as a series of six overlapping modes, of which the newest, the "helping mode" begins (he thinks) in the mid-twentieth century and results in a child "who is gentle, sincere, never depressed, never imitative or group-oriented, strong-willed, and unintimidated by authority." Few adults would deny as individuals that they sought to adopt a helping mode in their relationships with the children who share their lives and their cities, even though they might feel less confident that it would produce this particular combination of attributes. But our question in this book is whether the city, as a human institution, adopts a helping mode towards its young citizens, or whether Paul Goodman was right when he declared years ago that "the city, under inevitable modern conditions, can no longer be dealt with practically by children" because "concealed technology, family mobility, loss of the country, loss of neighbourhood tradition, and eating up of the play space have taken away the real environment".

A child is . . . well, a child is what you recognise as a child, and I am going to be equally evasive in defining the city. Traditionally there are differences between the British and American usage of the word. The expansive founding fathers of some Western town may have named it as the city it never quite became. Sleepy British towns that happen to contain an Anglican cathedral are called cities, and indeed this may be just, for as Leslie Lane once remarked, "Canterbury and St Davids are cities in a way that hundreds of large nineteenth and twentieth century towns are not." A city is loosely defined as a human settlement larger than a town, and there are already seventy-five cities with populations greater than a million. Soweto, whose children were provoked into revolt in June 1976, has over a million inhabitants, but is known as a township. It is estimated that by the end of the century the greater part of the world's population will be living in million-size cities.

But the distinctions between city, suburb, small town and village, grow less tenable as the years go by. In what sense is the village-dweller who commutes to the city, and whose children commute to the nearest urban school, to be thought of as a villager? Claus Moser and William Scott in their study of *British Towns* warn us that "One is all too ready to speak of *the* urban dweller, *the* urban pattern, *the* urban way of life without appreciating the variations found both within and between the cities." There are more similarities between urban and rural life in Britain that between urban life in Britain and urban life in Burma. There is much more in common in the experiences of children in affluent families, rural or urban, than in those of rich and poor children in the same city. In practice it is more sensible to think of the city region than of the city itself and it is only fiscal and administrative realities that persuade us that the city as an entity still exists. These considerations profoundly affect the viability of cities but our considerations of the lives of children should not be limited by some obsolete political boundary.

As a third disclaimer I should warn the reader that this book is not the product of interviews in depth with a random sample of a thousand children in a hundred cities. Much might be learned from such an enterprise, but not acted upon. I have met a great many people who have found fulfilment in trying to meet the needs of city children, from Alex Bloom to Marjorie Allen of Hurtwood. Their motivation came, I am convinced, not from statistical surveys, but from empathy, from their own and other people's recollections, and from sympathetic observation of what children actually do. Everyone has been a child, and the philosopher Gaston Bachelard devoted a book *The Poetics of Space* to evoking, through daydream, meditation and the resonance of the evocations of others, the newness of childhood experience of the environment. "After twenty years," he says, "in spite of all the other anonymous staircases, we would recapture the reflexes of the 'first stairway', we would not stumble on that rather high step. The house's entire being would open up, faithful to our own being. We would push the door that creaks with the same gesture, we would find our way in the dark to the distant attic. The feel of the tiniest latch has remained in our hands . . . We are the diagram of the functions of inhabiting that particular house, and all the other houses are but variations on a fundamental theme. The word habit is too worn a word to express this passionate liason of our bodies, which do not forget, with an unforgettable house." It is with this kind of experienced reality that I am trying to entice the reader to stand in the footprints of the contemporary urban child.

There is a final apology to be made. I have referred to the generalised child as *he*, when I meant *he or she*, since I can scarcely use the word *it*. But even granted that it is conventional to use the male pronoun to subsume both sexes, and granted that my own experience as individual, as parent and as teacher has been confined to boyhood, I have been made conscious in compiling this book that very often when I use the word *he*, this is what I mean. Boys *do* experience, explore and exploit the environment much more than girls do. They are also, in all but one vital respect, much more exposed to its hazards. Some of the implications of the differing environmental experiences of boys and girls are discussed in this book.

In attempting to convey the intensity, variety and ingenuity of the experience of urban childhood, the photographs are probably more effective than the text, and I am especially indebted to Ann Golzen who instantly grasped what pictures were needed and went out and took them. I am grateful too to the other photographers and especially to Becky Young and to Sally and Richard Greenhill. I also have a debt to innumerable children and adults who have talked to me about their environmental experiences and to all those people whose written accounts I have gratefully looted. Anyone writing on a theme like this must be conscious of an indebtedness to Iona and Peter Opie. It is hard to imagine that they have not said the last word on children's games. I am certain too that Paul Goodman was the first to articulate the misgivings of many who have been concerned with the obstacles faced by the children of our cities in attempting to grow up. John and Elizabeth Newson's long-term study of children growing up in an English city is going to be increasingly important for anyone examining urban childhood, as is the National Child Development Study directed by Mia Kellmer-Pringle of the National Children's Bureau. I must also acknowledge my indebtedness to the work of Kevin Lynch and his colleagues.

Godfrey Golzen first suggested this book, and I owe much for particular insights and items of information to Eileen Adams, Joe Benjamin, Jeff Bishop, Pauline Crabbe, Lois Craig, Felicity Craven, Aase Eriksen, Anthony Fyson, Roger Hart, Muffy Henderson, Brian Goodey, Robin Moore, Rose Tanner and David Uzzell.

It would be impossible to write about childhood without exploiting one's own family and I am conscious of what I owe to my wife Harriet Ward, and to five children of the city, Alan Balfour, Douglas Balfour, Barney Unwin, Tom Unwin and Ben Ward.

PICTURE ACKNOWLEDGEMENTS:

All photographs not otherwise credited here are by Ann Golzen
Page **6** Fox Photo Library; **8** South Street Reporter, South Street Seaport Museum, New York; **8/9** New York Public Picture Library; **12** Illustrated London News, 1871; **23** Paul Ritter; **26** Schools Council Publications. Map reproduced by permission of the artist; **30** Angus McLewin; **34** The Guardian; **36** Michael Abrahams; **46** United Nations; **48** Shelter; **51** Pat Crooke; **53** John Hillelson Agency: Marylin Silverstone Magnum; **57** Race Today; **59** Richard and Sally Greenhill; **61** Barnardo Photo Library; **63** Richard Constable/Yorkshire Television; **65** Richard and Sally Greenhill; **74** Becky Young; **77** (top) Pat Crooke; **77** (bottom) Becky Young; **80** *London Street Arabs* by Mrs H. M. Stanley; **80/1** Becky Young; **83** (top) Becky Young; **83** (bottom) Michael Abrahams; **85** (top and middle) Becky Young; **90/1** Becky Young; **92/3** (top) Pat Crooke; **92** Mansell Collection; **92/3** (bottom) Fox Photos; **94** Becky Young; **94** (top), **98/9** (bottom) Richard and Sally Greenhill; **103** Michael Abrahams; **108** Richard and Sally Greenhill; **115** Richard and Sally Greenhill; **119** (bottom) Bill Binzen; **120** Richard and Sally Greenhill; **121**, **124** (top) Becky Young; **124** (bottom) Keystone Press Agency; **126** Michael Abrahams; **128/9** Whiffin Collection; **130** Richard and Sally Greenhill; **135** (middle) Sheffield Family Service Unit; **139** (top) W Lascome; **139** (left) Jonathan Hunt; **140** Richard and Sally Greenhill; **150** Bob Pugh; **159** Richard and Sally Greenhill; **160** Richard and Sally Greenhill; **162** Mrs H. M. Stanley; **163** Pat Crooke; **170** (top) Ruth Berenbaum; **173** Richard and Sally Greenhill; **178/9** Richard and Sally Greenhill; **179** (left) Jeff Bishop; **184/5** (bottom) Mrs H. M. Stanley; **186** Richard and Sally Greenhill; **193** Fiona Cantell; **194** Michael Abraham/Inter-Action Trust, London; **198** J. P. Harpe; **202** Hungarian Tourist Board; **207** Richard and Sally Greenhill; **208** Peter Dunne/Thomson Regional Newspapers Ltd.

TEXT ACKNOWLEDGEMENTS: Grateful acknowledgement is made to the authors and publishers of all the works quoted in the text. These are listed together with all other sources and references in the notes beginning on page 212.

Perhaps it is this demand, strong and insistent in some, shrunken to vague wishes in others, which constitutes the "ideal environment", the private dream behind our public acts, compounded as it is of myth and "genuine recovery of forgotten experience." The particular intensity with which people recall their childhood, even when their evocation bears little relation to the reality, is one of the reasons why the first pages of autobiographies are usually more interesting than the last. Another is the relationship of their picture of home and family with their view of society and the external environment. Lionel Trilling identifies "the great modern theme" as that of "the child's elemental emotions and familial trusts being violated by the ideas and institutions of modern life" and he notes that

"Haunted as we are by unquiet dreams of peace and wholeness, we are eager and quick to find them embodied in another people. Other peoples may have for us the same beautiful integrity that, from childhood on, we are taught to find in some period of our national or ethnic pasts. Truth, we feel, must *somewhere* be embodied in man. Ever since the nineteenth century, we have been fixing on one kind of person or another, one group of people or another, to satisfy our yearning . . . everyone searching for innocence, for simplicity and integrity of life."

You can scarcely open a book or a conversation without bumping into the echoes of someone's private dreams. Here, for instance, is Orwell's glimpse-through-a-window of the "perfect symmetry" of ordinary family life: "Especially on winter evenings after tea, when the fire glows in the open range and dances mirrored in the steel fender, when Father, in shirtsleeves, sits in the rocking chair at one side of the fire, reading the racing finals, and Mother sits on the other with her sewing, and the children are happy with a pennorth of mint humbugs, and the dog lolls roasting himself on the rag mat." It is like one of those carefully composed tableaux in a folk museum, full of lovingly assembled bygones and bits and pieces salvaged from demolished streets.

From another culture, Vladimir Dudintsev evoked the same memory: "In Galitski's home and family everything was permeated by a particular kind of lovable simplicity which cannot be imitated or faked and therefore is not often met with. It was a family where there were many children, where everything was clean but lying about untidily, where the furniture was simple and inexpensive, and where generous helpings are served at table."

Outside the household, this ideal landscape is subject to the same conventions. Although Britain is an urban nation, or perhaps because it is, there is a persistent tradition that puts our lost personal landscape in a rural past. Thomas Burke discovered that even Kate Greenaway, "of the rustic name, who lived all her mental life, her real life, in a world of daisy-chains and cherry-blossom and maypoles and sun-bonnets, was born at, of all places, Hoxton, and brought up at Islington . . ." Raymond Williams, who traces the rural myth through its literary expression, notes how the lost idyll of the pastoral convention is always set in the past, usually not the very distant past, but simply in the childhood of its author. Writing of the "identification with the people among whom he grew up; an attachment to the place, the landscape, in which we first lived and learned to see", he confesses that "the only landscape I ever see in dreams is the Black Mountain in which I was born."

And even if we come from the Black Country instead of the Black Mountain, the enormous weight of literary convention, filtered through school books, pop songs and margarine adverts, postulates a childhood piping down the valleys wild, rather than roaming the city streets, still less the quiet avenues of the suburbs. "I wish to have rural strength and religion for my children" grumbled Emerson, "and I wish city facility and polish. I find with chagrin that I cannot have both." It is idle to dogmatise about the relative virtues of these alternative childhood environments, since our very assessment of them depends upon their myths rather than on reality. By now too we have lived long enough in an urban world for a nostalgic myth of *urban* life to have been nourished by literature and reminiscence. Raymond Williams sees common characteristics in both kinds of evocation:

"We have seen how often an idea of the country is an idea of childhood: not only the local memories, or the ideally shared communal memory, but the feel of childhood: of delighted absorption in our own world, from which eventually, in the course of growing up, we are distanced and separated, so that it and the world become things we observe. In Wordsworth and Clare, and in many other writers, this structure of feeling is poetically expressed, and we have seen how often it is then converted into illusory ideas of the rural past: those successive and endlessly recessive 'happy Englands of my boyhood'. But what is interesting now is that we have had enough stories, and memories of urban childhoods to perceive the same patterns. The old urban working class community; the delights of corner-shops, gas lamps, horsecabs, trams, piestalls: all gone, it seems, in successive generations. These urban ways and objects seem to have, in the literature, the same real emotional substance as the brooks, commons, hedges, cottages, festivals of the rural scene."

He suggests in fact that just like the sentimentalised rural idyll, there is an urban myth of paradise lost. The Yiddish writer Y. Y. Varshavsky evokes "the warm, cosy room, the fire dancing in the stove, and the little ones learning the *alef-beys* in the traditional sing-song." Maurice Samuel, thinking no doubt of other, harsher descriptions of *stetl* life, sees this as yet another example of "the miraculous capacity of children for wringing happiness out of the most disheartening circumstances" in co-operation with "the equally miraculous transforming power of time."

Does this mean that those of us who claim that the modern re-developed urban environment is so attenuated, so lacking in significant landmarks from a child's point of view, that the modern city child is deprived, are simply the victims of yet another nostalgic illusion? Anyone who looks at one of those pairs of photographs of Main Street, Anywhere in 1900 and Main Street, Anywhere in 1975, will feel that something has been lost. But then photography is the most poignantly nostalgic of all arts. What do we read into the faces of the children in the same old pictures? When we romanticise the past the social historians are at our elbow to remind us, as Peter Laslett does, that "Englishmen in 1901 had to face the disconcerting fact that destitution was still an outstanding feature of fully industrialised society, with a working class perpetually liable to social and material degradation. More than half of all the children of working men were in this dreadful condition, which meant 40 per cent of all the children in the country. These were the scrawny, dirty, hungry, ragged, verminous boys and girls who were to grow up into the working class of twentieth-century England." The difference between the child in the British or American city in the last

century and today is that the modern child survives while his predecessor very frequently did not. But once we go beyond the statistical steps to survival owed to sanitation, water supply and preventive medicine, and attempt to look qualitatively at the lives the modern city offers to its children, doubts and worries emerge. We begin to think that there *is* a difference between the slums of hope and the slums of despair, and between being poor and being part of a culture of poverty. The rich crop of autobiographical reminiscence from the inner East End of London, for example, throws up observations and judgements which could not possibly be made by contemporary children. Dolly Scannell, who was a girl in the nineteen-twenties, writes "Limehouse was my favourite place, near the lovely river and ships, tall houses down narrow causeways, a churchyard all grey and dreamlike with a pond in the grounds full of beautifully coloured goldfish. I could have lived at Limehouse for ever." When Louis Heren called his autobiography *Growing Up Poor in London*, his mother objected that it should have been called *Growing Up Among the Poor in London*. His was a fatherless family in Shadwell, a part of the East End which any social investigator, then or now, would regard as isolated and deprived. By any of the usual criteria of welfare agencies he was not only poor but "at risk". Yet he can say of his experience as a boy round about 1930:

"life was not so very different from that of children better off or living in a rural village. We had much the same pastimes, and played cricket and football on cinder pitches in the New Park as well as the asphalt school playground and the street. On balance, we were probably better off than ordinary country children. The schools and the local Carnegie Library were very good, and of course there was London which we roamed as far as the Museums in Exhibition Road. Our mother used to make up sandwiches and give us fourpence for the Underground fare to South Kensington, but we would pocket the money and ride free on the backs of lorries and the few remaining horse-drawn carts."

There are children growing up in Shadwell today who are as talented as Mr Heren (who is foreign editor of *The Times*) as we know from Chris Searle's anthologies of *Stepney Words*, but none of them could conceivably write in such terms of their childhood environment. Something has been lost.

Perhaps the most sensitive account of this environmental loss comes from Stuart Hall and his colleagues at the Centre for Contemporary Cultural Studies at Birmingham. They develop the notion of a continual and consistent "negotiation" between urban working-class culture and the dominant culture, in which it has "won space" in the city. The working-class neighbourhood, they say:

"which assumes its 'traditional' form in and after the 1880s, represents one, distinctive, example of the outcome of negotiation between the classes. In it, the different strata of the working-class have won space for their own forms of life. The values of this corporate culture are registered everywhere, in material and social forms, in the shapes and uses of things, in patterns of recreation and leisure, in the relations between people and the character of communal spaces. These spaces are both physical (the networks of streets, houses, corner shops, pubs and parks) and social (the networks of kin, friendship, work and neighbourly relationships). Over

London Street Scene 1930s

Market Slip, New York,

such spaces the class has come to exert those 'informal social controls' which redefine and reappropriate them for the groups which live in them: a web of rights and obligations, intimacies and distances, embodying in its real textures and structures 'the sense of solidarity, local loyalties and traditions'. These are the 'rights', not of ownership or force, but of territorial and cultural possessions, the customary occupation of the 'sitting tenant'. The institutions are, of course, cross-cut and penetrated by outside forces. The structures of work and workplace, near or far, link the local labour force to wider economic forces and movements. Not far away are the bustling commercial high streets, with their chain stores and supermarkets, linking the home to the wider economy through trade and consumption. Through these structures, the neighbourhood is socially and economically *bounded*. At one level— the horizontal—are all those ties which bind spaces and institutions to locality, neighbourhood, local culture and tradition. At another level—the vertical—are those structures which tie them to dominant institutions and cultures. The local school is a classic instance of such 'double-binding'. It is the *local* school, next to houses, streets and shops where generations of working-class children have been 'schooled', and where the ties of friendship, peer-group and marriage are forged and unmade. Yet in terms of vertical relationships, the school has stood for kinds of learning, types of discipline and authority relations, affirmed experiences quite at variance with the local culture . . ."

This is the framework into which all those reminiscences of urban childhood fit. "It was like a village in those days" explain old ladies into the primary school children's tape-recorders, and they say it of the most unlikely places. Robert Roberts writing of his childhood in Salford quite unselfconsciously finds himself talking of "our village", and of course Limehouse and Shadwell are parts of the London Borough of Tower Hamlets. *Once There Was a Village* is the title of Yuri Kapralov's account of

New York Street Scene 1930s

8

et Slip, New York, 1974

the death throes of the East Village in New York, east of Avenue B. Perhaps it is no longer in the dying working-class districts of the cities of Europe and North America, but in newer communities elsewhere, that communities comprehensible to their children are growing. In an international study, funded by UNESCO, A. M. Battro and E. J. Ellis interviewed children between the ages of eleven and fourteen in Villas Las Rosas on the urban fringe of the city of Salta in North East Argentina. In spite of its name, and of the fact that all its streets are named after flowers, Las Rosas consists of "standard houses, put down according to a rather haphazard plan on an old garbage dump next to the penitentiary", but in the view of its children it has "blossomed into a coherent society and place." They repeatedly volunteered the view that Las Rosas was "nice" friendly, protected and "fun" "They talk of neighbourhood friends, and emphasize the Villa's trees (there are not really too many), its plaza, and its paved streets (in fact there are few). They say they prefer their own area to others in the city. The believe things will change for the better. Most of them expect to live in the Villa when they grow up."

The children of Las Rosas continually mentioned the ten-day Christmas pageant which draws spectators from all over the city. "On the hill, the neighbours' association is building a swimming pool, and one or two of the boys helped clear the land for it. They await its completion eagerly but impatiently, since progress is slow. Most of the small standard houses in the Villa have been added onto, and many of them boast decorated facades, elaborate front walls, and patterned sidewalks . . . The Las Rosas yards are full of house extensions, chicken yards, work areas and vine-covered dining places . . . Las Rosas has the appearance of a hopeful and active community, however meagre its means. Children play a small but recognisable part in community action."

9

2
Happy Habitat Revisited

"The problem is not static but dynamic. A certain amount of change and novelty is an essential prerequisite for the enjoyment of the days and years of our lives. The task of environmental design is not to provide a terminal retirement home for our civilisation, but to guide the evolution of our surroundings in such a manner that we may find delight and assurance both in the process and in the stages it takes us through . . . Whether our urban designers like it or not, the members of our species will always have to go through childhood before growing up."

ALBERT E. PARR

Albert Eide Parr is the retired director of the American Museum of Natural History, and he actually had the nerve to address a meeting on the topic of "The Happy Habitat". Imagine his effrontery in suggesting that the function of the city might be the promotion not merely of business, not solely of entertainment, nor even of public safety, but of happiness. Never since the eighteenth century when William Godwin began a book with the resounding affirmation that "The true object of education, like that of any other moral process, is the generation of happiness" has so bold a claim been made. Accustomed to the idea that happiness is a matter of personal adjustment, personal relations, sexual compatibility or fulfillment in work, we feel that we have been sold short when Mr Parr blandly tells us that "when love for locale is common and strong among the inhabitants and quickly strikes the visitors, we know that we are in an environment offering fertile ground for the seeds of happiness."

This would not have seemed an exaggerated claim in antiquity, when Plato declared that while the city *arises* for the sake of life, it *is* for the sake of good life. And in terms of the individual's experience of the city, Albert Parr reminds us that "our minds have needs of sensory intake quite similar to our bodily appetite for food," and he reminds us too that our "most basic demand upon the environment is that it must offer a sufficiently rich, fine-grained, enduring, and varied diversity of forms and colours to offer satisfactory stimulus fields for all its inhabitants."

Time and again when I have discussed the theme of this book with American students of the built environment, they have dug into their brief-cases, handbags or filing cabinets to produce a copy of that same Albert Parr's article "The Child in the City: Urbanity and the Urban Scene" in which he describes his own childhood experience in a Norwegian seaport at the turn of the century:

"Not as a chore, but as an eagerly desired pleasure, I was fairly often entrusted with the task of buying fish and bringing it home alone. This involved the following: walking to the station in five to ten minutes; buying a ticket; watching train with coal-burning steam locomotive pull in; boarding train; riding across long bridge over shallows separating small-boat harbour (on the right) from ship's harbour (on the left), including small naval base with torpedo boats; continuing through a tunnel; leaving train at terminal, sometimes dawdling to look at railroad equipment; walking by and sometimes entering fisheries museum; passing central town park where military band played during mid-day break; strolling by central shopping and business district, or, alternatively, passing fire station with horses at ease under suspended harnesses, ready to go, and continuing past centuries-old town hall and other ancient buildings; exploration of fish market and fishing fleet; selection of fish; haggling about price; purchase and return home."

Bernard Rudofsky, who like my informants, instantly grasps the significance of this story in his book *Streets for People*, points out that the important thing is that young Albert was four years old at the time. He sees that not only were the streets safe for a very young child, but that the stimuli of the urban environment were such that the child could read and do sums long before he attained school age. Street signs and shop signs had reached him at an optical rather than a verbal level. And if little Albert had been in a modern kindergarten, his teacher would have learned from Piaget (by way of his interpretors) that he could not possibly have attained the necessary spatial skills by that age.

Rudofsky contrasts the environmental experience of Albert Parr with that described by Joseph Lyford as the typical learning situation of the New York child on his way to school. He will learn, Mr Lyford says,

"to identify an alcoholic before he hears him speak and spot any one of a variety of homosexuals. He has seen at close range the transactions that take place between men and women in hallways or on corners between Broadway and Amsterdam Avenue. He may know that a certain grocery store is the local 'drop' for a police game, he will have seen policemen accepting money from street pedlars, storekeepers and contractors. He knows that a red welt on the inside of the forearm is the entry point of a hypodermic needle and he understands at least a few words of the language of the junkie and the hustlers."

Somewhere between these two extremes is the characteristic environmental experience of the modern city child. No present day child of a similar age has that freedom of the streets that Dr Parr recalls from infancy, precisely because the streets are not safe, but the characteristic peril is not from the mugger or molester. It is simply from the motorist. Similarly those elements of inner city life from which one would prefer to screen the young have become much more dominant simply because the multiplicity of self-policing uses of the street, classically celebrated by Jane Jacobs, have dwindled. The inner city residential population, and so of course the child population, has fallen dramatically. Other elements—big business or bad business—dominate. Friends of mine, reared in Soho in the pre-war days when that district in the heart of the city supported four primary schools, lived a childhood of village innocence, playing with penny tops and marbles on its pavements and moving with the immunity of acknowledged citizens through streets which then, as now, had lurid reputations.

The difference between the nineteen-thirties and the nineteen-seventies is that today the illicit, transient, child population of Soho is greater than the official school-attending juvenile population. In 1975 a Member of Parliament, describing the boys who slept in cardboard boxes in shop doorways and alleys because they had nowhere else to go, said, "I will take any member round Soho where the boxes are and lift the lids." What kind of difference has there been since the nineteen-hundreds? One old man, brought up in central London, whose family slept five to a bed in two rooms just when Dr Parr was exploring the happy habitat of his boyhood, recalls how the Salvation Army man "used to go down the mewses and stables and lift up the tarpaulins to see if there was any derelict children under."

He illustrates the difficulty we have in trying to draw valid conclusions from Albert Parr's evidence. For he too had the freedom of the streets,

London School Board Officials Capture Truants at 2.40 am, 1871

begging or stealing, dodging the policemen, or wandering aimlessly just in case there was something to be found in the gutter: "We used to walk the streets all night at times . . . miles and miles all along Tottenham Court Road, Oxford Street, all along the gutters . . . We used to walk from King's Cross to Hampstead Heath. And it was fun of the fair in happy Hampstead in those days." Fun of the fair to watch but not to join in. There is a point at which the stimulation and excitement provided by the environment becomes secondary to the imperatives of survival. This old man, in his childhood, was at the turning point. Below him was destitution. At his level, ferret-eyed in the gutter which might provide a few dropped coins, or at the back doors of the bakeries which might provide a stale loaf, the city was a foraging ground, just as it is today for the *kangalis* of Calcutta. "At night you can see these small boys rummaging among the great stinking middens that are dumped on Bentinck Street or at the start of Lower Chitpore Road. They are collecting bones with fragments of meat sticking to them, scraps of green vegetables that have been discarded as refuse, spoonsful of rice that have been scraped from the half-finished plates of wealthy diners."

But beyond survival level, and anyone who knows poor children knows how precariously above survival level, sensory experience and random pleasure takes over. The girls a generation younger and a subclass more secure would make the same uphill journey as the old man simply to bring back, as John Betjeman noticed, "sheaves of drooping dandelions to the courts of Kentish Town." Simon Jenkins, an acute observer of the London scene remarks that "When Charles Dickens walked as a boy from Camden Town to work in a blacking factory behind Charing Cross, the walk was a continuous encounter with every variety of human being. The pavements were alive with people and he would get to know, and be known by, them all. There were the old people sitting outside doors in St Martin's Lane, stallholders shouting at him in Seven Dials, children, tramps and beggars recognising him as he passed, friends he came to know well, enemies he made detours to avoid. A huge range of activities went on before his eyes—buying, selling, exchanging, displaying, mending, cajoling, courting, procuring, bribing, and simply meeting people. All London was laid out on the pavement, and you didn't have to be introduced to it first."

He asks what kind of thematic material Dickens could have derived from a stroll along Victoria Street, or through the Barbican, or up the Finchley Road. He might well have asked what kind of environmental stimulation a child would gain from a walk through the aridly rebuilt or run-down semi-derelict inner city main streets of our towns and cities today. The rebuilt city, as Jane Jacobs complained, has "junked the basic function of the city street, and with it, necessarily, the freedom of the city."

Does the modern city provide the young explorer with the range of sensations that it gave for example to the young Maxim Gorki wandering wide-eyed through the streets of Nijni-Novgorod or the young Walt Whitman who loved to give himself up to the delicious sensations of loafing all day in the streets of Manhatten? You may say that potential writers were extra sensitive to the sights and sounds of the city, but collectors of oral history gather every day recollections which, even allowing for the distorting mirror of memory, reveal a street which was, in Rudofsky's phrase, "an open book, superbly illustrated, thoroughly familiar, yet inexhaustible."

There were echoes of Plato, Godwin and Albert Parr in the evocative newspaper headline "Textbook City Fails to Make Happiness". It referred in fact to the city of Sheffield, whose problems were being discussed at the National Conference on Educational Disadvantage by its chief education officer, Michael Harrison. According to *The Guardian*, "Sheffield, regarded as the national model of a cohesive working-class city, with the most progressive modern education, now has more unhappy children in its schools than it did five years ago. Mr Harrison's claim is understood to be based on a survey of 25 per cent of the Sheffield school population, an exceptionally large sample. Results so far are disclosing that family breakdown, among other things is 'spectacularly up' on 1970, when an initial survey was made. Mr Harrison said that family breakdown could be one of the main reasons for the unhappiness the survey found. Among the other possibilities were an increase in one-parent families, domestic stress and stress arising from inflation and worry about employment prospects. Mr Harrison's speech was desperately pessimistic about local government's ability to discover, plan for or solve such problems. He could not claim, he said, that Sheffield administrators were familiar with 'the realities of life' in different parts of the city. Until there was 'some sort of rapprochement between the school and the community', it would be difficult to approach the problem of disadvantage." The report went on to quote Mr Harrison's confession that no one knew whether it was anti-cultural attitudes, the high rates of pay now available in unskilled jobs, or other forces which caused the undoubted apathy among many parents about educational opportunity which leads their children to under-achieve. There was also, he said, a need to think more about the way in which authorities were upsetting people by rehousing policies unmotivated by sociological knowledge. "I have never yet seen a plan which talks in intelligent terms about people," he said. "It always talks of the space they will occupy and the quality of life—but without defining what that is . . ."

Only the last point in his catalogue of possible reasons for the unhappiness of Sheffield children, has to do with the experience of the physical environment, and I believe it is a very significant point. But in general terms his worries paralleled those reported from London. A team of psychologists from the Institute of Psychiatry at the Maudsley Hospital examined nearly 1,700 ten-year-olds in an inner London borough and compared them with 1,300 children of the same age on the Isle of Wight, a predominantly rural area. No immigrant children were included, and parents and teachers were also questioned. The findings were that by comparison with a very small percentage in the Isle of Wight, 25.4 per cent of the inner London children showed signs of psychiatric disturbance, and according to Professor Michael Rutter, these disorders ranged from sleep disturbances, neurotic crying or fear of school, to chronic fighting or stealing—enough to make the child unhappy and hamper the progress of his or her work in the classroom. When Dr Rutter presented his findings at the Centre for Urban Educational Studies in London, there were rumblings in the audience that the methodology was full of anti-working-class value-judgements. These misgivings seemed to me to obscure the real implications of all such investigations. You can sum it up in the phrase "happy families move out".

Skilled, affluent, secure and stable families tend to leave the inner city with the result that it is inevitable that the city population contains a higher proportion of families that are disadvantaged in one way or another, and that from the point of view of the children of these families neither the education system nor the environment itself compensates for this disadvantage except in a minority of instances, even though the anecdotal evidence implies that it once did. There is evidence, however, that this was always true of the slums of metropolitan cities. Thus the urban historian H. J. Dyos calculates that "in the worst slums of London the proportion of Londoners to the rest was above that which obtained in London as a whole. So as well as the slums acting as a zone of transition for rural migrants and incomers from smaller towns and cities, assimilating them to the urban system, they also represented the results of a process by which those relatively less competent to compete in the urban system drifted downwards into the least advantageous locations."

It would be surprising if the comparative studies made in cities throughout the world did *not* show that children from poor housing had poorer physical and mental health and development and of course lower educational attainments than children from adequate housing. The housing itself is just one aspect of the poverty that creeps into every aspect of the child's life. When the family is re-housed and the culture of poverty remains, casting its blight on the new estate too, we look for other factors in the urban home, beyond overcrowding, dampness or lack of sanitary amenities: the emotional or psychological problems of parents, the poor health, depression and irritability that accompany poverty, the absence of a wage-earning parent, the especial strains on single parents. Is poverty in the modern city worse, or harder to bear, than in the teeming cities of the last century? It depends whether you measure it in death rates or in life expectations.

It is certainly harder to bear when you can see that other people have got out of it. Thus the novelist Alan Sillitoe remarks, "When there is widespread poverty, people help each other in order to survive, but when poverty is patchy, uneven, and separated in its unevenness, they lose faith in unity, they acquire a sense of guilt, and this is worst of all because it is unnecessary, underserved, and undermines even further their self-respect. This accretion of guilt far outweighs the encouragement they are supposed to get from seeing other people less poor, whose example they are expected to follow . . ."

The boy or girl in the familiar background of poverty and deprivation is more and more isolated from the world of the successful and self-confident as time goes by. My wife once coined a profound aphorism in trying to define this isolation: "As the threshold of competence rises, the pool of inadequacy increases." The organisation of retail distribution, the organisation of work, the commercialisation of leisure, and the changed scale of the modern city, all demand a higher level of competence and know-how than was required of the poor city dweller in the past. You have to be cleverer to cope.

While Mr Harrison was talking about the unhappiness of Sheffield children and Professor Rutter was talking about the unhappiness of London children, I was talking to teachers in Glasgow about that city's problems. I was in a district of the city, a clearance area—though of course you could get the impression that the whole of the city of Glasgow was a clearance area— which I had first visited thirty years earlier, when for the first and last time in living memory, because of the war, there was full employment there. I remember, even in that situation, being accosted continually by barefoot boys chanting "Gie us a penny Mister", a cry which has haunted the streets of Glasgow for a century and a half. The overspill of a full pay packet was very unevenly distributed even then.

We know that it was possible for a poor child in pre-war Glasgow to live a life of great joy and fulfilment, as Molly Weir's autobiography and many other reminiscences of those who succeeded testify. But a far more typical view is that of Alasdair Maclean. "The Glasgow slum districts of my 1930s boyhood," he writes, "were unbelievable places. I used to think, after I had escaped, that one of them should be kept as a contribution to evolutionary theory, proof of how a jungle environment operating on a given stock through a process of natural selection will eventually produce animals."

When I first came to this particular part of his native city, there were areas with residential densities of between 700 and 800 people to the acre, and the whole emphasis of postwar housing policy has been to rehouse them either in the enormous municipal estates on the fringe or in the New Towns beyond. The dramatic fall in Glasgow's population (1,057,679 in 1961 down to 897,848 in 1971) has reflected the effectiveness not only of official policy but also of the magnet of the hope of a better life elsewhere, as is evident in the numbers of Glaswegians among the runaway young or the derelict old in English cities. Matt McGinn, a bard who often reflects very accurately the city's mood sings "I've packed up my bags and must go/ I'm headin' for Swindon or maybe for London/ In search of a livin' I'll go."

In this particular district of the city a continuous programme of redevelopment by the Corporation has been in progress for years. There were three-storey walk-up flats built in the years just before the war, more built in the post-war years, as well as the tower block of the last decade. And there were some of the remaining traditional Glasgow tenement houses of four or five storeys, some still occupied, some being demolished at the moment. In the middle of the area I arrived at the shabby premises of the Free School, run by a teacher with the impeccable academic qualifications demanded by the Scottish education system, who chose to use his talents in this alternative institution because he had lost faith in the official system. He was, needless to say, in trouble with the local education authority because the old building he occupied did not comply with the regulations as to the appropriate number of lavatories for each sex. Opposite his school, emerging from the ground, was the structure of the vast new secondary school which would combine the existing schools of the area.

But will this new building mean that either the unofficial community school or the truancy centre (an "intermediate school for casual attenders" run by a remarkable priest in association with one of the existing secondary schools) will no longer be needed? An official report by the Scottish Education Department's inspectors on the effect of raising the school leaving age suggests the opposite, and declares frankly that the schools had ignored the needs of less able pupils in favour of examination courses with the result that many pupils became disenchanted and simply stayed away.

Just round the corner was the new primary school. It was a brand new building, open-plan, carpeted, quiet, civilised, and even in these hard times in the education industry, amply stocked with all the attractive paraphenalia of junior teaching, although the first thing the Corporation had to do once it had taken over the building was to fit wire grilles to doors and windows and arrange for security men with dogs to do their night patrols once the janitor had gone off duty. The headmistress was quite obviously one of those marvels of the teaching profession, efficient, tough-minded and tender-hearted, who had first taught in the district twenty years earlier. I asked her what differences she perceived between those days and now. She replied that when she first taught there she had noticed among the children the effects of poor feeding, poor clothing, scabies, impetigo, nits, dental decay and ringworm. And she said that today it was just the same except for the absence of ringworm.

I asked whether she could discern a difference between the families in the old tenement blocks and those in the relatively new corporation flats. She replied that in the old tenement blocks there tended to be families who were in work, who remained as a family unit, and who paid their rent. Perhaps it would be true to say that in that particular district, everybody with the ability to get out had got out, and the perfectly sanitary corporation flats there (which incidently looked to me to have had no real attention to maintenance since they were built) had become the homes of the lame ducks of official policy who had not the ability to move out. The families in the notorious old tenements opted *not* to move there.

The secondary school headmaster said much the same. It was curious, he thought, that those parents who still lived in the old 'single-end' tenements with the sink on the landing and the 'cludgie' on the common stair, would send their children to school cleaner and better nourished that those from the postwar flats which at least provided those facilities which the Medical Officer of Health regarded as essential for the good life.

These are unpalatable observations for those who hold to the faith of the social engineering professions that bigger and better schools or bigger and better units of housing or more expert and intensive social work will modify the culture of poverty. When I met Roger Starr, the Housing Administrator for New York, whose problems make those of Sheffield or Glasgow seem like minor local difficulties, he asked rhetorically, "To what extent can government intervene to change *people*? Should a concern for human welfare drive government itself to impose specific behavioural patterns on those who are neither certifiably insane nor provably guilty of a criminal offence?" The British government's answer has been clearly stated (on paper at least). Reporting to the 1976 United Nations Conference on the Human Habitat on its various palliative experiments in deprived inner city areas, like Urban Aid and the Community Development Projects, it declares that they "have confirmed beyond doubt that the inner city's decline results from an external economic process, not from any change in the behaviour patterns of the inhabitants."

Looking at the experience of the city from the point of view of its child inhabitants, I think there is another factor: the scope and limits of one's own actions. During the period of mushroom growth in the cities of Britain and America in the 19th century, you get the impression that the child always had something to do, something to engage him in the experience of living. It is easy to see that he usually had too much to do: that he had to consider himself lucky to work for intolerable hours at some dreary labour which was beyond his strength and earned a pittance. Or that he was engaged in a desperate struggle to get food for himself and his family. But he was not trapped in a situation where there was nothing economically rational for him

to do and where his whole background and culture prevented him from benefitting from the expensively provided education machine, beyond the tender atmosphere of the infants school.

The child who grows up in the poverty belt of the British or American city today is caught in a cage in which there is not even the illusion of freedom of action to change his situation, except of course in activities outside the law. Self-confidence and purposeful self-respect drain away from these children as they grow up because there is no way which makes sense to them, of becoming involved, except in a predatory way, in their own city.

Sometimes there are glimpses which show the way towards this kind of involvement. When I mentioned to Roger Starr the instance of 'The Renigades', a Spanish-American teenage gang who had been entrusted with the rehabilitation of a landlord-abandoned apartment house in New York, he groaned. He was the man who had to authorise the bills. But was this not an instance of giving the young real responsibilities and opportunities which would give them a place in the city? The Glasgow priest who runs the truancy centre remarked that the last thing which his pupils (or the pupils of the school whose drop-outs he caters for) regard as important is a job—or indeed the very idea of going to work. Partly for the very obvious reason that in the decaying city with its decaying economy, the jobs do not exist, but partly, according to the secondary school headmaster, that so large a proportion of his pupils belong to families totally dependent on welfare handouts that there is no model to emulate.

But he told me in the next breath that when another of the old tenement houses fell to the demolition contractor's ball and chain, the cry would go up, "Tenny doon!" and the boys would hire a horse and cart, for £5 a day, and collect whatever metal was sticking out of the pile of rubble and sell it to the scrap metal merchants. In spite of the fact that the lead flashings, gutters and pipework had already been garnered by the professional lead-thieves, the priest told me that the boys were usually agreeably surprised at how much they could earn this way.

"I'm not saying they *should* be doing this" he said, but I could see that he admired them and was concerned with the existential value of childhood experiences. And sure enough, as I was being ferried back to the city centre in a Scottish Education Department car, (they happen to be the same make and colour as the ones used by Glasgow CID) we kept passing and being repassed by a horse and cart with four boys and a nosebag aboard. They looked at us, not apprehensively, but with curiosity, as they got through the traffic jams more rapidly.

They were between twelve and fourteen years old. They knew how to get hold of, and manipulate in dense traffic, a horse-drawn vehicle, and how to pilot it through the city to some entrepreneur who had a market for the last of the metallic rubbish of the old inner city. It is interesting to think that, like the gypsies, (called an "important element" by the chairman of the British Scrap Federation) they are part of an industry which has an estimated turnover of £125m. and saves an estimated £200m. in foreign exchange. Were they the final generation of children who actually had a function in the inner city?

3
How the Child Sees the City

"Is it the mindlessness of childhood that opens up the world? Today nothing happens in a gas station. I'm eager to leave, to get where I'm going, and the station, like some huge paper cutout, or a Hollywood set, is simply a facade. But at thirteen, sitting with my back against the wall, it was a marvellous place to be. The delicious smell of gasoline, the cars coming and going, the fresh air hose, the half-heard voices buzzing in the background—these things hung musically in the air, filling me with a sense of well being. In ten minutes my psyche would be topped up like the tanks of the automobiles."   FRANK CONROY

This account from Frank Conroy's autobiographical novel *Stop-time* describing the experience of idling at the gas station is used by Yi-Fu Tuan to illustrate the way in which "unburdened by worldly cares, unfettered by learning, free of ingrained habit, negligent of time, the child is open to the world." This capacity for vivid sensory experience, commonplace among children is an aspect of the world that the adult has lost, not just because the senses are dulled by familiarity, but because there is an actual measurable physical decline in sensitivity to taste, to smells, to colour and to sound.

What meaning has the structure of the city for the child citizen? Any reader searching among his early recollections will recall how his own perception of his physical surroundings expanded from the floor, walls and furniture of the room in the house or apartment in which he grew up, its links with other rooms, the steps, stairs, yard, garden, front door, street, shops, and public park. He probably does not remember how he put them together into some concept of the home and its relationship with the outside world, nor what gaps remained for years in his mental map of the city.

Further recollection will lead him to reflect that the environmental experience of the child *must* be different simply because of the difference of scale. Obviously the younger the child the closer his eyelevel is to the ground, and this is one of the reasons why the floorscape—the texture and subdivisions of flooring and paving, as well as changes of level in steps and curves (small enough to step over for an adult, big enough to sit on for a child)—is very much more significant for the young. Kevin Lynch and A. K. Lukashok asked adults what they remembered from their city childhood and they named particularly the floor of their environment, the tactile rather than the visual qualities of their surroundings. When he was teaching architecture at Nottingham, Paul Ritter got his students to mock-up a room two-and-a-half times actual size, just to remind us what a child's-eye-view was really like. Erected in the Co-op Education Centre there, it brought gasps of astonishment from the visitors. Because we grow so slowly, we have completely forgotten—even though we see our own children doing it—how we used, without any fuss, to move around stools, boxes or upturned buckets just to be able to reach the light-switch, the door latch, shelves, cupboards or window sills.

At a less obvious level, the child in his perception of the world, has a more varied experience, just because it is not focussed through the lens of existing mental associations, just because it is indiscriminate. As Yi-Fu Tuan puts it, in adult life "the gain is subtlety, the loss is richness." He suggests that, growing older, we substitute appreciation for direct sensory experience, the most important element of appreciation being remembrance. But the child has little to remember: "Because the child's world is so full of miracles, the word miracle can have no precise meaning for him." Moreover, lacking

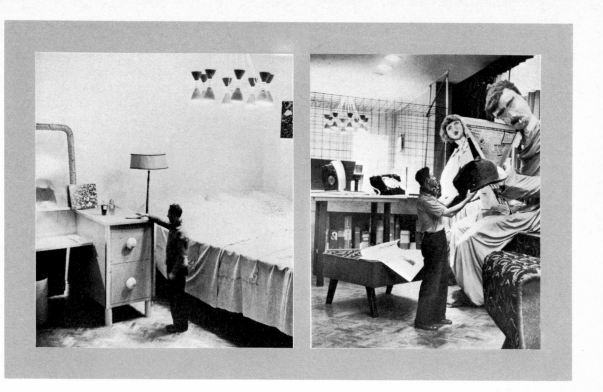

*Children's Eye View:
Rooms built by Paul Ritter
and his students in
Nottingham in 1959, 2¼
times normal size*

social awareness, his perception of the environment is not "tainted" by social considerations. He has not acquired that selective vision that distinguishes the beauty of the flowers from that of the weeds. Yi-Fu Tuan stresses again in his book *Topophilia* that "a child, from about seven or eight years old to his early teens, lives in this vivid world much of the time." We might ask, since ordinary observation suggests that for much of the time many children seem oblivious to their surroundings, being involved in some personal or social activity which is even more absorbing, what the child actually does with this wealth of vivid environmental impressions. How does he assemble it into an image of the city? Paul Shephard, thinking of what he calls "the halcyon acme of juvenile fulfillment—the idyllic and practical age of ten" remarks that "space in juvenile life is structured differently than at later ages; it is much more critically defined. It is intensely concerned with paths and boundaries, with hiding places and other special places for particular things.

Such experimental insights as we have about the child's perception of the built environment come—as so often happens in creative research—from the mutual accommodation of ideas from quite separate theoretical approaches. There is a thriving academic industry in environmental psychology and the study of our perceptions of the environment, which brings together two traditions of investigation: firstly the *cognitive mappers*, exemplified by Kevin Lynch, and secondly the *developmentalists*, exemplified by Jean Piaget.

It was Lynch who in his book *The Image of the City*, introduced us to the notion that we structure out personal concept of the city around certain elements. These were

(1) *Paths*, which are "the channels along which the observer customarily,

occasionally, or potentially moves . . . People observe the city while moving through it and along these paths the other environmental elements are arranged and related . . .''

(2) *Edges*, which are "the linear elements not used or considered as paths by the observer . . . such edges may be barriers, more or less penetrable, which close one region off from another; or they may be seams, lines along which two regions are related and jointed together . . .''

(3) *Districts*, which are "medium-to-large sections of the city, conceived of as having two-dimensional extent, which the observer mentally enters 'inside of' and which are recognisable as having some common identifying character . . .''

(4) *Nodes*, which are "the strategic spots in a city into which an observer can enter, and which are the intensive foci to and from which he is travelling . . . The concept of node is related to the concept of path, since functions are typically the convergence of paths, events on a journey. . . .''

(5) *Landmarks*, which are another type of point reference but in this case the observer does not enter within them, they are external. They are usually a rather simply defined physical object: building, sign, store or mountain.''

It was Piaget, the Swiss psychologist who has greatly influenced educational theory, who in a series of books set out a developmental theory of the child's conception of space. In the first stage, roughly between the ages of five and nine, the child grasps what are known as "topological" relationships which are those of (1) proximity or nearness, (2) separation, (3) order, or spatial succession, (4) enclosure or surrounding, and (5) continuity. This is the *pre-operational* stage, and it implies that the child "may be able to negotiate successfully sequences or routes, but cannot reverse these, hypothesise about them or add to them in any major way." In the second stage, around the ages of nine to thirteen, the child comprehends "projective space", and as Jeff Bishop interprets it in environmental terms, "the child now understands and is able to operate successfully amongst a series of known relationships and sequences of objects and situations. He therefore can now reverse his route to school while standing in school and can successfully negotiate alternatives, combinations and extensions of his route provided that they involve reshuffling of known sequences, rather than the deduction of new ones or large gaps between existing ones. At this stage the child can successfully represent correctly the sequence of events on a given familiar route, e.g. home to school, with a good level of scale and directional accuracy." This is known as the *concrete operational* stage.

The final stage in Piaget's terms is reached round about the age of thirteen and is known as the *formal operational* stage, when the child can comprehend Euclidean space, when the child can conceive of spatial relationships in the abstract, and can hypothesise about them by reference not to a series of bits, but to an overall abstract grid. For Piaget, "At the outset, the co-ordinates of Euclidean space are no more than a vast network embracing all objects and consist merely of relations of order applied simultaneously to all three dimensions; left-right, above-below and before-behind, applied to each object simultaneously, thus linking them in three directions, along straight lines parallel to each other in one dimension and intersecting those belonging to the other two dimensions at right-angles."

The young lions of environmental perception, who have over the last decade enlarged our understanding of the way children see the city, are

24

iconoclastic about the old masters who laid the foundations for their work. They point out that the original American research into the nature of the cognitive maps of the environment which we are all said to carry around in our heads, was done with populations who were adult, middle-class, articulate and car-driving. They point out that Lynch's original work, while drawing upon what Kenneth Boulding calls the "spatial image" and the "relational image", ignores those components of our picture of the city which he calls the "value image" and the "emotional image." They point out that Piaget's studies of children's perception were done indoors, in a classroom, without the stimulus or imaginative interest of work in the environment itself. They point out that the "level of abstraction" children can cope with at different ages ignore the potentialities of imaginative teaching designed to make these abstractions comprehensible. Educational orthodoxy used to hold for example that there was some age before which it was pointless to teach the use of maps because children would not have made the leap from visual to symbolic representation of the environment. Roger Hart told me of the work he did in this field with children in the third grade (seven to eight year olds) in an inner city district of Worcester, Massachusetts. Using low altitude vertical aerial photographs in A4-sized sheets (Ozalid prints of which could be made for a few cents each) Hart and the class built up the map of the city on the classroom floor. He asked the children to bring in their matchbox-toy model cars which are made on an appropriate scale for the maps. Then everyone set out on the map to find the way to the city centre. This led them to difficulties of traffic congestion and of finding a place to park. It also resulted in crashes and in the need to get an ambulance through the traffic and back to St Vincent's Hospital.

Brian Goodey and his former colleagues at the Centre for Urban and Regional Studies at Birmingham have carried out some equally simple and pleasurable work in a British context using sketch-maps drawn by both adults and children. With the co-operation of a local newspaper, they inserted in a week-end edition a map of central Birmingham with the middle left out, so that respondents, who were assessed by age, sex, occupation and mode of travel, could fill in their mental maps of the missing bit. The maps established the very simple and fundamental truth that people's conception of the central city differed according to their age, social status and life-style. You might regard this as so obvious as to need no proving, but if you look at the redevelopment of central Birmingham, or of virtually any other British city, you can see that the unspoken assumption has been made that the city exists for one particular kind of citizen: the adult, male, white-collar, out-of-town car-user.

In an inner-city district of the same city David Spencer and John Lloyd applied a variety of techniques to gain "a child's eye view of Small Heath", working with Infant (age five to seven), Junior (age seven to eleven) and Secondary (age eleven to eighteen) schools. The technique used with the nine–ten year olds and with 13–15 year olds was that of obtaining from them free-recall sketch maps of the route from home to school. Several hundred of such maps were aggregated to provide composite maps, the elements shown on which were classified as housing, shops, entertainments, public services, open spaces, industries, cars and roadside objects. In the drawings and written work obtained from the infants, much attention was given to people, animals, birds, vegetation and natural phenomena. Buildings, roads and

roadside objects were seen by the infants especially in relation to human activities, particularly pupils' own homes, friends' and neighbours' houses and "people waiting to cross the road assisted by wardens". The experimenters concluded that young children see the environment primarily in human and natural terms since the human and natural elements appeared only occasionally in the work of the juniors and very rarely in that of the seniors.

The American investigators Robert Maurer and James C. Baxter characterise the "impressive differences" between children's environmental imagery and that of adults as "a quality of intricacy and attention to detail . . . the individuality of individual houses, interest in animals, the unnerving confrontation with huge streets and bothersome trains." They used mapping techniques to gauge the perceptions of neighbourhood and city of Black, Mexican and "Anglo" American children, and concluded that the Anglo children had a more complex imagery and life-style than the others. Their maps of their neighbourhood showed more unique features, their concept of the neighbourhood was wider, showing familiarity with a greater area, their maps of the whole city were closer to reality, they listed a greater variety of play preferences. Maurer and Baxter attributed this to the greater mobility of the Anglo children through access to more varied transport, to the fact that their mothers were more likely to be at home during the day, giving more parental stimulation, to the fact that their friends were scattered more widely, giving motives for travel and awareness of a greater segment of the city.

Working with architectural students from Kingston Polytechnic, Jeff Bishop analysed both for content and mapping style, the maps drawn by 180 children between the ages of nine and sixteen in the East Coast port of Harwich. Their findings were similar to those obtained in American cities. Walkers, needless to say, provided more detail than bus riders or those who habitually travelled in their parents' cars. They found a remarkably sudden shift in the mapping style at the age of eleven, and, indeed, a difference between that of the eleven year olds who were in their final primary school year and those who were in their first year at the secondary school. The only explanation for this was that the secondary school children had begun to have formal geography lessons and had been taught to change to a more sophisticated style of representation. When Eileen Adams asked eleven-year-olds at Pimlico School in inner London to draw maps of the journey to school, she found that children living on estates of blocks of flats, drew more detailed and more accurate maps than those who lived in streets of houses. She was puzzled by this, since she assumed that the flat-dwelling child would have a less intimate familiarity with the external environment. Discussing the maps with the class, the explanation emerged. Each estate had a large painted map at its entrance, showing the names and dispositions of the blocks and their relationship with the surrounding streets.

But the most significant thing to come out of Jeff Bishop's work in Harwich, was the comparison of the children's maps with those of adults. In the middle of the port there is a lighthouse which featured as a significant landmark in all the maps drawn by adults. But none of the Harwich children showed the lighthouse on their maps, though many showed the public lavatory which stands at its base. Things which were important to them included kiosks, hoardings and other bits of unconsidered clutter in the

Stages in Map Making At the age of eight, the young child draws scenes as pictures. Buildings appear in side view, and there is little idea of distance in relation to height. The ten-year-old is beginning to draw scenes in plan form. Some buildings, however, still appear in side view. Most children by the age of thirteen can draw a map or plan. (From Schools Council Project: History, Geography and Social Science 8–13) Pictorial Map of the journey to school, changing trains at Oxford Circus, by Rachel, aged 11. (Produced as part of the Front Door Project, directed by Eileen Adams, at Pimlico School, London) street. One item that frequently recurred in their maps (and was totally ignored in those of adults) was a telephone connection box—a large metal object on the footpath with a fluted base. Obviously, as a feature for hiding behind or climbing on, this kind of obstruction has a value for children in their use of the street. What planners call "non-conforming users", or places which the adult eye just does not see, have importance in the children's maps too. There was for example the council refuse depot, noted by many of the children as the place where they wash down the dustmen's lorries.

The building of the Kingston Polytechnic where Jeff Bishop used to work stands between the river and the road. Walking past the place "where Daddy works" with his five year old son, he found to his surprise that the boy could identify the window of his room on the seventh floor, through remembering the view from the window. Now how could this be true of a child in Piaget's pre-operational stage? Well of course, Bishop explains, Piaget was working with children in a room, and drew conclusions about three-dimensional ability from two-dimensional tasks. Furthermore these tasks were not meaningful to the children performing them: they were not related to the real, actual environment of the child. Bruner has stressed the importance of the amount of interaction between the child and his environment, and another American researcher, Gary Moore, has developed an interactionist theory, emphasising that interaction and familiarity with the environment are the crucial factors in a child's progress along Piaget's stages. Age, sex and class he finds less important. David Stea, also in the United States, has worked on toy-modelling techniques with children of three years upwards. The models were capable of being arranged to form a community, with houses, streets, shops, a fire-station and so on, and with these, three-year-olds have demonstrated their ability to understand linear systems in correct sequence, while of course if Piaget were to be interpreted in the age-specific way in which his theories are taught in the teachers' colleges, an eight-year-old couldn't find his way home from school.

But how often, Bishop asks, do we give children an opportunity to show us what they know about the space in which they move around? How often do we let them lead *us* home from school instead of us leading them? During the building of a new stand at Chelsea Football Club's ground at Stamford Bridge, he seized the opportunity to garner cognitive maps of the streets around the club, in terms of whether the mapper was a resident supporter of Chelsea, or a resident non-supporter, a non-resident supporter, or a non-resident non-supporter. From this study of the maps they produced he reached the conclusion that motivation is an important factor in the perception of the environment, which may also depend on the circumstances of involvement, which he suggests may not be the same for the attender at a regular game as for the boy who plays truant on a Wednesday afternoon to see the reserves play. He also concludes that not everybody—of any age—actually reaches the final stage of Piaget's developmental sequence. Nothing in all this work, he thinks, actually refutes Piaget's stages, but it does indicate that they can be reached much earlier or much later than the age-related categories of his interpreters suggest.

There is also evidence that spatial ability can be well ahead of visual and graphic ability. (Trevor Higginbottom, Director of the Schools Council Project on Geography for the Young School Leaver, told me that the work it includes on cognitive mapping—one of the first examples of the techniques of the environmental psychologists reaching the regular curriculum—produces remarkable work from those children considered to be the least able.) It is part of the orthodoxy of child development that girls are abler than boys of the same age in verbal ability, while boys' spatial ability is far greater than that of girls. The work of the cognitive mappers is cited to confirm this. John Brierley, reporting tests which involve proficiency in the manipulation of spatial relationships indicating the greater average ability of boys even from the age of two, argues that it is very likely that visuo-spatial proficiency is under the control of the sex chromosome-hormone machinery and has its roots in the right hemisphere development of the brain. His conclusion is that "for practical purposes at school these findings strengthen the importance of systematic exposure of girls to early experience with toys, sand, water and boxes, which introduce numerical and spatial relationships, for doing so might well improve mathematical ability later on."

Experiments with children in several different cultures, the best known of which are those reported by Erik Erikson, indicate that given a selection of wooden blocks, boys tend to build towers whereas girls build enclosed spaces. Boys produce streets, walls and facades with movement *outside* the buildings. Girls produce furniture arrangements with people in a static situation inside buildings. Erikson, with his psycho-analytical approach, concludes that "the dominance of genital modes over the modalities of spatial organisation reflects a profound difference in the sense of space in the two sexes . . ." The kind of experimental evidence on which this statement is based, can be repeated in any home or any classroom containing boys and girls. Often the results are too true to be good: they tend to be such an over-confirmation of the psychologists' findings that teachers are embarrassed in presenting them. But if we are convinced by the idea of innate differences, we have to admit that they are powerfully reinforced by the different assumptions made in the upbringing of boys and girls, and by the evidence of Bishop and others that spatial ability, as tested, relates strongly to motivation and to familiarity. The significance of this is discussed in a later chapter.

The most ambitious attempt to evaluate the relationship between children and the urban environment was undertaken in the early 1970s in a project directed by Kevin Lynch for UNESCO. This was concerned with children of eleven to fourteen years in the city of Salta in Argentina (where their findings have been mentioned in Chapter One); in the western suburbs of Melbourne, Australia; in Toluca, a provincial capital in Mexico and in Ecatepec, a largely dweller-built settlement on the northern fringe of Mexico City; in two contrasted neighbourhoods in Warsaw, and two similarly contrasted neighbourhoods of another Polish city, Cracow.

Some interesting contrasts emerged from the maps of their neighbourhood and city that the children produced. In the case of the Polish housing projects, the focus of the maps was on the outdoor play spaces used by the children between "the blank ranges of apartments", and adult features were largely ignored. Their maps of the whole city showed islands of activity linked by "bridges" of public transport, but the central city children of the two cities in Poland, "produced much more systematic and accurate maps, based on rather elaborate street networks, and full of shops, institutions, places of entertainment, and historical memorials. They are more diverse in the area they cover and the elements they contain." The

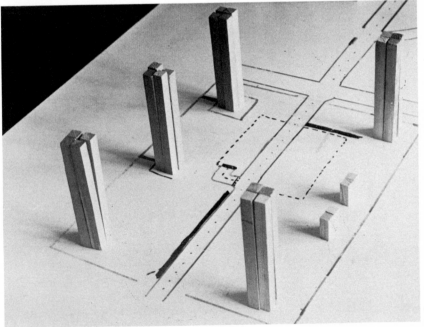

investigators in Poland describe the "hunger" for activity and stimulus of the children in the outlying estates, while the children of the central districts "who are quite aware of their advantageous access to city excitements are hungry for outdoor space."

In the case of the Colonia San Augustin at Ecatepec, Mexico, "one group (mostly boys) represent the environment as a map of streets and blocks, schematic and lacking sensuous detail, a key to the location of activities, a down-to-earth image of a highly repetitive environment. The other group (mostly girls) make pictorial representations, showing shops, parks and green areas, full of details embellished with textures, ornaments and splashes of colour."

What is very clear from the UNESCO study of these older children is that their picture of the city and their own part of it is conditioned by the esteem in which it is held by their elders. The Melbourne children for example were certainly the most affluent in this international sample, they were "tall, well dressed, almost mature, apparently full of vitality" but they see themselves as the bottom of society, and "if these Australians have hopes for themselves or their children, it is to be somebody else, and to get away." The Argentine children, on the other hand, are quite obviously conscious of being members of a community with "features which make it amenable to change at their scale of possibility." Only three of the interviewed children there thought they would leave the area in the future. Only three of the Melbourne children thought they would remain.

Alone in the UNESCO survey, the children of Ecatepec, the dweller-built settlement outside Mexico City "consistently named their school as a favourite place, and gave it a loving emphasis on their maps." The suggestions they made to the interviewers "reflect a genuine concern for their families, as well as their own future, and an empathy for fellow residents of the colonia." They were the poorest children in the survey, and to the adult researchers their environment was harsh, bleak and monotonous, and it is obvious from their report that they were puzzled by the unique affection for their school displayed in the maps, drawings and interviews of the children of Ecatepec. "This must be a tribute to the public education in that place," they surmise. No such tribute would be offered by the children of an equivalently poor district in Detroit, Boston, London or Manchester, though it might have been made there many years ago.

To know better how the child sees the city, it would have helped if the UNESCO project had contained some similar investigations in several of the exploding cities of Asia and Africa. I think it likely that this would have underlined the comparison between the social environment in a mature city like Melbourne and in the emergent urban areas like Ecatepec. The parents of the children of the Colonia San Augustin are poor rural migrants who have made the leap from rural hopelessness into the inner city slums, the *vecindades*, of Mexico City. Once they had got used to the urban system, they moved to a squatter settlement on the fringe of the city. In many such Latin-American settlements the parents have built their own school and hired their own teachers. For their children life is visibly improving, "there is less dust now, houses that used to be shanties are fully constructed, one does not have to go outside the colonia for certain services. . . ." The parents in the working-class outskirts of western Melbourne, with an infinitely higher standard of living, are conscious that they haven't quite made it. The stigmatisation of the district where they live communicates itself to the children. In this place where "football clubs and schools have two-metre-high wire mesh fence around the periphery topped with barbed wire" and where parks are "flat featureless tracts of haphazardly grassed unused land" the local authorities believe that "space for organised team sport is what is most urgently needed, despite the lack of use of what already exists."

It is hard, no doubt, for those who have devoted themselves to campaigning for physical space for the young in the city, a claim which is certainly self-justifying, to accustom themselves to the idea that, very early in life, another, more urgent and more difficultly-met demand arises, for *social* space; the demand of the city's children to be a part of the city's life.

4

Antiquarians, Explorers, Neophiliacs

" 'The kids don't notice.' What does a bit of dirt matter to children? Or a broken floorboard, damp in the walls? Or sharing a bed with their brothers and sisters? Or nowhere to wash? Children never look so happy as when they're in some kind of mess. And aren't children adaptable? Would it bother a child moving to another house or flat? Time and again, people will tell you how resilient children are. 'The kids don't notice'. They're great survivors. But the kids *do* notice.. . .."

MICHAEL LOCKE and MOIRA CONSTABLE

One of our myths about urbanisation is the idea that rural poverty is more tolerable than poverty in the city. If it were true the rural poor all over the world would not be flocking to the cities. "The touching picture of country people leaving neat and pretty thatched cottages for the sins and slums of the city is easily dispelled by a closer look at the pretty cottages" remarks Enid Gauldie, examining the history of working class housing in Britain and concluding that our rural slums were of a horror unsurpassed by the rookeries of London. The rural hovels of our ancestors were for sleeping in and little else. Boswell, in the Hebrides, noted that "the good people here had no notion that a man could have any occasion but for a mere sleeping place." Life was lived outside. For exactly the same reason the urban poor lived in the street. Many years ago the Newcastle writer Jack Common pointed out, as of course Mayhew had done in the last century that it was the use of the street that made working class life tolerable:

"... you can usually deduce your fellow-Briton's class status from the way he regards the street. To some it is merely a communication between one spot and another, a channel or runway to guide your feet or your wheels when you are going places. To others it's where you live. The average working-class house is a small and inconvenient place. Nobody wants to put up with the noise of children in it more than they have to—out they go, then, into the street. Similarly, a man can't do any casual entertaining there, not so as to suit him. If his pals call, they all go out together—down the street, that is, to the boozer. Even the women find it a pleasanter change if they want company to go and stand on the doorstep. Add these up and you get a most characteristic working-class scene: crowds of kids flying here and there across the road; boys and youths by the shop-windows and the corner-ends; men strolling the pavements or sitting shirt-sleeved by the doors; and the women in their aprons taking a breather in a bit of gossip 'next-door'. These people live in the street."

It is a pattern of street-use which the architecture of municipal re-housing has done its best to destroy, but for children it still exists, and not only for poor children. An extensive and long-term study of urban childhood by Drs John and Elizabeth Newson of the Child Development Research Unit at Nottingham University, notes that it is not only working-class children for whom the street is a vital resource, "a majority of middle-class children, almost all of whom have gardens, choose and are allowed to play in the street some of the time." They conclude, however, that "at the lower end of the class scale parents expect the child to pursue the busy and active part of his life *outside* the home, and then come in to relax; whereas at the upper end he is expected to 'let off steam' physically for relaxation outside, and then come in and get on with something more serious and creative."

The Newson study is intended to follow a representative sample of children in a typical British city from infancy to late adolescence and apart from its value as an anatomy of the process of child-rearing it provides innumerable vignettes of the way in which this is affected by the physical influence of the city home. The three volumes issued so far give a picture of 700 Nottingham children through interviews with their mothers, at the ages of one, four and seven. The families involved are divided, according to parental occupation, into five social classes, from "professional" to "unskilled", and into three housing types, "central area", "council estate", and "suburban". Not surprisingly in class I and II 80 per cent of the families of four year olds were found in the suburbs and six per cent in the central area, while in class V (unskilled) only 17 per cent were in suburban housing, while 45 per cent were in the central area. Looking at their material from the point of view of the environmental psychologist, Charles Mercer has extracted a series of seven propositions from the data on working-class four year olds, none of which applies to the middle class four year olds:

(1) The working-class child lives in a more crowded environment—more siblings and less space.
(2) The play of the working-class child must perforce take place in the street or other communal areas and *not* on the home territory.
(3) The working-class child is therefore more likely to come into contact with all sorts and a greater number of children.
(4) The working-class child's choice of friends is not guided by the parents, as all children play on communal areas.
(5) For the same reason the play of the working-class child is not generally supervised by adults.
(6) The working-class parent is reluctant to interfere in children's play, because this may lead to conflict with other parents who are also neighbours.
(7) Conflict with neighbours is less easily tolerated in the working-class environment because of the greater propinquity of families and the fact that working-class parents could not help but come into contact with the offended neighbours and meanwhile the children would have made it up anyway.

By the time the Newson children had reached seven they had made the transition from being relatively homebound to being school-children spending much of the day in an environment away from home. Seven-year-olds, the Newsons remark, "have many interests which tempt them to the next street and beyond, with the adventurousness to follow such temptations. The fact that they go to and from school each day familiarises them with short journeys, and widens the circle of children they know by sight, who in turn act as lures away from their home territory." The question they asked the 700 mothers concerning the children's use of the external environment, was the very simple one "Would you call him an indoor child or an outdoor child?" The answers revealed both class and sex differences: "Sixty per cent of children overall are described as outdoor children, but this rises to 71 per cent in class V and drops to 44 per cent in class I and II . . . Overall, more boys than girls are said to be outdoor (67 per cent against 52 per cent)" They add that "a further class weighting is given by the material circumstances of the family, which we noted as being relevant to how far the child was likely to be physically 'off out' among the poor group, or retained within the family circle. Descending the social scale, the accommodation dwindles while the family size increases, so that the mother is less able to tolerate children playing indoors and it quite simply becomes necessary to regard the street as overspill space. Furthermore, as one moves up the scale, the child is much more likely to have some place in the house which belongs to him, where he can keep his own things; this immediately means that indoor play is both more positively encouraged and more inherently attractive for the child further up the class scale."

It is when you think about the implications of the Newson findings that you begin to understand the impact of housing policy upon the poor who in the past have 'won space' from the dominant culture in the sense outlined in Chapter One, but who have systematically been deprived of control over their living space, even though space standards and sanitary standards are higher in the new housing *project* (US) or *scheme* (UK). The relatively affluent, with the freedom of choice that money can buy, select the suburban street, where their children can be, at will, indoor or outdoor kids. The poor of the inner city, who over generations, have evolved a code of practice which seeks to make life tolerable for themselves or their offspring, have been the victims of the decisions of others whose values do not include a consideration of the psychic damage they inflict. When the rich live in the city, they have that space that enables their children to choose their personal balance between indoors and outdoors, and they have the network of contacts, the chequebooks and the know-how with which to enrich the environmental experience of their children.

In Albert Street, Canton, Cardiff, I knocked at the door of one of the few houses which still had curtains in the windows—one which still had windows in fact, and met Mr and Mrs Simms and their 13-year-old son, the last inhabitants. "I was born in this street" Mr Simms said. "We all were. My grand-parents lived here, and my parents were born here too. We children were in and out of each other's houses, and you can't imagine the fun we had, looking at the place now." In his back yard, beyond the dahlias and rhubarb, he opened a hutch and brought out his ferret, draping the creature round his neck and re-assuring me, "She won't bite you while I'm here. When I was a kid, it wasn't only ferrets. We had rabbits and chickens. It was like living in the country."

Skiffle in the Street,
Salford, Lancashire, 1958

He reminisced about the former occupants of the deserted houses all around. This one, whose pigeon house with its fretted decoration still stood, that one whose pear trees cropped so heavily and would again this year, with no-one left to eat them ("Many's the pear I nicked from that tree when I was a boy"); that other one who had always organised street parties with tables, benches and bunting all down the street on occasions of national rejoicing. "We were like one big family" he said, but now of course those neighbours were scattered to the winds in the new estates outside the city.

His own children had grown up in dereliction and decay, and in his view the Corporation had waged a war of attrition against a whole neighbourhood, steadily depriving it of its amenities. Pubs and chip shops had closed, street lights were not maintained, the pavement was unsafe. Vandals and petty thieves were looting the adjoining houses and had frequently broken into his. His neighbours used to be his childhood friends. Now the only neighbours were rats, winos, vagrants and lead thieves. "And can you tell me one single way in which my boy's life will be better out on the estate than it would have been here?"

The same story is told in every British city. The traditional culture of the street is recalled in innumerable recollections from an earlier generation than that of Mr Simms. As history they have to be treated with caution. Robert Roberts remarks that when he talked during the 'thirties and 'forties with people who were already mature by 1914, "they criticised the then fairly recent past, faculties alert, with what seemed like objectivity." But by the 'sixties, "myths had developed, prejudices about the present had set hard; these same critics, in ripe old age, now saw the Edwardian era through a golden haze." Nevertheless, one factual theme emerged, as much from the recordings made by school children interviewing old inhabitants about the past of their district, as from innumerable published autobiographies. This was the freedom to move. Our views on the historical inevitability or political desirability of the decline of the private landlord in Britain have blinded us to an aspect of the housing situation of our grandparents, which profoundly affected the environmental experiences of children. When private renting was the norm, there was a considerable freedom of choice in the housing market, even for very poor families, and this resulted in a degree of dweller satisfaction which is much rarer when a multiplicity of landlords has given way to the local authority.

"In the thirties", recalls Elizabeth Ring, "there was no such thing as a housing shortage. For from five shillings to five pounds a week there were rooms for all." Jack Common says of his childhood in Newcastle, "At that time, families were always moving. There were houses to let everywhere." Arthur Newton says of Hackney in East London, "To change houses was easy then." Mollie Weir from Glasgow describes with relish the many moves of her childhood and her mother's fondness for "flitting", which in her family's context did not imply a "moonlight flit". "How different everything looked," she says, "even if we'd only moved to the next close, which my mother did twice, for we knew our houses so intimately that the slightest variation in a lobby or a window-frame, or the size of a fireplace, was of enormous significance. Everybody loved a flitting . . ."

From a totally different background, the East End of London, A. S. Jasper in *A Hoxton Childhood* describes a whole series of childhood environments, starting in August 1910 when "We were living at number three Clinger Street, Hoxton, in a hovel on the ground floor. It comprised two rooms with a kitchen, with an outside lavatory, which also served the family upstairs." By p. 15 "It was agreed that Mother would try to find a bigger house. In those days it was easy; one had only to go to an agent, pay the first week's rent and move in. On more than one occasion my father came home late, drunk as usual, and was told by the next-door neighbour we 'didn't live there any more'. We had owed so much rent but the fact was that we had to have a larger house. My mother duly found and inspected a house in Salisbury Street, New North Road. It wasn't a bad area and I always remember it was the nicest house we ever had." And he describes with gusto how they set about redecorating it: "Wallpaper was about threepence a roll; a ball of whitening and boiled size made whitewash for the ceilings." But bad times came again, and on p. 39 "Our new abode was Ebenezer Buildings, Rotherfield Street. What a dump it was after the nice little house we had just left!" Soon his mother and sister went house-hunting again and decided on a house in Loanda Street, by the side of the Regents Canal near the bridge in Kingsland Road. But a little later "Everything was getting too much for Mum and she reckoned the house had a curse on it. The only way out was to move again. This time she found a house in Scawfell Street. This wasn't far from Loanda Street. It certainly looked a road with some life in it, which was what we were used to. Loanda Street was a drab place of flat-fronted houses where everyone closed their doors. There wasn't the friendliness." By p. 88 "We were now in 1917 and we were on the move again. Why, I cannot remember. This time we moved to Shepherdess Walk, off City Road. It was a very large house let off in flats. We had a ground floor and a basement flat consisting of five large rooms and a scullery . . ." Not many pages later, in September 1918 "We now lived in a very nice place in the main road. The rooms were large and there was always something going on." But in the following year, the man who owned the dairy downstairs "shocked us by saying he was going to sell the dairy and we would have to quit the flat. He told us he had a house at Walthamstow we could rent and he would pay all the expenses if we would move. In 1919 Walthamstow to us was like moving to the country. The whole family discussed the matter and it was agreed they would go and see the place . . ." So a couple of pages later they moved. "It was a small house just off the High Street. The rent was eight shillings a week. I was beginning to like our new surroundings. For a penny you could get to Epping Forest, and this was all so different to the slums of Hoxton and Bethnal Green. My friend Dave would come some weekends and we had some good times together in the forest."

Thus there were eight moves in Mr Jasper's childhood between the ages of four and fourteen. The moves were intimately related to shifts and changes in the family's minimal income and to the family size—whether his sister's husband was living with them or not, and so on. And the final move had brought the family right out of the inner city and into the ampler opportunities provided by the leafy suburbs. In both these instances there glows through the pages what teachers are trained to call an "affective relationship" between the family and its housing. This was not the result of staying in one house or street for a lifetime as was the case with Mr Simms (for both families I have taken as examples seem to have been quite extravagantly fond of moving); it was the result of having, even among the very poor, some degree of consumer choice. Changes in family circumstances as well as aesthetic preferences were reflected in a move which was, for the children ar least, a family adventure. Neither were they the families of skilled artisans. Miss Weir's father died when she was a baby and Mr Jasper's father was a drunken casual labourer. Both were effectively one-parent families.

Today, when the population of Glasgow or of Inner London is dramatically lower than it was in their childhood, the element of freedom of choice in housing that their families had, has totally disappeared. They would either be stuck in one particular bit of run-down accommodation in the fast-dwindling private landlord sector, or if they were lucky they would be equally immobile in the flat the council had provided (as suitable for unsatisfactory tenants) waiting years for a transfer, or if they were unlucky, they would be parked, as happens in some London boroughs, in low-grade "bed-and-breakfast" hotels which have to be vacated during the daytime, so that in the school holidays for example, the children would be wandering, rather than exploring, the streets from morning to night. Incredibly, some children alleged to be in the "care" of the local authority *in loco parentis*, are dumped in overnight hotels in this way, through lack of anywhere else to put them.

Perhaps children and adults too, might be divided between the *antiquarians*, who cherish an environment precisely because of its associations with continuity and familiarity, like Mr Simms, *explorers* like Miss Weir and Mr Jasper, who though they are very far from the migratory elite of the professional classes, positively enjoy and savour the change from one home to another in a known habitat, and the *neophiliacs* for whom the past smelt of decay and deprivation, while the new present promises hope and a more expansive life. Just as there is a consolation in being the most recent of many generations to occupy a building, so there is a promise in being the first to experience its newness, and this promise is strengthened and confirmed when the new environment is ampler and more spacious than the old. A Post Office worker who moved from Islington in inner London (where his family of four lived insecurely in two rooms with shared facilities) to the expanding town of Swindon, told me of the difference in his children's lives that a self-contained house with a garden had made. "They used to be frightened to use the toilet on the landing" he said, "because they never knew what they would find there. It wasn't that people were dirty, it was just that so many people went there." His remark illustrated the medical conclusion that constipation is a working class disease, environmental in its origins.

Space, and the luxury of a room of one's own, are the positive advantages of the new or rebuilt environment, beautifully caught by Hazel Robbins, aged seven, who moved from inner to outer Birmingham:

"I like my house I am liveing in now better than my old house because it is nicer and I have three bedrooms and in my garden I have lots of flowers and I have a livingroom and a kitchen has well and I have a bathroom and a toilet to and I like it very much to and in my liveingroom I have a fire place and a book case to and a stereo recordplayer and two tables to and in my kitchen I have a gas stove and a fridge and some cubs to and in my bathroom I have a bath and a sink has well and I like my house because it is big and the bigis room are the liveing room and the kitchen and they are both and my curtains and the small bedroom is my bedroom."

Hazel's pleasure in the new environment leaps out of the page, and for her all the new domestic equipment (the "cubs" she refers to must be the ice cubes in the new refrigerator) is part of the new life-style that accompanies the move to the ampler life of the suburb. It is doubtful whether in later life she will recollect with fond nostalgia the days before the move. It is tempting to read some significance in her use of 'I' and 'my', where many English children would refer to 'us' and 'our' in these circumstances. (Many an only child will refer to 'our mum' or 'our dad', thinking of the family as a unit rather than of the individual's possessiveness.) Consequently Hazel is unable to give any special significance to her own curtains and her own bedroom. She is just at the age when, according to the environmental psychologists, having a room of one's own becomes important, a need which accelerates as time goes by.

Hazel is a neophiliac. She rejoices in the new. When the UNESCO investigators, A. M. Battro and E. J. Ellis walked around the Argentine city of Salta with Raul (12) and Patricia (13) the children's comments on what to antiquarian eyes was the most picturesque part of the city, expressed a clear preference for newness, neatness and tidiness. "A beautiful street must be a street with wide sidewalks, well-painted facades, clean and with modern houses. Everything that looks untidy, such as wires, rickety doors, worn steps, deteriorating signs, old adobe houses, must be eliminated." This does not mean, the observers comment, "that the child does not know the aesthetic value of the ancient convent, he would even 'like to live there' if it were a private house, but what most attracts his attention is the recent coat of paint that distinguishes it from other antique houses semi-abandoned or converted into cheap grocery stores."

For the explorer, apart from the excitement of change and the new experience it brings, the personal satisfactions to be won from an environment include the extent to which it can be used and manipulated, and the extent to which it contains useable rubbish, the detritus of packing-cases, crates, bits of rope and old timber, off-cuts and old wheels, that used to accummulate when there was a shop on every corner and a small factory or workshop down the bottom of the alley. In Bute Town, Cardiff—another district of the same city where Mr Simms and his son championed the values of the traditional culture, which were being eliminated before their eyes by the city authorities—a devoted primary school teacher had evolved a programme of local studies to ensure that her class, equipped with cameras, were thoroughly familiar with their neighbourhood. Her ten-year-olds took the visiting specialist in environmental education around the locality with their Instamatics clicking. They stopped at the community centre, two mosques and the geriatric hospital (housed in the old Seaman's Mission from the days when Cardiff was a living port) snapping away where the visitor would have been abashed to intrude.

"This is the factory where my Mam works." Click went the camera as Mam emerged to greet them. "Look, there's my Dad" and click went the camera again as the child's father came round the corner in his lorry. The educator was delighted. Wasn't this an area where the working lives of the parents were accessible to the educative lives of the children, and wasn't this something unique and precious in modern urban life? He was quite right. It is rare for the mother to be able to leave her workbench when summoned to greet her child and her classmates, and it is rare for the father, high up in his cab, to be delighted by the appearance of his own child in the group standing on the corner. But in this instance the educator's contact with the environment as experienced by the children went further. Because once the class had taken him round their route of the recorded environment they said goodbye. "But where are you going now?" he asked. "Where we always go," they replied. "Can't I come too?"

So, more gratified than shy, they took him into their unofficial play-spaces. There was an almost mischievous glee among the children as they took him into the scarey area of town, through alleys, ginnels and tunnels into the district which had no longer an official existence. The council had here spent one-and-a-half day's labour by three men in bricking up the doors and windows of each of the abandoned houses, but they still sustained a population, the inebriates, the junkies and some bewildered homeless people, who along with the bloated dead domestic animals, provided the setting for the use the children made of these abandoned streets. It was here and here alone, that they were able to *use* the environment in a kind of caricature of the way an earlier generation had used their streets. Here, and here alone they were able to indulge their appetite for either building or destroying. Their human encounters in this sector of the city were those which the educator would have most wished to spare them. But just because the adult users of this no-man's-land were unofficial inhabitants too, they were not a threat to the children's determined use of the area as an adventure playground, a place where anything might be discovered, decomposed furniture and old gas ovens, timber for bonfires and bricks for improvised buildings. It is here that tiles and slates can be ripped off roofs, panels hammered out of old doors, bushes ripped out of old backyards. For the interloping educator, apart from its present squalor, the area was full of the pathetic mementoes of human occupation, the remaining hints that generations had been born, lived and died here. For the children it was a place of eerie encounters, forbidden games, and for the acting out of destructive passions.

5
Privacy and Isolation

"At some stages parents are aware that their children would dearly like a room of their own. At yet other ages children may appear to create separate places for themselves and their friends, places into which the intrusion of an adult is a profanity. To my knowledge, no researcher has attempted to trace the development from the den made with a cardboard box under the kitchen table by the three year old, to the den made at the bottom of the garden out of branches by the nine year old, to the 'private' room of the teenager, to the study, library or den of the adult. There are clearly similarities in these different uses of space but differences in the way in which these places take on their form and meaning at the different stages in development."   DAVID CANTER

The quest for personal privacy and the sense of social isolation are not opposites in the experience of the urban child. The same child who is most deprived of a private and personal place is likely to be the child who is most isolated socially. Inner city teachers, even very experienced ones, are so accustomed to mobility, freedom of access to transport and social competence in getting around, that they are continually surprised that so many of the children they teach lead lives confined to a few streets or blocks. A survey conducted for the Community Relations Commission found that just under half of the children under five in the Handsworth district of Birmingham *never* went out to play. "They have no access, either exclusive or shared, to play spaces at the front or back of the house and their parents feared for their safety if they let them out."

Describing an infants' school in Islington in North London, Sue Cameron remarks that "The experience of many of these children during the first five years of their lives has been so limited that they come to school like so many blank pages. Near the school is a park and a busy Underground station, but many of the children have never been inside the park and some of them don't know what a tube train looks like. Asked what they did at the week-end, they usually say they just stayed at home." Even when we assume that they *must* have been around by the time they reach thirteen or fourteen, we find that such children's world is fantastically restricted. Teachers in a school on a housing estate in Bristol told me of the shock with which they learned that some of their teen-age pupils had never been to the centre of the city. Teachers in the London borough of Brent told me of 13 and 14 year olds who had never seen the Thames; teachers in the boroughs of Lambeth and Southwark, in schools a few hundred yards from the River told me of pupils who had never crossed it.

It is difficult to convey the psychological isolation of the deprived urban child, though readers of George Dennison's account of the First Street School, may gather something of its implication, and of the paradox that many city children are just not hooked onto those "educational networks of fantastic riches and variety" that the city through its very existence provides. The hero of Vittorio de Seta's *Diary of a School Teacher* found that his pupils in a working-class suburb of Rome "did not feel that they belonged to the big city" and when he took the class to explore the ancient heart of the city, they were "like tourists in their own town." Even the adolescents of Kevin Lynch's UNESCO study, were, in his view, the victims of "experimental starvation". He found that distance is not the essential restriction on the movement of young adolescents away from their local areas. More important is the mixture of parental control, personal fear

and a lack of knowledge of how to get about, as well as the availability and cost of public transport. "It is thus not surprising that many of the children speak constantly of boredom. There seems to be little to do or see that is new."

Innumerable studies of delinquent or potentially delinquent children in the world's cities stress their insecurity and isolation. Aryeh Leissner, with experience of both New York and Tel Aviv, remarks that "street club workers were constantly aware of the feelings of isolation which pervaded the atmosphere." He says of the latter city that "the young, as well as the adults of these poor communities identify themselves as inhabitants of their own immediate neighbourhoods. But they say that they are 'going to Tel Aviv', when they leave their own areas to attend to some business in other parts of the city, sometimes only a few minutes' walk or a short bus ride away. They distinguish between shops, cinemas, cafes, etc., in their own neighbourhood and 'in Tel Aviv'. Although their own communities are geographically and administratively integral parts of the City of Tel Aviv, the people who live in these communities do not seem to feel as if they are."

In Chicago, J. F. Short and F. L. Strodtbeck noted that "the range of gang boys' physical movements is severely restricted" not only for fear of other gangs, but also because of a "more general lack of social assurance." James Patrick found the same "social disability" in the Glasgow boys he observed.

Much of a child's time is spent waiting, for mother or father, or for something to happen

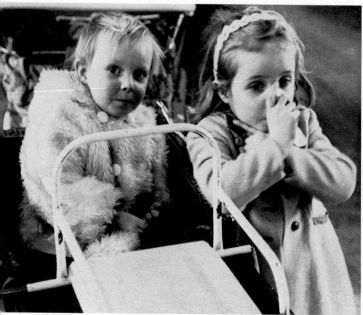

For the black city boys interviewed by Florence Ladd, "home" was a landscape of interiors rather than of streets, and Lee Rainwater has evolved a "house-as-haven" theory of home, based on fear of the outside. All the same, for Claude Brown, in *Manchild in the Promised Land*, "I always thought of Harlem as home, but I never thought of Harlem as being in the house. To me, home was the streets." But only the streets of a narrowly-defined district. How far did he stray from home?

Rangoon

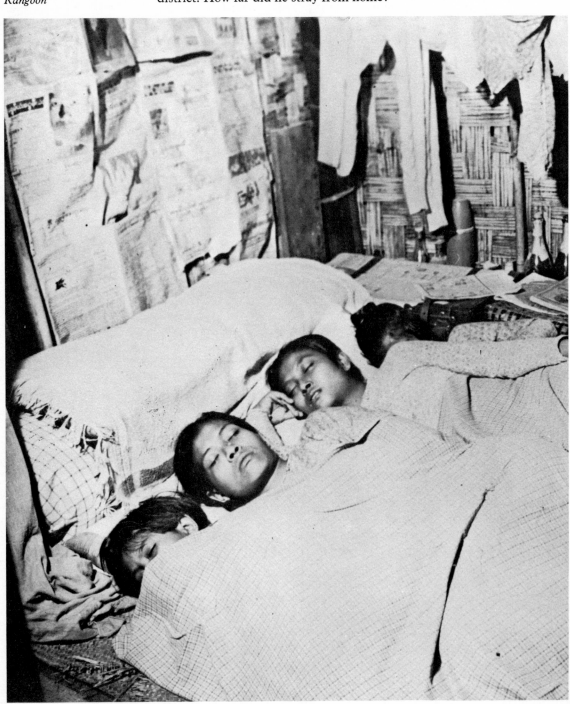

The lack of social assurance certainly does amount to a social disability for many city children. Some children steal, not because they have no access to the purchase money, but because they find it a less arduous transaction than the verbal encounter with the seller. They move like strangers through their own city, so that one is forced to admire those cheerful rogues who know every inch of it backwards and get involved in much more serious and sophisticated offences, just because they have absorbed the structure and functions of the city.

The poor child, who is usually the most isolated from the life of the city *as a city*, is also, paradoxically, the child who is denied the solace of solitude. He is seldom alone; he is the child who is least likely to have a bedroom or a bed to himself. In many of the cities of the world, the very concept of privacy for the child is meaningless. What sense does it make in Hong Kong or Manila to speak of the child's right to privacy? We may suggest that people don't miss what they have never experienced, and there is evidence that different cultures have different concepts of personal space, though even in the poorest of cities, one of the things that wealth buys is privacy. Gaston Bachelard pitied those children, who lacking a room of their own to go and cry in, had to sulk in the corner of the living room, though the boys interviewed by Florence Ladd, because their bedrooms were shared, mentioned the living room or sitting room as a place where one might be alone.

What does privacy actually mean to the child? Maxine Wolfe and Robert Laufer of the City University of New York have been investigating the concept of privacy in childhood and adolescence, by questioning children aged between five and 17. Not surprisingly, they found that the idea became more complex with age, but they found four major meanings at all ages. The first was that of being alone and uninterrupted, or of being able to be alone. The second was that of controlling access to information—being able to have secrets. Once the child goes to school, he is able to reveal some things to one set of adults, the parents, and other things to others, the teachers, and to differentiate between siblings and other children in the disclosure and withholding of information. The third meaning was that of "no one bothering me", and the fourth was that of controlling access to spaces. Three of these four meanings were given more frequently by those children who had their own rooms—being alone, no-one bothering me, and controlling access to spaces ("no one being able to go into my room; no one can come in unless I want them to"). Keeping secrets, and not telling what you are thinking, were available to all groups, though this aspect of privacy, the control of information, is obviously important to those children who were not able to secure it physically. The researchers point out that "a child who has never had a room of his own may not define privacy as a physical separation from others but may develop techniques of psychological withdrawal. A child in a small town, once aware that control of personal history is impossible, may not see this as a relevant aspect of privacy."

The comparison with the situation of the small town child raises the question of the relative isolation and privacy of children, all along the rural-urban continuum. We assume that the country child is more isolated, but he is usually part of a far more homogeneous community, just as he was in the "village in the city" when urban communities were more stable. We assume that he had more privacy, but as Maxine Wolfe and Robert Laufer suggest,

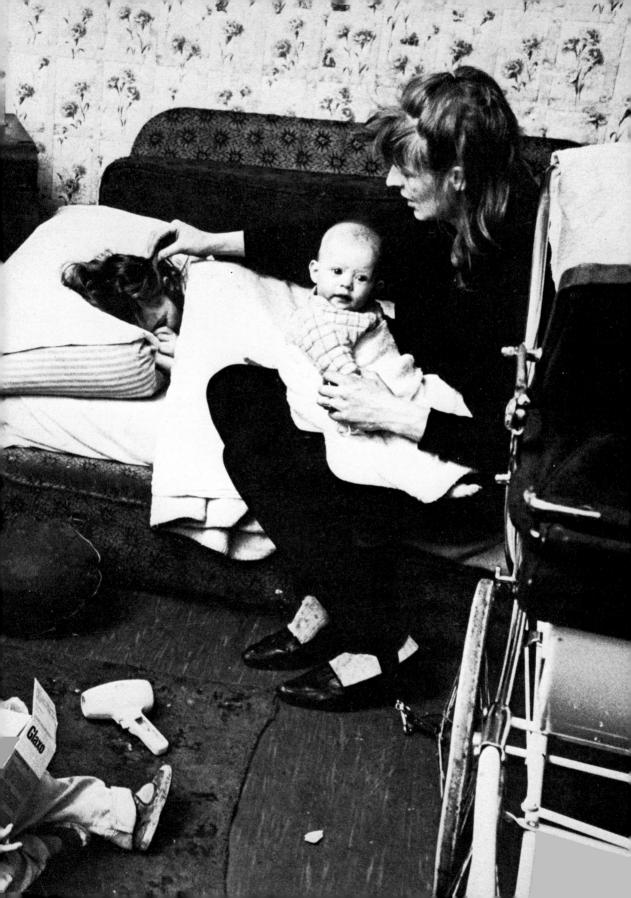

"if city children walk around the corner or a few streets away from home there is a high probability they will not be known. The child living in a small town may have to go further (i.e. into the woods) to achieve the same type of privacy."

The isolated child in the city is unfamiliar with the public transport system, with the use of the telephone, with the public library service, with eliciting information from strangers, with the norms of behaviour in cafes and restaurants, with planning his activities in advance, with articulating or responding to requests outside the immediate family circle. The reader might well ask whether such a child really exists, and the answer from any inner city teacher would be that children as isolated as this from the mainstream of urban life, exist in very large numbers. Various attempts are made to provide an explanation for their isolation: the idea of a "culture of poverty", the idea of a "cycle of deprivation", and the idea of a "restricted language code." Each of these explanations has its passionate opponents, who see them as modern versions of the Victorian equation of poverty with sin, the idea that the poverty of the poor is their own fault, or as an assumption of the superiority of middle class values.

But if we simply want to know why so large a proportion of inner city children grow up unable to manipulate their environment in the way that is taken for granted in the middle class home, we are bound to look for explanations in the social isolation of the home of the modern inner city child, soberly analysed by Martin Deutsch in these terms: "Visually, the urban slum and its overcrowded apartments offer the child a minimal range of stimuli. There are usually few if any pictures on the wall, and the objects in the household, be they toys, furniture, or utensils, tend to be sparse, repetitive, and lacking in form and colour variations. The sparsity of objects and lack of diversity of home artifacts which are available and meaningful to the child, in addition to the unavailability of individualised training, gives the child few opportunities to manipulate and organise the visual properties of his environment and thus perceptually to organise and discriminate the nuances of that environment . . . It is true, as has been pointed out frequently, that the pioneer child didn't have many playthings either. But he had a more active responsibility towards the environment and a great variety of growing plants and other natural resources as well as a stable family that assumed a primary role for the education and training of the child."

The tragedy of the isolated city child, and the dilemma of all our efforts to alleviate his deprivation were most poignantly expressed by John and Elizabeth Newson as they reached the third stage of their long-term study of child-rearing in an English city. They remarked that they are continually asked to specify how children should be brought up, while they have never claimed to be capable of giving such advice. They have, however, reached a conclusion: "Parents at the upper end of the social scale are more inclined *on principle* to use democratically based, highly verbal means of control, and this kind of discipline is likely to produce personalities who can both identify successfully with the system and use it to their own ends later on. At the bottom end of the scale, in the unskilled group, parents choose *on principle* to use a highly authoritarian, mainly non-verbal means of control, in which words are used more to threaten and bamboozle the child into obedience than to make him understand the rationale behind social behaviour: and this seems likely to result in a personality who can neither identify with nor beat the system. In short, privileged parents, by using the methods that they prefer, produce children who expect as of right to be privileged and who are very well equipped to realise these expectations; while deprived parents, also by *using the methods that they prefer*, will probably produce children who expect nothing and are not equipped to do anything about it. Thus the child born into the lowest social bracket has everything stacked against him *including his parents' principles of child upbringing*."

This is a bleak conclusion, made all the more pointed by the fact that it is the outcome of many years of investigation and reflection. It underlines the vital compensatory role of nursery education, of efforts to improve the quality of child-minding, and of all those attempts, in and out of the schools, to enlarge the environmental experience and capability of inner city children. But it also leads us to speculate on the difference between the "slums of hope" and the "slums of despair". Oscar Lewis, who invented the concept of the culture of poverty, remarked that in Cuba, or in the squatter cities of Peru, Turkey, Athens, Hong Kong and Brazil, there are millions of poor people, but little sign of the culture of poverty. For the child in such places there are few of the blessings of privacy, but we may speculate that there is little of the crippling isolation that envelopes the poor child in the rich cities.

Street scene in Mombasa

Adrift in the City

"In the meantime I wait for my clients. Let the children—our examiners—come with their hot hands and fragrant round heads, their laced shoes that swing like pendulums, and the smiles they display like medals, their atavistic fears and amazing ability to learn, their obsessions and cajoleries, their relentless selfishness and irresistible weakness, their vulnerable docility and their mirror images of our own depravity. . . .

"Let the runaways come, those caught after nights spent in the woods, in confessionals, cotton bales, sandboxes, or empty pigsties; the boy who is inconsolable because his mother has moved him to the floor to make room in bed for her new lover; the girl who was going to put her half-sister's eye out with a red-hot poker but dropped it at the last minute; the youth whose father chased him around the yard with a knife and almost caught him when a pious widow next door tripped the father up with her broomstick, pulled the boy in, and laughed and cried, and covered him with kisses while he ate and slept. . . .

"Let all the others come, those whom no amount of candy, tears, and toy trains can keep at home, who climb out of the window, toss their school bags into the cellar, hide stolen money under their inner soles, arm themselves with compass, kitchen knife, paper mask, and flashlight, and set out for the border, for new worlds across the sea, but end up in jail. . . ."   GEORGE KONRAD

The city is an irresistible magnet. For the young in small towns and villages where nothing ever happens, it pulls with the promise of variety and excitement. It draws those who chafe against the daily round and common task, those who feel that they can no longer stand Mum and Dad and the constraints they represent, those who know that back there in Deadsville there are going to be no jobs and no prospects, that nothing is *ever* going to happen.

When Theodore Dreiser was a child in Evansville, Indiana, his older brother came back from Chicago and declared, "You never saw such a place! . . . That's the place for a family, where they can do something and get along! Not stuck off in a little hole like this! Why, say, there must be four or five hundred thousand people there! And the shops! And the high buildings!"

Literature, tradition and the conventional wisdom have sanctified the small town, in Europe, America and the rest of the world. The town was small enough to be home: "not just the house but all the town. That is why childhood in the small towns is different from childhood in the city. Everything is home." To Eric Sevareid everything was home, and for Page Smith, even the "bad boys" of the small town were pranksters rather than delinquents, and to his eyes the town "offered the boy an extraordinary degree of freedom within the security. A suburban neighbourhood might rival the town in the secure world that enwombed the growing boy, but it was generally a world of barriers, of barred exits, of nurses and solicitous aunts."

He goes on, "In every recollection of the town we find the symbol of water. In its classic form it is the old swimming hole or the broad Mississippi of Tom Sawyer or Huck Finn. It is the symbol for freedom and also for mystery and perhaps for something deeper. In the swimming hole, clothes and the conventions of the town are discarded. The adult world is rejected in this unique arena which custom has allowed as the American boy's special preserve. The pond, the lake, the river, the swamp, the stream; it is as though here the small-town boy is dimly aware that he touches the source of

Opposite: *Calcutta*

life—dangerous, strangely loving and enfolding."

Dangerous and enfolding, but tolerating rather than loving, the analogy of water fits the city too. *Town Swamps* was the title George Godwin gave to his study of the city in the eighteen-fifties. Immersed in the city, symbol too, of freedom, mystery and the discarding of small-town conventions and assumptions, you sink or swim. The thoughtful youngster in a small town or provincial city, unless he has a foothold on the escalator of higher education, knows exactly the job prospects awaiting him if he stays at home. Armies are recruited this way. For the boy from an Egyptian village the army is an education, an initiation into sophisticated urban habits, an opportunity to acquire saleable skills. But you don't have to go to collapsing traditional societies to see the same phenomena. A young soldier from South Shields said to me, "I reckoned I had only two choices: to become a hippy or to join the army. When I go home, not that I always do go home when I have leave, I meet the boys who were at school with me. The ones who are still there are drawing social security and I just have to buy them drinks. The others have gone to Newcastle or London."

As juvenile unemployment grows, the flight, not only of the young who have left school, but of those who simply abandon school, home and parents, because these seem no longer relevant to their needs, set out for the big glowing city, like moths fluttering towards the light. In the late nineteen-sixties they came from the stricken cities of Northern Ireland, from Scotland and the North East. By the mid-1970s they were coming from a much wider and more dispersed series of home towns. What jobs are open to the school-leavers of Herefordshire, for example, in the summers of the late seventies? In the hinterland of other world cities, the same juvenile migration is far more obvious.

Their elders, from Italy, Spain, Portugal, Greece, Yugoslavia, Turkey, and North Africa, flocked to the industrial conurbations of Western Europe to provide labour for the jobs the natives were no longer willing to undertake themselves. Those who returned, bringing the hard-earned consumer goods of the big city, showed those who remained, as well as their children, what they had missed. The situation was beautifully and bitterly described by Guy de Maupassant in his story of the peasant families who "laboriously tilled the unfruitful soil to rear their children. All of them were brought up with difficulty on soup and potatoes and fresh air." A rich lady seeing the youngest of the Tuvache children grubbing around in the dust, took a fancy to him, plied him with pennies, sweets and kisses, and finally sought the reluctant parents' agreement to his adoption. Indignantly they refused, but she was more successful with the Vallin family next door. Little Jean Vallin was adopted, and years later returned to visit his parents, who proudly displayed him to the priest, the schoolmaster and the mayor. Charlot Tuvache watched sourly from the doorway of his parents' cottage, listening to their tut-tutting about the family next door. "Fools" he said in the darkening porch, "It's parents like you who bring unhappiness to their children."

The rich lady, Mme d'Hubières, is the city beckoning the young, for opportunities, experiences and joys they never thought could be theirs. Everything, from hoary traditions like Dick Whittington to the latest tv advertisements, persuades the present day Tuvache kids that the big city is where the action is and every kind of chance and excitement is to be found.

The reality is totally different of course, but perhaps the surprising thing is not how many young people make the enormous emotional and psychological leap to the big city, and with such inadequate preparation for the experience, but how many resist its magnetic attraction because the ties of family and familiarity, of place and reassuring routine are sufficient to hold them in an environment which has pathetically little to offer. Spend an afternoon on early closing day in an English or Scottish provincial town, and ask what it has to offer the young. A hundred years ago George R. Sims (author of Christmas Day in the Workhouse) met a hopeful pair at Highgate nearing their destination as they saw the city lights, and wrote the ballad that brought him, but not them, fame and fortune:

O cruel lamps of London, if tears your light could drown,
Your victims' eyes would weep them, O lights of London Town!

Its American equivalent, from 1877, had words and music by the Rev. Robert Lowry, pastor of Plainfield, New Jersey. Kenneth Allsop called it the song that impaled America, because it "stated a commonplace truth at precisely the emotional pitch at which it is felt by us all." It was "Where Is My Wand'ring Boy Tonight?" and considering the vast numbers of children in the United States who leave home every year, its success was predictable. "In 1932 a Chicago University research team reported for the Children's Bureau that there were probably 200,000 juvenile hobos then in movement on America's highways and railroads—and then apologetically adjusted their estimate to that appalling sum of half a million . . ." Most of those interviewed by the busy sociologists of the day said they had left home so that there would be one less mouth to feed. More than half came from homes broken by death, separation and divorce. Most of them, Thomas Minehan found, remained within five hundred miles of home doing the circuit from city to city, forced to keep moving by relief policies which were harder on juveniles than on older vagrants. Allsop says that "Where an adult was given six meals and two nights' lodging, the boy tramp got one of each. (A girl tramp was sent to jail.) By forcing the youngsters out of town and onward, the relief men argued, they were forcing them back home. In reality, because few had homes, they were being forced into beggary and theft."

Over forty years later in the mid-1970s there were estimated to be not half a million, but a million runaway children in the United States, with an average age of fourteen. Few were driven by hunger or poverty. Indeed, the motives they reported to solicitous interviewers—usually a mild parental rebuke—seem a trivial reason for finding one's way thousands of miles to the cities of the West Coast just to hang around begging for change from passers-by. The issue only gets highlighted because of some tragedy—the murders of missing girls in Tucson, Arizona in 1966 or of missing boys in Houston, Texas in 1973—when weary policemen explain that in any city there are so many child runaways, many not reported to the police, that it is pointless to investigate each case, when the child is probably somewhere in the San Francisco Bay waiting for, or perhaps ignoring the message on the pinboard: Come home. All is forgiven.

It is easy to homilise about the decline of family solidarity, and to stress that one sixth of the children of the United States are growing up in one-parent families (as are one tenth of the children of Britain) but the American child is also the heir to an immense and exhilarating tradition of Get Up and Go, Go West Young Man, folklore which is reinforced every decade. Apart from the rags to riches myths of the 19th century there has been the romanticised legend of the hobo, the vast migrations of the depression years, *On the Road* in the fifties, the pilgrimage to Haight-Ashbury in the sixties, and a great chorus of railroad songs, folk, rock, country-and-western and pop which cry out that to have beat one's way from Frisco Bay to the rockbound coasts of Maine, is a kind of *wanderjahre* or initiation rite which everybody goes through. Everybody doesn't of course, and perhaps we should wonder, not at the numbers of American children who take off, but at the number who resist the pressure to do so in favour of the daily round, the common task, the ordinary domestic affections and local ties.

If you're not involved, if the parental heartaches are not yours, you wonder, not only at the foolhardiness of the kids in taking off, but at the independence and intrepidness that leaves them as survivors in the city thousands of miles away. The children we never hear about are those who make out on their own, the ones who don't fall into the hands of exploiters, the police or the social agencies. "The Helping Hand Strikes Again!" as John Holt remarks, and wanting to stress the *competence* of children, he tells us about the Italian twins who came to the school in Colorado where he first taught. "When they were very small, at most four or five years old, during World War II, their parents had disappeared—killed or taken prisoner. Somehow these two small boys had managed to live and survive for several years, in a large city, in a country terribly torn and dislocated by war, in the midst of great poverty and privation—*all by themselves*. They had apparently found or made some sort of shelter for themselves in a graveyard and lived by begging and stealing what they needed. Only after several years of this life were they discovered and brought under the wing of the state." The twins were not like those feral children found in the woods. When an American adopted them and brought them home, Holt found them "friendly, lively, curious, enthusiastic" and "quick, strong and well coordinated, by far the best soccer players in the school."

John Holt has to emphasise, for the sake of idiot readers, that he is not in favour of infants living alone in graveyards, but the story is worth considering in the light of those pampered children who can stand everything except being pampered. It was, curiously enough, a pair of twin boys, aged 15 not five, who made headlines in the British press because they succeeded in "evading" help from the social services department of an English city for more than a year. Their borough's assistant director for casework whose office was 200 yards from the boys' home explained "We were not told these boys were living alone and even their teachers did not know. The boys have admitted that they used forged notes to explain why they were not at school. The neighbours were apparently aware of the situation but nobody told us." And the chairman of his committee complained that the boys "deliberately and successfully avoided their situation becoming known to the council." Nobody mentioned the thousands of pounds the pair saved the council by refraining from being taken into care or suggested that they were entitled to some kind of pay-out as a reward.

The drifting child population always was considered a menace to the city.

"Operation Beggar" in Bombay 1976. Three thousand people, including many children, were rounded up by the police. The children were sent by the authorities to train as agricultural labour in the interior of the state of Maharashtra

In 1703 and 1717 vagrant, begging and thieving boys in the streets of London were rounded up and shipped off to Virginia, following the precedent of a century earlier when, Joseph Hawes tells us, "the Virginia Company made arrangements with the Common Council of London to have 100 young vagrants collected from the streets of London and sent to Virginia in 1618. The Virginians were glad to have the children, and in 1619 they persuaded the Common Council to send a hundred more."

Henry Fielding, in his capacity as a London magistrate, remarked of the children who had come before him in the year 1755–6 that "these deserted Boys were Thieves from Necessity, their Sisters are Whores from the same cause; and having the same education with their wretched Brothers, join the Thief to the Prostitute . . . The lives of the Father being often shortened by their Intemperance, a Mother is left with many helpless Children, to be supplied by her Industry: whose resource for maintenance is either the Wash Tub, Green Stack or Barrow. What must become of the Daughters of Such Women, where Poverty and Illiterateness conspire to expose them to every Temptation? And they often become Prostitutes from Necessity before their Passions can have any share in their Guilt . . ."

Mr Hawes carefully follows this theme through the cities of 19th century America. The Common Council of New York City were begged by the Rev. John Stanton in 1812 to "make an attempt to rescue from indolence, vice and danger, the hundreds of vagrant children and youth, who day and night invade our streets," and in 1826 in Boston, the Rev. Joseph Tuckerman complained about the "hordes of young boys who thronged the streets and at times disrupted the operations of the city market" while by 1849, George W. Mansell, chief of police in New York, reported to the Mayor calling attention to "the constantly increasing numbers of vagrant, idle and vicious children" who swarmed in the public places of the city. "Their numbers are almost incredible . . ."

In the same year in London, Albert Smith reported in a graphic vignette not on the attractions of crime and vice for the horde of children adrift in the city, but on the magic of show-biz:

"As you pass through one of those low, densely-populated districts of London you will be struck by the swarms of children everywhere collected. These children are not altogether the result of over-fecundity of the inhabitants. Their parents live huddled up in dirty single rooms, repelling all attempts to improve their condition and, whenever the rain is not actually pouring down in torrents, they turn their children out to find means of amusement and subsistence, in the streets. Picture such a bit of waste ground on a fine afternoon, alive with children. Among the revellers there is a boy, who for the last five minutes has been hanging by his legs to a bit of temporary railing, with his hair sweeping the ground. On quitting it, he goes to a retired corner of the plot, and, gravely putting his head and hands upon the ground, at a short distance from the wall, turns his heels up in the air, until he touches the house with his feet. This accomplished, he whistles a melody, claps his shoeless soles together, goes through certain telegraphic evolutions with his legs, and then calmly resumes his normal position . . . This boy is destined to become an Acrobat—at a more advanced period of his life to perform feats of suppleness and agility in the mud of the streets, the sawdust of the circus, or the turf of a race-course. The young Olympian gradually learns his business. He first of all runs away from home and joins a troup of these agile wanderers to whom he serves an apprenticeship. It is his task, whilst sufficiently light and slender, to be tossed about on the elevated feet of a 'Professor'—to form the top figure of the living column or pyramid, or to have his heels twisted round his neck, and then to be thrown about or worn as a turban by the strongest man of the party. Next, in his hobbledehoy state of transition—when he has grown too big for the business just named, his office is to clear the ring with the large balls at the end of a cord, and to solicit the contributions of the spectators. And finally, he proves his fibres to be as firmly braced as those of his companions and comes out in the ocre cotton tights, the rusty-spangled braces, and the fillet of blackened silver-cord, as the perfect Acrobat."

From Gavarni the acrobat to Edith Piaf, to have started as a street entertainer as a child is part of the folklore of the entertainment industry. Boys still do cartwheels for pennies in the shopping mall of Düsseldorf and dive for the tourist's small change in the harbours of the East. When Andie Clerk was a ten-year-old in Liverpool, he worked for a queue entertainer: "He was what in the world of gymnasts was known as a good catcher. He'd chuck me up, somersault me and catch me, and if the crowd looked promising, I'd have to do a double one. 'I'll give yer an extra fling an' mind yer over twice,' he'd say, and he'd give me a good hiding when the folks had gone in, if I partly missed the second turn and was awkward for him to catch. I became so supple that I'd go down backwards and pick up ha'pennies in my mouth from the street which he invited people to put down. As long as there were ha'pennies coming, there I'd got to stop, picking them up and he'd take them from me. I don't think I liked it, my mouth and lips were dirty and nasty as I tried to get hold of the coins." Travelling theatrical companies and music hall or vaudeville acts, when they needed children to

Opposite: *Pakistani Boy Dancer*

58

complete the act, used to take them off the street. "Fred Carno in his week in town would take some kids straight off the street to complete the reality of his show. And I knew a kid that Harry Tate engaged one Monday morning for the week, nightly for the six-thirty and eight-forty shows and three shows on Saturday, when the kid would be given ten shillings and depart feeling like a millionaire."

A chance in a million certainly: the intoxicating contact with the world of entertainment, the glamour of being part of it in the theatre of the street are and always were, illusions for the children of the street, but they are part of its myth for observers and street kids alike. Hence the Bogota daily *El Tiempo* has a cartoon of Copetin, the archetypal *gamine*, and hence too José Mauro de Vasconcelos' novel *O Meu Pé de Laranja Lima*, about Zezé, "the most ingenious entrepreneur among the shoe-shine boys of the city, superb at conning rich customers, untiring in his efforts to help support his huge, hungry, angry, penniless family, and absolutely unable to curb his infinities of leftover energy and inspiration," which was the best-selling novel in Brazil in the early nineteen-seventies. A hundred years earlier in London and New York there was a similar vogue for books like the novels of Horatio Alger or his English equivalents. In the English genre the city waifs usually died of hunger and cold, but in their innocent virtue were an inspiration to all around them; in the American versions they had that plucky get-up-and-go character which ensured, as it does with Copetin or Zezé, that they will be among the survivors.

To a child's hopeful vision, the myth is true. Mayhew found that the children of the street could not bear the restraints of a more secure existence, and Sarita Kendall writes today of the real life Copetinos of Bogota that "freedom and adventure are the chief attractions of the streets—*gamines* who have described their lives to me emphasise the excitement and the independence above all, dwelling on the misery only when they expected to get a tip," while a present-day Indian social worker, Jailakshmi, says "slum children are free birds, they want to be free all the time." Well over a century ago a 12-year-old street trader answered Mayhew's question with, "No, I wouldn't like to go to school, nor to be in a shop, nor be anybody's servant but my own."

The Victorians respected this fiery independence, except for the convicted child who was to have his spirit crushed in prison or reformatory, because it fitted the ideology of self-help. Thus the Children's Aid Society in New York, which disapproved of indiscriminate alms-giving as perpetuating pauperism, provided a Newsboys' Lodging House for paperboys and shoeshine boys, with evening classes as well as beds and meals, for which the boys were obliged to pay. James McGregor set up a Shoeblack Society in London in 1851 to house the boys who supported themselves by cleaning the shoes of visitors to the Great Exhibition, and in 1868 Dr Barnardo organised a Woodchopping Brigade. Such occupations for vagrant children were more susceptible to literary romanticisation than the more characteristic trades of begging, crossing-sweeping, theft, prostitution, or the variety of "street-finders" listed by Mayhew: the bone-grubbers, rag-gatherers, pure-finders, cigar-end and old wood collectors, dredgermen, mudlarks and sewer-hunters.

The visitor to the cities of Asia, Africa and Latin America, swarming with children, scratches his head and wonders why the scene has a kind of

*Dr Barnardo's
Woodchopping Brigade*

familiarity. Slowly it dawns on him that he has been prepared for the scene by Tom Jones and Oliver Twist. When he doesn't get this feeling he knows he is in a police state, and the children are out there in enormous black townships like Soweto, or that they dare not show themselves for fear of the police. The late Robin Copping went to Ecuador to collect zoological specimens and found that the authorities in Quito and Guayaquil imposed a 9 pm curfew on unaccompanied children. He set up clubs for the street children where, besides meals, they were paid to attend classes, to compensate them for loss of earnings. When Richard Holloway went to Addis Ababa he found that the boys of eight to fourteen who throng the city from the countryside perpetually "live on the defensive", but that "when the possibilities of attending school were presented to them these were eagerly accepted. They tended to identify themselves as scholars and therefore a cut above their former associates still on the street." When Mike Francis of International Children's Aid sought in Dacca to provide facilities for some of the hundreds of children thrown out on the streets as a result of social upheaval and poverty, and living at the mercy of gangs specialising in prostitution and slavery, he found that much of his time was spent in trying to secure the release of untried children from the Central Jail, where their lives were even more perilous than in the streets.

In the cities of the poor world, it is, Richard Holloway remarks, "important to understand that street boys are extremely realistic about the world they live in. However wretched life is on the streets they are keenly aware that the city holds the promise of much more for them than their original feudal farms." But it is also important to understand that the runaway children of the rich world have the same conviction. And in the tightly organised Western city they are *obliged* to disappear into one or other of the urban sub-cultures. Imagine a runaway child from Strathclyde who had the naivety to present himself at a London comprehensive school to ask for an education. In the first place he wouldn't be wanted, and in the second, the initial telephone call made on his behalf would be to the police. The example never actually arises because the first thing the child has discovered is that the system is something to be avoided, or at most exploited, rather than to be used.

A variety of networks are at the disposal of the runaway child who knows the passwords and links. Those who don't know them learn very rapidly, or fall very soon into the hands of the police. One is the world of squatting, which in London has become absolutely essential to the young incomer of any age since the cheap rented room has disappeared. Another is the drug subculture, another is the world of clubs and discos, and the final one is that of prostitution. The migrant juvenile has pathetically few assets to exploit, so it is not surprising that one of them is catering for minority sexual tastes. The prostitution of young girls was one of the unmentionable commonplaces of the Victorian city, made mentionable by the trial of the crusading journalist W. T. Stead in 1885 following his series of articles "The Maiden Tribute of Modern Babylon". Kellow Chesney says that "According to the chaplain of Clerkenwell Jail, the appeal of immaturity had so increased by the early 'eighties that, where it had once been common for child prostitutes to ape the appearance of adults, it was now grown prostitutes who got themselves up to look like children."

The event which brought home to a wide public in Britain truths known to any observer of the city scene, was the Yorkshire television programme "Johnny Go Home". This grew from the experience of two members of the firm's documentary team who, leaving a film cutting room off Wardour Street in the early hours of the morning, stumbled over two young boys asleep on the pavement. Asked what they were doing there in the depth of winter, the boys replied, "We live here". John Willis, who eventually directed the programme, recalled that "Next day, everybody at the documentary department had nagging doubts. Everyone knows about winos, squatters and tramps. But these were healthy young boys, and although only half a dozen sentences had been exchanged with them, what struck us was their acceptance of the essential normality of their existence."

The situation in British cities is that hostels run by official or reputable voluntary bodies are not available for "children", which in the legal sense means anyone under seventeen. It would in fact be illegal to make such provision. The large number of vagrant children, many of them runaways from Scotland and the North-East, have no official existence in London. There was more provision for them in Victorian times than today. Then as now, they arrived at the main line stations which were the hunting ground of the charitable organisations then, and of "Bishop" Roger Gleaves and his assistants a hundred years later.

The first part of Mr Willis's film picked out just a few of the young wanderers from the West End. One was Annie, who began to leave home for a few days at a time, sleeping on the Circle Line, when she was 10. At 12 she became a junkie, later she was raped, and by now she had been through eleven institutions, always running away. Sixteen when the film was made, she got her breakfast from the nuns in Blandford Street and spent her days

"bottling for a busker" (collecting the money for a street musician). Another was Nicholas, a boy prostitute who, after wandering homeless for a week, found it possible to make £80 in a few hours, charging £5 for 'tossing off' his clients. "It was a frightening experience at first but it dawned on me that it was an easy way to get money. It's a boring and lonely life. Others don't like you if you're 'one of them' ". Yet another was Tommy, who ran away from his parents' home in Glasgow. He had been picked up at Euston Station, used for pornographic photographs and thrown out again. Then he was collected by Gleaves and installed in one of his chain of hostels at Lambeth, and sent to register for social security payments giving his age as 17.

The £9 a week was collected by Gleaves for each inmate. They lived in squalor on canned beans and old frozen food. Mr Willis's story would have ended there, but when the television crew went back to the hostel to get more film, they found it full of police investigating the brutal murder of a 19-year-old resident, by three employees of Roger Gleaves. The second part of their film investigated the events surrounding his death, and it ended back in Piccadilly to comment that the children drifting there were getting younger every year, and to watch Johnny, just 11, finding his way to the bright lights.

The viewers were not told Johnny's story, but when John Willis and the executive producer Michael Deakin recounted the background to the film they explained Johnny's mode of survival in the city. "To describe Johnny as a truant would be mild. Quite simply he cannot remember when he last went to school . . . When he swaggers down the street in the Elephant and Castle where he lives, other kids' mothers turn their heads. He is at once pretty and masculine, an irresistible combination in a young boy." He lived with his drunken father in two squalid rooms, and "A couple of years ago he evolved a pattern of life, better adapted to surviving in so uncaring an environment, and up till now it has succeeded in making him both happy and, after a very special fashion, educated." After his father had gone to work, Johnny would climb over the back fence to see his friend Ernie, an ex-boy prostitute in his middle twenties, to go up west. "They all treated Johnny as though he were one of them, and an adult. Better still, they admitted him to a club, a society of people who lived outside the regulations of what they called straight society. In their world people stole, or ripped things off, naturally and logically." When Ernie was arrested for a car theft, Johnny was devastated, and went again to the West End to see what would turn up.

The situation revealed to a vast public by "Johnny Go Home" received immense public discussion, if only for its revelation of how Roger Gleaves was able to exploit the welfare system, and take in the Charity Commissioners, the Department of Health and Social Security, the police, the probation service, several borough councils and a prison governor. It led to demands for better advice back home for children likely to flee to London, and for a more effective travellers' aid service at the London stations as well as demands for the closing of amusement arcades in the West End where the runaways congregated and were picked up. Official guesses at the time the film was made assumed the number of vagrant children in London to be between 25,000 and 30,000. The police in their "juvenile sweeps" of the West End round up and send home a dozen a week, usually the least experienced. But another twenty arrive in London every day. Those who are sent home seldom stay home. Tommy for example was taken back to his home by the television company. Di Burgess says, "We took him back to his parents' council flat on one of those grim estates just outside Glasgow. His parents were good, down-to-earth Glaswegians who genuinely didn't know where he was and worried about him. But it didn't work. He wouldn't even stay the night." What happens to the runaways in the end? Deakin and Willis concluded that "for a surprising number of the cases we followed, in the end things turned out better for the kids than we at least had ever expected."

In all the acres of sanctimonious comment that the episode provoked, the wisest summing up came from Don Busby, the editor of a homosexual newspaper who remarked that the more sheltered members of the viewing public "would be very likely to identify the monster Gleaves with all those men who befriend boys. Indeed one of the major effects of the programme is that it has now made it difficult for *anyone* to befriend these boys apart from the authorities. In fact the greater percentage are running away from local authority 'Care' homes because they are unhappy there . . . Why do so many boys run away? This is the question which should have been asked. Almost all boys run away because they are starved of affection. It is not surprising that they will respond to the affection offered by the first stranger who comes along. The social services attempt to 'look after' their economic and moral needs, but are incapable of satisfying their basic emotional needs. Johnny doesn't *want* to go home."

Cartwheels for pennies in Düsseldorf

7
A Suburban Afternoon

"Like the theatre stage, it is a self-contained world furnished with a number of properties of a kind and variety that together make up what I am calling the suburban style. But it is not a flat backcloth; it is a panorama in depth as well as breadth as the spectator moves before it. Instead of facing the scene from beyond the footlights, or even from the stage itself, our pilgrim to suburbia must be thought of as having somehow stepped inside it. In the same way that Alice, dreaming in front of the looking-glass, found herself translated into the world beyond it, or that a child, gazing through the eye-hole of a Victorian peep-show, might imagine himself suddenly projected within the box, with its strange brightly coloured world all round him, so the pilgrim visiting suburbia finds he is no longer looking at the picture from outside. The well-furnished scene has become a kind of well-stocked jungle— not a fearsome one, because stocked with tame trees, tame houses and tame gardens—but one from which all other worlds are shut out. Suburbia has closed in round him, and is so completely a world of its own that it is the untidy, incalculable city from which he had come, or the countryside with its frightening expanse of sky, that seem strange and unreal."

J. M. RICHARDS

Most people don't enter the suburb as pilgrims, for if they do not live in one as adults, they are likely to have spent their childhood in one. One definition of the suburb might be that it is the child-rearing sector of the city. It is here that families, except for the rich, the very poor and the transitional, bring up their young. I was reared in a suburb and I expect that the reader was too. The parental motive in moving to the suburb is likely to have been the same: to buy more space for family living while remaining within reach of work. The suburb is born, of course, of the transport revolution. Railway, tram, bus and private car have each opened up more territory for the city worker, while land developers, private and public, have sought to ensure that the yearning for a family house and garden can be met there at almost all levels of income.

In the nineteenth century the central districts of the city had a swarming child population. Reformers were shocked by, and feared, the juvenile mob. Our own century has seen a continuous decline in the child population of the inner city. Fifty years ago Roderick McKenzie noted that "The school census shows an absolute decline in the number of children of school age in the central districts of the city although the total population for this area has shown an increase for each decade. It is obvious then, that the settler type of population, the married couples with children, withdraw from the centre of the city while the more mobile and less responsible adults herd together in the hotel and apartment regions near the heart of the community." He was thinking of the American city, but his observation is equally true of population movements in British cities, where, as H. J. Dyos remarked of his studies of the Victorian suburb, the motivation for moving out of town "derived something also from the repulsiveness of some of the aspects of life as it had to be lived in the centre of the city." The inner city becomes more and more a place which excludes the children of those who have any choice as to where they live. "London no more a city of children" said a newspaper headline of 1974. "No kids in ghost town of 1985" said another in the following year, and in the year after that, the education authority began to take notice of the fact that its clientele was rapidly declining.

The movement of population to the suburbs has been such a characteristic of the cities of the Western world in this century that we can confidently say that by now the majority of urban children in Europe and North America are in fact suburban children. In the United States by the early 'sixties the suburban share of the metropolitan population had reached 50 per cent, and had become 57 per cent by 1970. "Furthermore" say the editors of *Suburbia in Transition*, "during 1970 America became a suburban nation: more people now live *around* central cities (37.6 per cent) than in them (31.4 per cent) or in rural areas (31 per cent)."

The suburb is the characteristic settlement pattern of the twentieth century, but has been the target of such a barrage of criticism—social, fiscal, aesthetic, political, ideological and snobbish—that in spite of the demolition of the suburban myth by the sociologists, it has passed into the folklore of the intelligentsia. As David Thorns remarks, "the continued existence of the myth is due as much as anything to the fact that the critics of the suburbs have become caught up in their own creation." In terms of the child's experience of the suburb there are differences between the suburbs of British and American cities, notably that the British child's experience is most frequently of one suburb rather than of the species, while if 50 per cent of American families move in five years, and if 20 per cent move in any one year, the American suburban child must sample several in the course of growing up.

The eleven-year-old narrator of Keith Waterhouse's *There is a Happy Land* who lives on a council estate outside the centre of a Yorkshire city, wanders from Coronation Grove, through Royal Park and crawls through a giant pipe—some kind of old sewer and finds himself in a road "with houses that had been there for ages, made out of stone." Unlike the wide grass-verged roads of the new estate "all the streets were just rough cobbles with sooty grass growing through them . . . We could only tell we were in the same town by the buses, all of them the same colour as our own." But then, up at the top of the road new houses were being built: "They looked all new and clean and my heart sank whenever I saw them because they were like the houses in our own street: corporation houses with front doors that seemed to be grinning through their letter boxes. It seemed that houses like ours were springing up all over the world."

This autobiographical novel was set in the least environmentally rewarding of suburban types: the British council estate, built since the first world war on the fringe of the city, the type to which the charge of sameness and monotony is most nearly true. It is hard to be just to the estate. As Enid Gauldie writes,

"If council estates, brooding bleakly at the edge of our towns and swamping pretty villages, seem to have done nothing but harm to the shape and appearance of towns, they can only fairly be contrasted to what they replaced, a kind of squalor, a kind of misery even the most disparaged of council schemes has not yet achieved. The tragedy is that, by the time the idea of compulsorily subsidised housing had been realised, it was almost too late for anything but wholesale destruction of a centuries-old environment, for the meanest replacement of it by the cheapest houses, the barest amenities, the bleakest layout."

The most influential factor was not, however, the limitations of the environment, but the incomes of the occupants. It was noted in the nineteen-thirties that the move to the new estate, while it provided the

increment of more space that accompanies suburban living, often brought a drop in nutrition, not just because of increased rents, but because of increased fares for the breadwinner and higher food prices (since the shop rents too were higher than in the inner city). Exactly the same unwanted result is found today in the estates on the fringes of Glasgow, Liverpool, Leeds or Cardiff. The experience of the child on the estate is bound to be affected by the family budget, but the way in which children are able to *use* the environment is quite different in a new and an old estate. When Becontree was built as the largest planned working-class suburb in the world, it exhibited all the symptoms of a community which had not found its identity and whose children have been considered as suffering in terms both of diet and of environmental satisfactions through the move from the inner city. Looked at again after thirty years, it presented quite different characteristics. Organisationally the network of community ties and organisations had flourished, physically the gardens, bushes and trees had grown; what it lacked was the social and physical variety that results from the accidental and un-planned growth of the suburb. It was the coming of the Ford works at Dagenham which saved Becontree. Many other estates on the fringes of cities had no such fortune, and have declined rather than matured.

The bonus given by the new estate to the child, is in the spaces that have not been absorbed. For Keith Waterhouse's *alter ego* there were the tusky fields, the rhubarb fields on the way to the woods and the quarry, and in the woods were the basins: "The basins were some like *holes* up in Clarkson's woods. They were like pits with water at the bottom, only this summer they had baked green at the bottom, all cracked. Everybody used to go up on their bikes and ride round inside them. There were about six basins altogether and you had to ride round each one of them, then climb the slope *out* of this basin into the next one. If you missed one out you were yellow. We used to call it the Wall of Death." Virtually all suburbs, in their early years, have such areas, left out of the development perhaps because of the liability to flood, which could, by default, be colonised by the young. In some it is the wood or coppice which provides tree-walks, tree-houses, and every kind of climbing and swinging activity. In others it is the pond or the river, like the hallowed American swimming hole, which besides rudimentary water sports gives the hope of fishing and of the collection of tadpoles, minnows, sticklebacks and newts.

The new suburban development provides the detritus of the agricultural industry as well as that of building. To reach the primary school I attended in its first year and mine, we would clamber through a hedge and over a ditch which some-one had spanned by the grid of an old harrow. Within a year or two, all trace of it had disappeared, apart from the fact that the trees in the back gardens of that road were older and taller than most. Seven years later, with a longer walk to my secondary school which again was as new as I was, the short cut was actually through a farmyard, Gaysham Hall, where pigs and chickens were still kept in an absent-minded way, as though the farmer had forgotten that he had sold off his land. A few years later you could not believe that this suburb had so recent an agricultural prehistory unless you could read the faint traces left behind. Instead there was a different kind of child's bounty in heaps of sand and gravel, the stacks of bricks and timber, the scaffold poles and drain pipes of innumerable building contractors.

The place that is *becoming*, the unfinished habitat, is rich in experiences and adventures for the child, just because of the plenitude of "unmake" bits of no-man's land which have ceased to be agricultural and have yet to become residential. There are secret places for solitude among the weeds and hillocks, gregarious places in hollows like Keith Waterhouse's basins, where the soil is worn smooth by feet and bicycle tyres and where some-one has looped a stolen length of rope round the branch of a tree and an impromptu playground develops, to disappear next year or the one after that when the builders move in. Even then there is the excitement of watching carpenters, bricklayers and concreters at work. The casually fenced suburban site is different from the construction job in the city itself, with its impenetrable hoardings and its warning notice "Guard dogs patrol this site." Between the builders and the kids in the suburb there is a wary truce rather than open war. A knot of boys hang around the concrete mixer waiting to be chased away. The foreman knows who built those crazy towers of bricks last night and who left footprints in the wet concrete.

In the new suburb too, the child is reminded of the poignancy of time and change. Almost before his eyes the habitat alters. The houses completed six months before that of his parents are the old houses, those built since his family arrived are forever the new ones, roads are paved, trees felled and views altered before his own eyes.

The 'reluctant' suburb—the village swallowed up in the expansion of the city—offers another kind of experience of time, because of its ancient nucleus, old shops, churchyard with ancient graves. Going *down* to the High Street (for the builders of the engulfed village did not build on the windy hillside where the new estates have grown) is quite different from going to the new shopping parade. The scale of the buildings changes, they are closer together with a more intimate texture, there is somewhere to shelter from the rain, there are alleys, old railings, accidental nooks.

The fully-mature suburb, where generations of children have been reared, has yet another atmosphere. Even when each house in the road started life almost identical with its neighbours, time has brought every kind of variation, not just in paint and foliage, but in conversions and modernisations, piecemeal rebuilding. From the back bedroom window the child sees beyond the patchwork of back-gardens with greenhouses, sheds, garages and back additions to the houses in the next street. In such a district too, there are enticing glimpses of *occupations*, more people are locally employed than in the dormitory areas further from the city centre. Nicholas Taylor notes that "It is one of the most important features of the social life of our suburbs that back alleyways and back gardens should give sanctuary to the specialised craftsman, who has very often operated there for generations. Close to where I live, in ordinary lower middle-class suburbs, we have knife-grinders, mica-splitters, Turkish Delight makers, security printers of postage stamps, and a Japanese food warehouse."

In fact the suburb in its maturity has all those characteristics of varied environmental experience we used to associate with the heart of the city. It has the qualities of imageability and legibility that Lynch sought in the city, it is a comprehensible setting for tempering experience to our powers. It is a setting very suitable for child-rearing, which is why so many parents choose it, as the world experienced in daily life expands from the perambulator journey to the park and the local shops, the walk to the primary school, the bus-ride to the secondary school or the town centre, the occasional trips "up town" to the entertainment centre of the city itself. The way in which this widening experience is given a structure in the child's life depends of course on individual circumstances. Is it a car-owning family? Has the child older brothers and sisters to tag along behind? Has he a bicycle and is he permitted to use it? Is the week punctuated with social engagements to which he goes as an individual rather than as part of the family: cub scouts or brownies, music lessons, dancing class, the Little League, the football club based on the public park, the Saturday morning picture show?

Even in the era of universal television "going to the pictures" still gives pleasure and delight, and in the days before its decline the weekly visit was a landmark in the lives of urban and suburban children. To be deprived of it as a punishment, or for lack of the price of admission, or through being stigmatised for bad behaviour by the management, was one of the tragedies of juvenile life. John Holloway recalls how "When the cinema was over, we always did the same thing; we bought fish and chips at a shop opposite, and walked down Harrington Road eating the food and re-living the film. Those walks home were among the happiest or at least the gayest moments of my whole childhood. After the cinema the daylight used to seem very white and bright, and I would be dazzled at first, but the naive magic of the film would spread over into it."

Another remembered thrill is that of the first time the child is allowed to come home alone after dark. The familiar streets are changed by the streetlamps, the privet or laurel bushes conceal mysteries, the familiar moons of other people's television are glimpsed through uncurtained windows, the security of home is just a few steps further on.

The biggest advantage enjoyed by the suburban child when his surroundings are compared with those of the inner city child, is the amount of public open space and of "unmake", the sites which are yet to be developed. James Kenward sees the suburb as simply being from the child's experience, between the shops and the fields. "If you walk for so many minutes in one direction you come to the shops, and if you walk for so many minutes in the other direction you come to the fields. More exactly, if you bisect a line with the shops at one end and the fields at the other you will find Suburbia."

Regarded as a childhood idyll, the suburb is at its best in mid-afternoon. It is quiet and still and the only sounds are the sounds of childhood: an occasional shout from the playing-fields of the secondary school, singing heard through the open windows of the primary school, and the cries of the small children in the public gardens as their mothers chat over their baby-carriages. It is the child-rearing sector of the city: its nursery. But it is precisely this aspect of the suburb which makes it seem an intolerable place for those who are neither nurses nor nurslings. To the adolescent or the young man or woman who is not involved in the family nest, it is a place of tedium and monotony where *nothing ever happens*.

Nevertheless, we are concerned with the suburb as an environment for children. Anne Kelly, asking herself whether the suburb is really a child's utopia, found that "a recent spot check in the Connecticut town of Darien— a suburb in every sense of the word—revealed that while some elementary and junior-high youngsters, if given their choice of the place they would like to live, might elect Majorca; Beloit, Wisconsin; New York City; Maine, or

California, the majority preferred a suburb like Darien. Of the seventy-eight children in the fourth, sixth and ninth grades questioned, all but three said they are happy with the suburban way of life."

In Britain, a densely populated country, where there just isn't room for suburbia on the American scale, the garden city, new town policy has on a limited scale, attempted to provide an alternative to suburban sprawl. Inspired by Ebenezer Howard, who sought an environment which would provide the benefits of both city and country, the vital difference between the new town and the suburb is that the new town provides jobs as well as homes, so that the breadwinner is not obliged to become a commuter into the central city. The whole purpose of Howard's advocacy of the garden city was to relieve the pressure on population and land values in the inner city, and the whole tragedy of what has happened since his day, has been that the cities, even while collaborating in this policy, have, with an eye to revenues and votes, sought to rehouse families within their own territory in high-density housing. It was in 1945, not in the decades of experience since then, that Frederic Osborn wrote to Lewis Mumford, "I don't think philanthropic housing people anywhere realise the irresistible strength of the impulse towards the family house and garden as prosperity increases: they think that the suburban trend can be reversed by large-scale multi-storey buildings in the downtown districts, which is not merely a pernicious belief from a human point of view, but a delusion. In a few years the multi-storey technique will prove unpopular and will peter out. Damage will be done to society by the trial, but probably all I can do is hasten the day of disillusion. If I have underestimated the complacency of the urban masses, the damage may amount to a disaster."

It *was* a disaster, and in the various autopsies on the Pruitt-Igoe housing in St Louis, which had to be blown up by the US army, I have yet to see one which fairly and squarely acknowledges that it was the activities, not of the tenants but of their children which doomed that project. In a less spectacular way, this is true of many high density inner city developments in Britain. In the 1950s Professor Peter Self remarked that it was "short-sighted and a trifle hypocritical to impose standards on council housing occupants which the rest of the community are busy rejecting," for the city fathers committed themselves to a policy of high densities which were a guarantee of future trouble.

The first decision of any family with the luxury of choice has been to opt for suburbia "for the sake of the children." Today, when the devastated inner districts of any British or American city bear witness to the need for rebuilding at densities which take note of the needs of children, Ebenezer Howard's vision of a many-centred city gains enormous relevance.

Can we imagine a city in which children are housed at a density which provides space for family life and activities, and at the same time offers contact with the world of work and with the variety of participatory activities as well as spectator entertainments which the contemporary urban child demands? Can we merge the obvious advantages of suburbia with the traditional advantages of the inner city? We probably could if we had the political will to burst the bubble of inner city land values.

8
Colonising
Small Spaces

London

Cape Town

London

Nairobi

Philadelphia

The Corner (Cape Town)

(London)

rb (France)

The Street Drain London Street Arabs, 1890

Philadelphia

Occasional Table

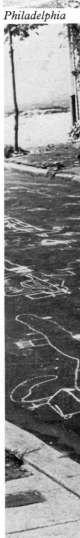

Chalking the Stre

London today

Using Slopes

Using Found Objects

Using Railings

The Pleasure of Climbing

9

Adapting the Imposed Environment

"The city parks, which are among the best monuments and legacies of our later nineteenth century municipalities—and valuable, useful, often beautiful though they are—have been far too much influenced by the standpoint natural to the prosperous city fathers who purchased them, and who took them over, like the mansion house parks they often were, each with its ring fence, jealously keeping it apart from a vulgar world. Their layout has as yet too much continued the tradition of the mansion-house drives, to which the people are admitted, on holidays, and by courtesy; and where the little girls may sit on the grass. But the boys? They are at most granted a cricket-pitch, or lent a space between football goals, but otherwise are jealously watched, as potential savages, who on the least symptom of their natural activities of wigwam building, cave-digging, stream-damming, and so on—must instantly be chivvied away, and are lucky if not handed over to the police.

"Now, if the writer has learned anything from a life largely occupied with nature-study and education, it is that these two need to be brought together, and this through nature-activities. But . . . we have been stamping out the very germs of these by our policeman-like repression, both in school and out of it, of these natural boyish instincts of vital self-education, however clumsy and awkward, or even mischievous and destructive when merely restrained, as they commonly have been, and still too much are. It is primarily for lack of this touch of first-hand rustic experience that we have forced young energy into hooliganism; or, even worse, depressed it below that level."
PATRICK GEDDES

One thing that observation of the behaviour of children makes clear, though it has only recently entered the world of reports and textbooks, and has yet to affect environmental policies, is that children *will* play everywhere and with anything. The provision that is made for their needs operates on one plane, but children operate on another. They will play wherever they happen to be, for as Arvid Bengtsson says, "play is a constant happening, a constant act of creation in the mind or in practice." A city that is really concerned with the needs of its young will make the whole environment accessible to them, because, whether invited to or not, they are going to use the whole environment.

The concept of the adventure playground grew out of observation of what children actually did on patches of waste land and on derelict areas and bomb sites. Joe Benjamin, a tireless pioneer in this field, laments that even the adventure playground concept has hardened into a kind of ideology in which "the swings and slides of the engineer have been replaced by those of the scrap merchant: the tubular steel climbing frame of the equipment manufacturer by the old telegraph pole or railway sleeper; the chain by the rope, the wood swing seat by an old tyre." Similarly Lady Marjorie Allen complained that American playgrounds were designed for insurance companies, and Paul Friedburg remarks that "we have taken the romance out of our parks because of our mania about maintenance."

Park and playground designers who usurp the creative capabilities of the very children who are intended to use their work by building play sculptures instead of providing the materials for children to make their own, or who have earnest conferences about the appropriate kind of fencing to use, should pause and think about the implications of Joe Benjamin's remark that "ideally there should be no fence; but when we reach that happy state we will have no need for adventure playgrounds." For the fenced-off child-ghetto sharpens the division between the worlds of adults and children, while Benjamin's whole case is that we should share the same world. "No matter how *we* might consider play potential in our present and future designs, children will continue to interpret this in their own way. The point is that the streets, the local service station, the housing estate stairway, indeed anything our urban community offers, is part of the natural habitat of the child. Our problem is not to design streets, housing, a petrol station or shops that can lend themselves to play, but to educate society to accept children on a participating basis." This explains why it was possible for Dennis Woods of North Carolina State University to deliver a paper with the title "Free the Children! Down with Playgrounds!"

Hermann Mattern of Berlin underlines his point, "One should be able to play everywhere, easily, loosely, and not forced into a 'playground' or 'park'. The failure of an urban environment can be measured in direct proportion to the number of 'playgrounds.'" Such an approach of course could easily be seized upon as a justification for *not* adapting the city parks to the needs of contemporary citizens, or for *not* creating pocket parks in vacant city sites, and for not redressing the glaring imbalance in the areas of public open space available to the inhabitants of rich and poor districts in the city. But it underlines the fact that we would have a clearer idea of the way the environment could be adapted for use by children if we looked at the way children actually use it.

If you ask adults about their happiest or most vivid recollections of city childhood they will seldom talk about the park or playground, but they will recall the vacant lot, the secret places behind billboards or hoardings. They will describe the delights of sand in the city, not so much the sandbox in the playground but the transient pile of sand dumped by builders in the street. In the Parc Monceau in Paris piles of sand are dropped in the avenues by the authorities, apparently expressly for the needs of children and are subsequently shovelled away for use elsewhere.

In whatever different ways the lives of children in the city have been regarded in time or space, there have always been adults watching, assessing and drawing conclusions from the games children play. We know this from the breadth of reference of Iona and Peter Opie's superlative account of *Children's Games in Street and Playground*. Their predecessor as encyclopaedist was Alice Gomme, whose two volumes on *The Traditional Games of England, Scotland and Ireland* were lampooned by Norman Douglas because of her conviction that the games she recorded were a survival of primitive rituals, but in fact she shared his pleasure in the sheer zest and variety of the games she and he observed in the London streets. For her they were a civilising influence, and in introducing her collection of *Children's Singing Games* she remarked "When one considers the conditions under which child-life exists in the courts of London and of other great cities, it is almost impossible to estimate too highly the influence which these games have for good on town-bred populations . . . Our reformers may learn a lesson from them, and perhaps see a way out of the dismal forebodings of what is to happen when the bulk of our population have deserted the country for the towns."

Norman Douglas himself, as we learn from his biographer, accumulated his magnificent collection (published in 1916) of *London Street Games*, from the boys he befriended in the London streets, as well as from their sisters, from their teachers and from unacknowledged predecessors like Lady

Gomme. When he looked back in 1931 on his book, what impressed him was "the inventiveness of the children. That is why I piled up the games into a breathless catalogue which, to obtain its full momentum and psychological effect, should be read through, *accelerando*, from beginning to end without a break. It is then that you fully realize the youngsters' inventive powers." Lady Gomme remarked in 1894 that "it is one of the misfortunes of present-day society that our children lose the influences derived from the natural playing of games." Norman Douglas asked, "I wonder how many of these games are still played?" Recent American students of street games echo his concern. Alan Milberg declares, truly, that "city or country, the true villain of the street game today is the car," while Arnold Arnold sees the function of his own compilation as that of keeping the games alive through the dark ages of children's street culture: "Crowding and lack of space, urbanisation, TV addiction, and an obsession with pumping information into children have robbed many of playfulness and essential play experiences . . . Children will be able to maintain their play lore unaided only when we have survived this age of cultural discontinuity and social isolation. I hope that this book will serve as a repository of the now interrupted game culture of childhood until that healthier day."

Uses of the Milk Crate

Our first impulse is to think they must all be right. Perhaps the car in the street and television in the home have destroyed the rich and varied accumulation of street games, recorded at the turn of the century in New York, Dublin or London. But the Opies are at our elbow to remind us that this belief in the decline of traditional games is itself a tradition, and they cite H. E. Bates, J. B. Priestley, Richard Church, Howard Spring "and other professional observers of the social scene" as falling victims to it. They found that 78 per cent of the chants that Norman Douglas recorded from his urchin friends in the first world war were still being chanted in 1959, and they are confident enough in their material to give us lists of those street games which really are diminishing and those which are growing in popularity. They found a marked decrease in the popularity of games which victimise one player and a possibly corresponding increase in those in which children fight on equal terms, a decrease in the ones which are most promoted by adults, and a continued flourishing of those which adults themselves are least likely to play well, or at least likely to encourage. They noted that "when children are herded together in the playground, which is where the educationalists and the psychologists and the social scientists gather to observe them, their play is markedly more aggressive than when they are in the street or in the wild places." They found that, when free of adult organisation, games were, according to your viewpoint, often extraordinarily naive or highly civilised. "They seldom need an umpire, they rarely trouble to keep scores, little significance is attached to who wins or loses, they do not require the stimulus of prizes, it does not seem to worry them if a game is not finished."

If you read Norman Douglas's book or the magnificent collection of the Opies, or best of all, if you find yourself an inconspicuous place, forget about time and all your pressing tasks, and simply watch and listen, you will develop a kind of reverence for the games of children, for their inexhaustible ingenuity, for the way in which the rules they devise are more subtle, less attuned to competition and more geared to enabling everyone to have a chance, than the team games devised for them by adults. They require a

minimum of equipment; even those which need a ball can often be played with one made of screwed up newspaper.

But they exploit any feature that the urban landscape happens to provide: end walls for ball games, kerbs, gutters, changes of level. Jeff Bishop, to illustrate the way contemporary designs (or absence of designs) for the play space around school buildings ignore the needs of the games which children actually play, drew up a list of environmental requirements:

Pirates (or Shipwrecks, Tree Touch, Tree Hee, Tree Tiggy) According to the environment, played using walls, fences, ledges, trees, roofs. All players except the person who is 'he' climb to the safety of walls etc. The chaser catches them without touching the ground (the sea). Requirements: continuous lines of walls or fences in a complex pattern, alternatively many mature or semi-mature trees close together.

Touch Wood, Touch Iron, Touch Colour (or Tig on Wood, Wood Tick, Tiggy on Iron, Dobby Colours). A chasing game in which the player is safe if he is touching wood etc. Touch colour (the Opies say) "prevails today probably because the architecture of contemporary school playgrounds efficiently eliminates trees and other signs of nature." Requirements: trees shrubs, metal fences, gates, colours.

Off-ground He (or Dobby-off-Ground, No Feet, Tig or High, Tuggy off-ground). As above, but anybody with feet off ground is safe. Requirements: ledges, railings, steps, mistakes, gulleys, plinths, sills, any sign of interest.

Shadow Touch (or Tig on Shadow). A chasing game in which only the child's shadow can be 'tigged'. Requirement: maximum exposure to sun.

Crusts and Crumbs (or Rats and Rabbits). Sides of a road are designated as Crusts or Crumbs. According to the name called by the 'caller' one side of children chases the other, attempting to catch them before they reach the safety of the pavement. Requirements: part of the staff car park kept clear of cars and with obvious pavements.

Wall to Wall (or Charlie, King Alley, Onefootoveryoumustgo). Children line up against one wall and run across at a signal to another wall, avoiding a 'catcher'. Requirements: two parallel walls preferably about 15 metres apart with level ground between.

Hide and Seek. Self-explanatory. Requirements: lots of corners, nooks, crannies, holes, trees, doors etc., everything the modern school yard does not have.

Every generation assumes that the street games of its youth have been destroyed by the modern city. Yet they survive, changing their form in innumerable adaptations to exploit environmental changes. The lifts of the tower block, the trolleys from the supermarket, are incorporated into the repertoire of playthings, often to the great discomfort of the adult world. The very outrageousness of some of the forms these adaptations take, surely suggests that children are demanding their share of the city and knocking for admission into this adult world which monopolises the city's toys and forgets, as Iona and Peter Opie keep reminding us, "that the most precious gift we can give to the young is social space: the necessary space—or privacy—in which to become human beings."

The American fire hydrant is an archetypal instance of the way children adapt the artifacts of the built environment. The torpid summer heat of a city like New York amazes and dismays European visitors. "The rich sleep in air-conditioned rooms," Cecil Beaton noted years ago, "but for the poor there is no alleviation from the baking streets at night; sleep is impossible, and they

Uses of the Fire Hydra

toss and turn all night long. Children lie naked in the streets, waiting for the water trucks to come past and spray them. Somebody will turn on a fire hydrant, and the children will have an extra bathe, until the policeman on the beat comes along.'' In British cities a fire hydrant is an inconspicuous object: there is a metal plate on a nearby wall indicating how many feet away the actual access cover is sunk into the pavement. But in American cities it is a punctuation mark in the street scene: a robust cast-iron bollard, amply proportioned with several projecting nozzles, capped off but ready for immediate use. A menace to drunks and a solace to dogs, the fire hydrant has entered into running battle between children and authority: a battle now largely won, for in many cities, as in Philadelphia, the opening of the hydrants is now authorised when the temperature reaches a certain level.

For Claes Oldenburg growing up in Chicago, ''those fire-plugs were a kind of monument, full of water, waiting to burst.'' For generations of New York children, as the sweltering summer draws on, the cry goes around,

"Who's got the spanner?" And when some plumber's child or some household with the foresight to have one in readiness, or to have made good use of the school metalwork shop, opens up the hydrant, the children of the whole neighbourhood are drawn to the spot, and, after the joy of the initial wetting devise elaborate rituals of splashing and squirting. Years ago it was the Italian and Jewish kids whose grandchildren now play in the pools of their suburban gardens. Today it is their black and Puerto Rican successors who perform this ritual with innumerable modifications. By the 1960s the activity was legitimised when the Police Athletic League of New York City, in streets closed off for play, provided sprinkler heads to replace perforated tin cans. But in Mayor Beame's New York of the 1970s the European visitor is still amazed that children can flood whole streets, with the cars swishing through as though there had been a cloudburst.

Richard Dattner admiringly observed the variety of activities revolving around the fire hydrant:

"The first is a game requiring quite a bit of strength from the little boys who are engaged in it. They stand in an orderly line on the dry side of the hydrant, waiting to take their turn on the firing line. The boy at the head of the line is channeling the water stream through a small can from which both ends have been cut. He can hit with great accuracy anything that moves within twenty-five yards. After a few seconds, the next boy in line moves to the front and the previous marksman takes his place at the rear of the line. Cars are the favourite targets, and the children have an uncanny ability to spot drivers who disapprove of their activity, giving them a full broadside shot. With a tremendous amount of water pressure at their command (it normally takes two firemen to handle a fire hose), the kids are suddenly a match for all the adults who have previously harassed them, and the soaking confrontation provides them with some measure of justice. Many drivers stop to inveigh against the children (from behind closed windows), but none is foolish enough to leave his sanctuary, and all eventually drive away. The few drivers who in a decent manner actually ask the children to lower the spray so they can pass are often rewarded by equally decent behaviour on the part of the youngsters.

Guayaquil, Ecuador

"Across the street, at the other end of the water stream, an entirely different game is in progress between cars. Here the object is to avoid the spray, primarily as a test of speed and skill against the accuracy of the amateur firemen and not at all to stay dry. (Few children want to be dry on a hot day, and those who do are careful to stay well down the block.) The spray is lowered and the kids edge closer within firing range, while the marksmen across the street exhibit a remarkable nonchalance. Suddenly a tin can is clamped over the stream, a great squeal goes up from the intended victims as they retreat, and shouts of victory or disappointment, depending on the outcome, rise from the dripping, smiling firemen. The cycle is repeated, with minor variations in cast and plot, all day long and into the night.

"Meanwhile, the water has accumulated in the gutters and is flowing towards the drain at the corner. Farther down the block a little boy has dammed the stream with some cobblestones (taken from the street), creating a lagoon; half-a-dozen children are wading in it or sunning themselves along the edge. Two girls on the sidewalk are following toy boats floating on the end of strings in the rapids just before the drain. A little boy squats over the drain and looks into the murky depths below, perhaps imagining subterranean encounters between sewer repairmen and giant alligators grown from Florida souvenirs flushed down toilets long ago. All this joy is usually quite illegal (and often a policeman comes to turn off the water. Sprinklers are available to decrease the water loss, but they are not the same—the spray can't be aimed and doesn't produce enough water to suitably flood the street."

Thames at Wapping in the 19

In the suburbs of course, a subdued version of the same pleasures can be provided with the garden hose in the back yard. Travellers on the District Line or the Southern suburban lines in London can see from the safe distance of the train how in summertime the hosepipe, insecurely attached to the tap over the kitchen sink, passes through the back doorway into the pocket-handkerchief back garden, filling the old galvanised iron wash-tub or the new inflatable paddling pool. Having soaked each other, the children happily squirt the family next door, or the upstairs windows, and the traveller through the close-packed inner suburbs reflects once again what an extension of freedom the tiniest back yard becomes.

Luckiest of all, from the child's point of view, are those cities on the coast, with a shoreline and beaches, but most cities have a river with varying provision for children's play, usually illicit. Not in the grand central area

EVENING CHRONICLE

LATE NIGHT FINAL

No. 29,265. Newcastle.   THURSDAY, JUNE 3, 1971   3p

IF SHE'S 2 TO 14...

'Water babies' hit the Civic Centre

By MARTIN HUCKERBY

DOZENS of children from the West End of Newcastle leapt into fountains at the Civic Centre today as part of a giant "swim-in" protest.

Shouting and yelling, fully dressed youngsters jumped into the cold pools in the centre of the council buildings.

Nearly 190 children carrying placards and banners marched chanting round the Civic Centre, forcing their way into the rates hall in spite of the efforts of council porters.

The "water babies" were all part of a protest organised by the West End Tenants' Association and the Noble Street Active Group in a bid to get the Snow Street swimming baths reopened.

And then they charged shrieking in to the big pools, splashing around happily to the consternation of council officials. Hundreds of city pent's workers stood at the windows watching.

Porters tried to get the kids out again, but it was like trying to dam a flood. More than a dozen police looked on, but took no action.

LAWN

Some of the children came equipped with towels, and changed into swimming costumes before leaping into the water.

They clambered on to the sculpture, in the middle of the footsteps, sitting astride the birds chanting slogans and ignoring warnings to get off.

In spite of the cold they sprinted around in the water for quarter of an hour before climbing out chilled but still cheerful.

Others played football on the immaculate lawn.

For the kids, it was cheer beginning to end, though one porter commented: "Half of them will end up in bed with pneumonia."

Mrs. Ann Blay, secretary of the West End Tenants, said that a big petition about the closing of the baths at Snow Street, Benwell, and at Snow Street, Westgate Hill, had been handed to the council earlier this year but nothing had been done.

THE message is in the medium and they're both water. An irresistible wave of marchers stormed the city's Civic Centre today with banners and placards.

The junior demonstrators were putting pressure on the council to re-open the Snow Street swimming baths.

And in the absence of a pool, the protesters, organised by the West End Tenants' Association, took over the ornamental pools at the centre.

But all good things must come to an end and a book rub-down, while adults sorted out their problems, marked the end of the "demo" for these children.

PLAY

The children had nowhere to swim now, she said, because mothers could not afford to swing their children to baths elsewhere.

The protesters also want more play facilities in the West End, including an indoor play centre at Noble Street.

If nothing was done to re-open the Snow Street baths, "we will come back again," threatened Mrs. Blay.

Ald. Arthur Grey, the leader of the city council, said the protest was "just exhibitionism."

Policeman hold a watching brief as one young demonstrator (top) fishes out a goldfish. More pictures—Page 3.

LATEST

WEST END TENANTS ASSOCIATION

ance Halprin's Portland Falls

In the first three decades of the century, dozens of photographs were taken of boys being chased out of the Serpentine lake in Hyde Park, London. They were thought very amusing, but no-one drew the conclusion that swimming should be allowed there until, in 1930, George Lansbury, a much-loved Labour politician, found that as President of the Board of Works he was in charge of the Royal Parks. Douglas Goldring recalls that "so mean was the attitude of the governing class that Lansbury had to fight tooth and nail against Tory obstruction to obtain for Londoners the right to bathe in their own Serpentine in their own park."

with its broad embankments and river walls, but down in the dockyards and wharves or upstream where the natural foreshore or something like it is retained, the river retains its playground function. In the Thames at Putney the children poke about for treasure trove on the river bed at low tide, down river at Wapping or Shadwell the boys splash around on the ancient steps. Back in the 1930s the Council used to bring barge-loads of sand to form a beach, but nowadays, even though the water is actually cleaner, a child who falls in is given a tetanus injection.

Municipal ponds and fountains are seldom intended for the delight of children. Nowadays they are usually the centre piece of traffic islands or the foreground of buildings of state. In ancient cities of course they are frequently colonised by children, especially where there is an industry of diving for the tourists' drachmae or centisimi. There are exceptions. When Lawrence Halprin designed the ponds and fountains at Portland, Oregon, he did it with *use* in mind. "We thought a great deal," he said, "about the feelings people have about water. There seems to be a deeply felt need to become involved with it. So we worked with the idea of allowing the people in the area—particularly the young people—to participate actively in using the fountains. And this idea influenced the process of design. It meant, for example, that the design could not have railings or, for that matter, any constraining elements that would by implication say 'stay out'. The very nature of the forms and boundaries had to imply 'come in, participate, get involved, please use.' The design had to be permissive and indeterminate, to the extent that we ourselves should not know what would emerge in the participation."

In the very week when he was describing this experience in his Annual Discourse at the Royal Institute of British Architects, the principle was being put into effect by the children of the North End at Newcastle-upon-Tyne. Nearly a hundred of them, carrying placards and chanting slogans, marched to the city's grandiose and expensive Civic Centre, (known locally as Dan's Castle, after T. Dan Smith, an ambitious civic dignitary subsequently jailed for corruption) making their way into the rates hall, invading the lawns, splashing around in the ornamental ponds, and clambering over the sculptures in the middle of the fountains. Their desecration of the shrine of civic grandeur wasn't a permanent take-over. It was part of a campaign to get the council to re-open a closed swimming bath at their own run-down end of the city. "Just exhibitionism," said the leader of the council.

Now everybody *knows* about the child's need for playing in water. It is certainly a photographer's cliché. The *Village Voice* remarks sardonically that the kids on Carlton Avenue and Adelphi Street in Brooklyn can shout "Hey Mister, take my picture", "with just the right amount of reverence and derision needed to be preserved in any great social document. Furthermore, there is a handy fire hydrant. Some insist this is as important to the genre as the tree is to Godot." Similarly there are dozens of photographs from the early years of this century of policemen or, preferably, policewomen, chasing little boys from the Serpentine in Hyde Park, but it was not until 1930, through the happy chance of having George Lansbury as President of the Board of Works, that bathing in the Serpentine was permitted. There were grave misgivings among the legislators when Lansbury's Lido was opened.

Leningrad

Philadelphia

To provide water play for children is administratively messy. It presents a health hazard (the pool on Boston Commons has to be drained and refilled every day in summer). It needs supervision. It is expensive to provide and maintain. Consequently it very seldom happens in sophisticated modern cities. In the cities of the poor world it happens naturally.

It also happens lethally of course. While no-one was ever drowned by a fire hydrant, it is statistically certain that children will die in the rivers, canals, wharves and creeks of our cities. What impossible equation between the responsibility to remove hazards and recognition of the need for excitement, risks and fun, can the administrators draw?

In Manchester, the Rochdale Canal, once a lifeline of the industrial revolution, was closed to traffic in 1952 and became a tip for every kind of rubbish and a danger. Fences and barbed wire were erected along its banks, but in spite of this a child was drowned on an average of once a year, partly because of the fences, since no-one was around to rescue them. Finally the city obtained powers to acquire the site as part of a strategy to reclaim the canals and river valleys of North Manchester to link them with existing parks as part of a continuous system of public open spaces. The first possible approach would have been to restore the canal for navigation, boating and fishing, but the planning officer, John Millar, found regretfully that "in the climate of the time it was quite unacceptable politically." The second possible approach was at the opposite extreme: put the flow of water which was necessary to feed the Bridgewater Canal into a culvert and simply fill in the Rochdale Canal. A simple and final solution administratively, but one which would do away for ever with the water and with the historical associations. The solution that was eventually adopted was to reduce the depth of water to one which would never exceed seven inches, keeping the appearance of the canal, and turning the locks into stepped cascades. The first part of the scheme to be opened was that in the densely-populated district of Miles Platting, and it soon became, as John Millar puts it, the largest paddling pool in Europe. "The population not only took to the landscaped areas along the towpath, but to the canal bed itself. The cascades quickly came to be used as shower baths, whilst a number of unfamiliar aquatic sports were devised within the pound areas."

There had been considerable misgivings and opposition to the solution that was adopted, and when the scheme and the landscape architects Derek Lovejoy and Partners were given a Civic Trust Award for its excellence, a storm broke. "Look at the vandalism that has happened," cried the opponents. "Look at the increased incidence of cut-feet cases in the local hospital. Look at the rubbish and filth that is still thrown into the canal, and is all the more visible because of the reduced depth. How can such an ill-judged experiment be considered worthy of an award?" The answer of course is that if Manchester wanted a cheaply maintained scheme, the uncreative solution of filling in the canal should have been adopted, and if it wanted to enhance the lives of its children, it should be prepared to meet the heavier costs of continual maintenance, of education to improve environmental standards, and above all, of taking positive steps to involve the local children in becoming wardens of their own playground, so that no-one would think of throwing bottles and old bike-frames in the sparkling cascades of the Rochdale Canal.

10
Play as Protest and Exploration

"Should such persistent choice of busy and provocative play-places alert us that all is not as appears in the ghettos of childhood? Children's deepest pleasure, as we shall see, is to be away in the wastelands, yet they do not care to separate themselves altogether from the adult world. In some forms of their play (or in certain moods), they seem deliberately to attract attention to themselves, screaming, scribbling on the pavements, smashing milk bottles, banging on doors, and getting in people's ways. A single group of children were able to name twenty games they played which involved running across the road. Are children, in some of their games, expressing something more than high spirits, something of which not even they, perhaps, are aware? No section of the community is more rooted to where it lives than the young. When children engage in 'Last Across' in front of a car is it just devilment that prompts the sport, or may it be some impulse of protest in the tribe?"

IONA and PETER OPIE

In their gentle and tentative way, Mr and Mrs Opie are drawing attention to the existence of a land-use conflict between children and adults. They cite innumerable historical instances: how in 1385 the Bishop of London complained of ball-games around St Paul's, how in 1447 the Bishop of Exeter complained of young people playing in the cloister during services, how boys had to be forbidden in 1332 from playing in the Palace of Westminster while Parliament was sitting, how in Stuart times a beadle had to be employed to whip away from the Royal Exchange "unlucky Boys with Toys and Balls" while in the 19th century "there were repeated complaints that the pavements of London were made impassable by children's shuttlecock and tipcat."

Paul Thomson sees it not just as territorial conflict or resistance, but as an outright war with adults. Children, he declares "like other social under-groups, have long protested against their position by resistance, sometimes open and sometimes hidden, a war with adults which parallels and echoes the wars between the classes and the sexes." He sees the various critical weaknesses of the child's position in this war: the rapid passage into an older age group, and the fact that "their point of conflict with the oppressing group is through the members of it whom they most value personally. For most children, parents are likely to be the best adults they know. It is this which makes their expressions of discontent against other adults, with whom they have less close bonds, such as neighbours, policemen and teachers—in universities as well as schools—of especial significance. They are expressions which need to be understood, not merely in terms of observed acts and stated issues, but as symbolic (and perhaps hopeless) protests against the entire system of adult control of society."

This element in play mingles of course, in the very same games with contrary aspects, the most obvious of which is imitation of the activities of the adult world and intense curiosity about its ways and secrets. All are linked with pleasure and excitement in activity itself and with the exploration of the nature of materials, structures and physical skills. The moment the child is free to *use* buildings, surfaces and changes of level for his own purposes, he becomes adept in employing them. As Steen Eiler Rasmussen says, "he seems to project his nerves, all his senses, deep into these lifeless objects. Confronted by a wall which is so high that he cannot reach up to feel the top, he nevertheless obtains an impression of what it is like by throwing a ball against it. In this way he discovers that it is entirely different from a tautly stretched piece of canvas or paper. With the help of the ball he receives an impression of the hardness and solidity of the wall."

Play is often *at the same time*, training in motor skills and sensory awareness, exercise and excitement, and warfare with the adult world, as well as providing a disturbing parody of this world. There are cities torn open by sectarian warfare, like Belfast or Beirut, where the play of children merges imperceptibly into the deadly games of adults. Joe Benjamin discusses the secret of imitative games of the eight to thirteen years olds:

"The Opies referred to American children playing 'Assassination' after the death of President Kennedy, and Berlin children 'shooting each other across miniature walls'. My own files include similar examples: Auschwitz children played 'Going to the Gas Chambers', Israeli children almost hanged an eight-year-old friend while playing 'The Eichman Trial', British children played at CND demonstrations, 'Train Robbers' (where the police always lose); others have played shoot-outs and ritual executions which they call 'Irish and Soldiers', and 'Weddings' where reality was achieved by breaking into a church and using the rector's prayer book, lighting the candles and wearing the choir's surplices. It is not suggested that these games should or can be stopped. But as they do involve social attitudes based on observation and imitation we can no longer afford to ignore them. We need to do more than merely pay lip-service to our moral obligations. Children are demanding this of us in that they are following the examples we set. We can neither—nor are we in a position to—punish nor admonish, but we can begin to understand. And in understanding, which we can achieve only on a basis of participation, children themselves will begin to understand us and the society in which we all live. This is what community work is about; what relationships are about; what learning is about; what growing up to maturity is about, and, therefore, what play is about."

One of the things that play is about, intermingled with all the others, is conflict with the adult world. Here is a group of children aged eight to eleven, who live in a municipal estate in South London, talking about their games to a sympathetic enquirer, Jenny Mills:

Child: We like playing tin soldiers here because the walls have got bumps in. There's a row of people along the wall and there's someone standing outside of us, and they have to throw the ball and try to hit us, but if they miss they just try again.
Jenny: Why does the wall being bumpy help?
Child: 'Cos it hits the ball away again. Then we play Knock Down Ginger. When we finish playing we press all the buttons in the lift and then the person that goes in the lift first goes to every single floor.
Jenny: Can you tell me what Knock Down Ginger is?
Child: Well you knock on the doors and then someone holds the lift and you run away and sometimes people chase you and sometimes they don't. And you can tie a string to one door and two doors are opposite each other and you knock on one door and they open the door and the other door knocker knocks. And sometimes we play He and Tin Can Tommy around here and hide in the flats.
Jenny: Can you tell me what that is?
Child: Well, you throw a tin and then you run and a person has to go and pick the tin up while you are hiding and the person has to try and find you. We play Run-Outs in the lifts. A team stays here and a team goes up in the lift and you can go to any floor you like and then the other team gets in the lift and they have to get the floor you're on and then they have to "Had Yer."

Using Waste Places, London

Peking

London

Another child took Mrs Mills up to the entrance to the 'Bus Station', which turned out to be the space in the roof for the lift motor room and the water storage tanks:

Child: This is the bus station I was telling you about. The little door in there, you open it and you climb up the steel ladder and then there's little square holes. You climb through and there's all birds wot fly at yer.
Jenny: And its a bit scarey, is it?
Child: Yes. 'Cos its all dark and you have to take a torch. And there's a little gap or hole at the top and you climb through there, and we go right over the humps and go to a wall and climb down a drainpipe.

Even in this densely built district the children had unerringly found a bit of waste ground, an area at the back of the church, where rubbish was left:

Child: The dump—we call it a dump—and the Vicar he comes out after you—and in the dump its got a lorry all burnt up and all old stuff and the fence knocked down and all the bushes, and it's got a boiler what you climb up to get over the wall.
Jenny: And where do you go from the wall?
Child: Along the wall and on to a flat roof on the vicarage sort of place, and then the Vicar comes out after you and he puts his dog out, howling to amuse yer, and he comes down some steps behind the wall here and then he traps yer. And when you go up there, there's the window thing and once it was broken—you know he fixed it— and it was broke though and when people got married we used to look through there and see them and see what they do when they sign the book, and we used to watch.

There is a universal character about the stories the children told Jenny Mills. The striking thing is not that high density living in apartment blocks has killed off the ancient ploys of childhood, but that they have been adapted by children to the new conditions of living. When high flats with lifts were imposed upon the urban working class household in Britain, it was not anticipated that the lifts would become a weapon in the war of children against the adult world, or, perhaps simply a plaything. The exasperating inconvenience this brings to adult residents is easy to imagine. One long-suffering tenant remarks, "They go in the lifts and they race each other up twenty floors. And the people in the block have a lot of trouble because you can wait twenty minutes. You get children playing in there and they press every button and it stops at every floor going down. Five minutes at each floor. It's just a play place for them really."

Others put it less mildly. Some residents have developed a bitter hostility towards the young, elderly people live in fear, and in one London housing estate the boys have actually found a way of travelling on the roof of the lift car, both imperilling their own lives and terrorising the occupants of the lift below their feet. There are several other adaptations to the new urban environment of ancient pranks. One trick is to collect all the doormats from outside a row of front doors along the access balcony of a block of flats and to pile them outside one particular door, or to exchange a worn mat for a new one, waiting to see what the inhabitants will do about it. Another is to tie a length of cotton round a milk bottle and suspend it over the access balcony from some-one's door knocker. Yet another brief and sensational delight is to buy and assemble a plastic model aeroplane, fill it with cotton wool and paraffin, ignite it and launch it from high up in a block of flats.

The little girls in Lambeth interviewed by Jenny Mills discovered that the bumpiness of the wall (caused by an architectural feature, the projection of a few courses of brickwork) gave an entrancing randomness in the angle at which their ball bounced back. They were discovering an environmental lesson immortalised by Steen Eiler Rasmussen, in discussing the way a ball gives the child an insight into the nature of a structure, its weight, solidity and texture:

"The enormous church of S. Maria Maggiore stands on one of Rome's seven famous hills. Originally the site was very unkempt, as can be seen in an old fresco painting in the Vatican. Later, the slopes were smoothed and articulated with a flight of steps up the apse of the basilica. The many tourists who are brought to the church on sight-seeing tours hardly notice the unique character of the surroundings. They simply check off one of the starred numbers in the guide-books and hasten on to the next one. But they do not experience the place in the way some boys I saw there a few years ago did. I imagine they were pupils from a nearby monastery school. They had a recess at eleven o'clock and employed the time playing a very special kind of ball game on the broad terrace at the top of the stairs. It was apparently a kind of football but they also utilized the wall in the game, as in squash—a curved wall, which they played against with great virtuosity. When the ball was *out*, it was most decidedly out, bouncing down all the steps and rolling several hundred feet further on with an eager boy rushing after it, in and out among motor cars and Vespas down near the great obelisk. I do not claim that these Italian youngsters learned more about architecture than the tourist did. But quite unconsciously they experienced certain basic elements of architecture: the horizontal planes and the vertical walls above the slopes. And they learned to play on these elements. As I sat in the shade watching them, I sensed the whole three-dimensional composition as never before. At a quarter past eleven the boys dashed off, shouting and laughing."

Yet another of the universal reactions between the city and the environment encountered as play is the exploration accompanied by fear and risk. Torn as we are between tolerance and repression, this is the kind of venture that worries us most. It was the "scarey" nature of the forbidden territory in the roof that was one of its attractions for the children interviewed by Jenny Mills. Similarly when at the symposium at Washington DC on Children, Nature and the Urban Environment, Simon Nicholson persuaded fifth graders from the nearby Stevens Elementary School to write about "Our city and the places where we play", in the hope of bringing some kind of reality to the proceedings, the children insisted on describing the derelict Scarey Dairy, where rats and broken glass were one of the attractions. The school board were unnecessarily embarrassed. The same pleasure in an environment the adults would rather not know about was revealed by the children from Bute Town, Cardiff, described in Chapter Four.

But the tacit licence to destroy extends beyond the dead area of the city into the surrounding district which is merely dying, and even into the district which, physically, is experiencing what was expected to be a rebirth. There are public housing projects, both new and old, where the war between children and adults for control of the environment has been lost by the adults, who will tell you that they dare not complain to the council or to the

police for fear of reprisals. The estate gets more and more like a battlefield, and just like the clearance area it replaces, it suffers from a progressive decline in standards of maintenance and of ordinary municipal services because of a fatalistic acceptance that whatever is done there will be spoilt by the children.

A headline in the *South London Press* reads, "Council decides to ban children on new estate to stop vandalism", and in those American cities which are experimenting with urban homesteading, one of the criteria for potential success or failure is the size of the child population of the district. In the city of Oslo the ownership and control of municipal housing estates was transferred from the city to the tenants, and in one of these estates there is a remarkable caretaker, employed by the tenants' co-operative. He has in fact a gold medal for caretaking. He employs the children of the estate to collect litter, to sweep up the leaves in the autumn and to clear the snow in winter. Fourier in his utopia, concluding that the love of dirt and the destructive passions he detected in children should be given some useful purpose, organised them into "little hordes" to act as public cleaners, to clean out the stables and attend to the animals. Like the Norwegian caretaker (whose own social function had been recognised by his gold medal) he was awarding them the dignity of performing a function in society.

Newcastle

This is not a matter to be taken lightly. The success or decline of housing projects depends, most of all, on winning the children. An enormous expenditure both in cash and in human happiness depends upon them. If I were asked to take you to a significantly unvandalised public housing project in London, I would take you to the Churchill Gardens estate by the riverside in Pimlico. This was begun in 1949, so that in terms of the terrifyingly rapid obsolescence of municipal housing, it is an old estate, even though it doesn't look it. Right from the start an active tenants' association negotiated with the council and its architects (Messrs Powell and Moya) about improvements to the design of later phases of the project, about the rights of tenants, and so on. The result is that today, with a tenants' organisation that is totally independent and operates its own licensed bar (where residents and caretaking staff meet as friends rather than as adversaries) every variety of interest among the young is catered for, from Olympic gymnastics to martial arts. The tenants' association itself, when it sees that the interests of its children are drifting in a certain direction, seeks out someone to pass on the appropriate skills. The tenants, and not the education authority or some welfare organisation, found the woman who teaches gymnastics, and their association is active in attempting to meet the whole range of interests in every age-group of its children.

The activists of the association take it for granted that they have a responsibility towards the children of the estate. I have met children there who were totally untouched by anything they did and who lived a life of jungle warfare against both their school and their home environment. Fortunately for their neighbours they were too few to disturb the harmony of the estate. In many urban situations the opposite is true. So many of the children are so totally alienated from their surroundings, their parents, their neighbours and their homes, that life is made untenable, or acutely miserable, for the other occupants. My sympathies are with the victims, but any afflicted urban community has to ask itself how it came to rear a generation which, for fun, but to its own disadvantage, would, for example,

burn away the plastic buttons on the lifts with gas lighters, or open the joints of the rising water main. It is all play, it is "just for a giggle" and it results in misery, expense and danger for others. The citizen may reflect on the vulnerability of mechanical services and the miscalculations of those who provided them, but he is bound most of all to reflect upon the vulnerability of a society which can no longer control its children but which accepts no responsibility for inducting them into the community, and which does not even recognise the need to find a place for them in its social life.

Juvenile vandalism is a phenomenon of the rich cities of the world. In the cities of the poor world artifacts are too precious to be wantonly destroyed. I asked Sally and Richard Greenhill, who have seen more of Chinese cities than most foreign visitors, about vandalism in China. No, it wasn't a Chinese problem, they replied, but they had been told in Shanghai that there had been an outburst of damage to lamp-posts. The culprits had been sent to work for three weeks in the lamp-post factory.

It led them to discuss the significance for children of the ethos of productive work in Chinese schools. At a primary school they visited in Nanking, the productive task of the school was the fabrication of the metal handrails for the boarding platforms of buses and the metal edges of the steps. So every bus they see in the street incorporates their handiwork.

In the derelict Surrey Docks in London, a woman called Hilary Peters succeeded in getting a lease on a patch of land and an old lock-house because she wanted to keep goats and chickens. Predictably she was plagued by marauding children. Realising what an experience it could be for Deptford kids to keep livestock and grow things, she decided to make them her allies. "The only way of coping with them," she remarks, "is to let them in." A few miles away in Spitalfields I climbed with Ron McCormick on to the roof of a rotting tenement Great Eastern Buildings. Two eleven-year-olds had built themselves a pigeon house and stocked it with birds. Next day the landlord ordered them to pull it down.

1
The
Specialist
City

"When I was six or seven the Boys' Brigade from the church round the corner used to parade round the streets with bugles and drums. I liked the sound and decided to join, which meant, as I found, that you had to go to Sunday School. I also found that you had to be a Senior to play the bugle. By the time I was eleven they gave me a bugle but by that time they were about to be disbanded. In any case I had seen a trumpet in a second-hand shop and was given it for my eighth birthday. My mother found a horn-player living nearby who gave me my first lessons. At my secondary school I started playing with other people and also joined the Centre for Young Musicians which meets on Saturdays. There I started in the Concert Band and have also played in the Training Orchestra and the Brass Ensemble. On Sundays I play jazz with some friends and sometimes I play with other friends in a brass band in parks. I often get asked to help out in all kinds of concerts, operas and churches. I earn money that way as well as with my paper round. I travel around a lot and this year I shall be touring America with the London Schools Symphony Orchestra."

FOURTEEN-YEAR-OLD LONDONER

All our generalisations about the city child are about the poor or deprived child. The child from a better-off, or simply a more sophisticated family is far better able to exploit the wonderful potential that any city offers. He had learned how to use its facilities. Blessed is the child, rich or poor, with a hobby or a skill or an all-consuming passion, for he or she is motivated to utilise the city as a generator of happiness. There are plenty of juvenile passions which are generators of misery for other people, but it remains true that the child who is hooked on to some network built around a shared activity has found ways of making the city work for him.

An enormous range of possible experiences and activities are open to the city child, and as always the household which is accustomed to planning ahead and knows where to look things up draws the maximum benefit from opportunities which are theoretically available to all the city's children. The child whose parents in New York buy the *Village Voice*, or in London buy *Time Out* with its 'Kidsboard' column, or know that you can ring 246 8007 to know what's on in Children's London, is made aware of an infinite range of things to do and places to go. When I asked James Stevens Curl, the author of *European Cities and Society*, which he thought was the best city in Europe for a child to grow up in, he replied "London, without any doubt," and a poll amongst much-travelled Americans revealed a similar opinion. One cannot accuse the Greater London Council, the London Boroughs or the great national museums centred on London, of failing to put on programmes of activities to stimulate the city's children. But the leader of the Inner London Education Authority remarked to me sadly that "Whatever new facility we provide, we know in advance that it's the middle class children who will draw the benefit." Significantly it is the quality newspapers and not the popular ones who find it worthwhile to include features on holiday events and activities for children.

Innumerable voluntary organisations and a great variety of local community associations organise fairs, carnivals and festivals which have sought to involve the young in the community. Sometimes they are reminded by the audiences that it takes more than greasepaint, funny hats and a didactic message to captivate the young, but their intentions are impeccable.

Among children themselves, powerfully pushed of course by commercial

interests, two great enthusiasms arise. In Britain these are football and pop music. The girls who follow around in the wake of the public appearances of a popular musician, from the airport to the recording studio and the concert halls of different cities, bring an enormous harvest for the record industry, but their devotion also acquaints them with the transport system, with the techniques of gaining admission to public performances, and (immensely important for the poor child) with the discipline of forward planning of personal activities. Exactly the same is observable among the followers of football, usually boys, who gain the same kind of incidental education. In finding their way to the football ground in a strange city, they accumulate fragments of the grimy industrial geography of the sport. They know their way about England in a way which is quite foreign to the British Tourist Authority.

Within the city the minority of children who actually play for a local or school team gather the same kind of transportation lore which opens up the means to using the city and discovering its routes and limits. No-one who has been astonished by the environmental ineptitude of the contemporary inner city child will minimise the personal importance of these incidental gains. The whole world of music in its many manifestations has the same result for the child musician, who gets to know the city's auditoria, the specialised shops and services which cater for their needs, as well of course as acquiring the self-confidence which accrues to the possessor of a skill and the cameraderie of the world of performers. From ballet to hang-gliding, gymnastics to coin-collecting, a specialist enthusiasm is the key to the exploitation of the city.

Fishing, for example, is an enormously popular yet almost invisible urban enthusiasm. At the week-ends the boys set off in the early morning with their rods, bait and sandwiches, for the rivers, ponds and reservoirs on the fringe of the city. They are meticulously informed in the lore and etiquette of the craft. They know where a license is required and where to obtain it, what may be taken from the river and what must be thrown back, and after the fisherman's contemplative day, come quietly home. Some children develop a passionate interest in transport itself. There are lovers of buses and trains with their encyclopaedic knowledge of depots, operating schedules and vehicles; and there are the dedicated cyclists and the girls in love with horses, who, if they know where, can gratify, even in the great city, their dreams of the saddle and the stable. The city can gratify the most esoteric enthusiasms, and the paradox is that the narrowest of interests can provide the child with the broadest of introductions to the art of making the city work.

Listen to Linda Whitney (14) describing her activities afloat in the inner city: "The Pirate Club has over 1,500 members. It is an open air club on the Camden Locks. It costs 3p to join and 3p for a whole week's rowing. The reason I go there is because there are lots of nice boys and they take you out in a boat and do the rowing. You can row two miles to Maida Vale tunnel, near Little Venice and back again. On the way you can see Regent's Park Zoo. We often stop to see the animals and birds. Anyone can join the club between the age of seven and sixteen. It's good fun except when you fall in the water. My brother once fell in. He untied his boat and went to jump. His boat had drifted away a little and he landed up in the canal. The thing I like about the club is it's so cheap. It is subsidised by the raids we do on the Jenny

Wren. Two of our skippers get into a boat. They go either side of the Jenny Wren, and the Captain of the club shouts out, "This is a pirate raid, throw your money in the two rowing boats." They don't have to throw in money but they usually do. Sometimes the money goes in the water. Once a 50 p piece went in. If a person falls in, they have lots of spare clothes and they put on the fire in the barge. They have lots of boats, boats for four people, boats for three and boats for two, or if you wish you can go in a canoe, but first you have to pass a test. It's quite easy. I've passed mine. If you have passed they put a 'T' on your Pirate Badge. It opens at 11 am and closes at 5.30 pm. It opens during the holidays and at weekends. It's somewhere to go and it keeps you fit and builds your muscles up."

Children's organisations, originally set up to rescue the child from the streets, or to win him for God or for the Nation or the Party, have probably failed to achieve these aims, which is just as well, but they have played an important part incidentally, in fostering the all-important urban know-how, in developing the habit of *using* the city. Whether it is the Boys' Brigade, the Scouts, the Little League or the Konsomol, the important instrumental lessons remain long after the ideology has been discarded.

When Paul Neuburg was a boy in Budapest and like all the other school-children of the city, joined the Red Flag Club, then actually run by the AVH, the State Security Corps, its ideology washed over him. "In fact it occurred to me to remember my socialist club with gratitude only when I emigrated to the West and found that there one had to pay for tickets to the pool and everything else". For him and the other boys it was simply "the thing that paid for our tickets to the swimming pool and our fares to and fro,

employed our coaches full time, gave us swimming trunks and bathing wraps, entered us for races and took us on a fortnight's holiday each summer. The loyalties that it bred, which we manifested in rooting for our team and shouting abuse at the referee during water-polo matches, had no more to do with State security than with crimson cloth, let alone socialism itself."

The first more-than-local uniformed organisation for boys, the Boys' Brigade, founded in Glasgow in 1883, rapidly spread throughout Britain. In a famous comment on its success Henry Drummond wrote, "Amazing and preposterous illusion! Call these boys 'boys' which they are, and ask them to sit up in a Sunday class and no power on earth will make them do it; but put a fivepenny cap on them and call them soldiers, which they are not, and you can order them about till midnight." It was evangelically Christian in motivation, and military in its appeal, but what former members recall was the chance to play fifes, bugles and drums. "If they had a big bass drum" remarks Frank Dawes, "the boy who was allowed to take it home to practice on had been accorded a great honour . . . there soon developed a sound quite unlike any other in the world; the sound of the local Boys' Brigade band."

It was the same with the scouts. When Baden-Powell wrote *Scouting for Boys*, spontaneously formed groups of scouts preceded any central organisation. The Scout movement's emphasis on woodcraft had been anticipated in the United States by Ernest Thompson Seton with his Woodcraft League at Summit, New Jersey in 1902. Critics of the Scouts in Britain have always drawn attention to the movement's official links with patriotism, militarism and religion. But the ethos from headquarters was often secondary to the uses made of the organisation by the kids. Louis Heren, for example, as a poor boy in the East End of London in the 1930s belonged to the 2nd City of London Sea Scouts which met in a derelict office building. "We were an odd lot," he recalls, "who had become sea scouts because there was no other way of getting near a boat" and he describes the troop as "a kibbutz, kongsi or commune of boys, an extraordinary self-governing, self-motivating and self-perpetuating group." Even when their headquarters was moved to Captain Scott's ship *Discovery*, moored on the Victoria Embankment in the heart of London, "amazingly, the independence and internal anarchy of the troop remained unimpaired".

In Britain John Hargrave, a Boy Scout Commissioner was expelled soon after the first world war for demanding a democratic organisation in the Boy Scouts and for the deletion of all the military and imperialist passages from the official handbook. This defection was followed by the foundation of the Woodcraft Folk under the auspices of the co-operative movement. And as recently as 1975 this body was under attack from the central office of the Conservative Party in Britain, with the complaint that its members (Elfins, aged 6 to 9, Pioneers, ages 10 to 12 and Venturers, aged 13 to 17) are exposed to lectures on Karl Marx and the Working Man's International. If this were anything like the whole truth about the Woodcraft Folk it would not today be a growing organisation, any more than would be the Scouts and Guides, who have tacitly abandoned those features of their original ideology and practice which would make them ridiculous to the contemporary urban child.

In the United States the Boy Scout movement is said to have been born when William D. Boyce, lost in London, was rescued by a scout who

impressed him with the creed of preparedness and helpfulness. Returning to Chicago he established the Boy Scouts of America in 1910, drawing upon the woodcraft movement set in motion by Ernest Thompson Seton and a variety of youth organisations. Its emphasis was on escaping from the debilitating influence of the city in favour of the great outdoors, but early in its history John Alexander explained that outdoor life was prescribed in order to enable the scout "to give the best he has to the city and community in which he lives".

The piety and worthy intentions that have always surrounded organisations for the child of the city conceal their actual usefulness for the child, usually the city boy, although the Girl Guides (and their junior organisation, the Brownies—originally Rosebuds) were founded in 1910 and in 1912 in the USA. Their real utility is in spacing out the week, in accustoming the member to forward planning, and to acquiring the habit of using the city's facilities. These are immense gains and in the internecine warfare of youth organisations the question of "Who joins?" has rightly been considered important. In the task of "rescuing" poverty-stricken children from the streets, Frank Dawes stresses the role of local boys' clubs. "It may be true that scouting, like the boys' brigades, tended to attract boys who were, as Waldo Eager puts it, 'in the comity of the nation, who attended church and chapel, had decent and orderly homes and, as a rule, accepted the usages of society.' Boys' clubs on the other hand, catered for working boys deprived of opportunities by poverty."

One veteran of the days when boys' clubs catered for boys who were working from the age of twelve or thirteen, describes the aura of the St John's College Mission at Walworth in south-east London, "The members fell into five classes, recognisable by their smell. The 'layers-on' and 'takers-off' from the big printing works smelled of printers' ink; boys from the boot factory smelled of blacking; those from the jam and pickle works smelled of raspberry jam for two months and of aromatic vinegar for ten; lads from the market smelled of fish and were covered with rough salt—a visitor said that sitting next to one at a boxing match was like clinging to the supports of a pier—and the fifth class of nondescripts, errand boys, beer bottlers and workers at the tan yards would and did smell of many things."

Canon Peter Green was looking back to the early years of the century from 1950. In the late 1950s when Dr Richard West was one of a galaxy of subsequently distinguished educators teaching the children or grandchildren of those boys at Walworth School, he found many of them so isolated in the locality that the school visit to the museums at South Kensington was their first trip to the north side of the River, so narrow was their experience of the city. By the 1970s teachers at the same secondary school were looking back nostalgically to the days when those smelly old industries were available as sources of employment for their school leavers.

The socialising and exploratory and enabling role of the club is as urgent a task in the contemporary city as it was in the city of the nineteenth century. But for thirty years or more the world of the youth club has been torn by dilemmas and doubts. The evangelical or didactic message, the assumptions of single-sex institutions, the emphasis on physical fitness, have all been rejected by the clientele. In the 1960s the concept arose of the "unclubbables", the assumption being that it was normal for adolescents to belong to a club and that there was something abnormal about those who did

Silversmiths

not. Coffee bars and cafes were started to attract them. Then this amorphous group became known as the "unattached" and this label shifted from the young to the youth worker. As John Ewen observes "From being a worker with the unattached, he gradually became known as a detached youth worker. It was not now the young people who were perceived as unattached, but rather the worker himself was detached from an institutionalised base. There seemed to be less conviction in the validity of young people's attachment to an institutionalised group or club, and more acceptance of the role of a worker who was free to work in the community without either the objective of relating clients to institutionalised provision, or a responsibility himself towards an institution." The final shift in ideology has been for this worker to become a facilitator, or what the French call an *animateur*, with the task of assisting the community itself to be more involved with the problems of its young, and the young to be more involved with the problems of their community.

It is easy to parody this approach and its assumption that there are some communities where these involvements occur naturally and others where a platoon of community workers have to be let loose on the unsuspecting inhabitants: social manipulation as yet another substitute for social justice. "Added to the traditional burdens of the poor" remark the authors of *The Wincroft Youth Project*, "there is now the weight of a bureaucracy that, ironically, is employed to serve them." The theory of community action as evolved by Saul Alinsky in the United States and by Richard Bryant in Britain defines the political impotence, or powerlessness, of the victim-community as *the* central problem. The Wincroft Project was a soberly-monitored exercise in detached youth work in a poor district of Manchester with 54 boys whose situation was thought to be typical of the adolescent years of many boys in the central slum areas of cities: "their social segregation from adults, their position at the base of the social pyramid, and their lack of a positive and helpful contact with the middle class are not unique, neither is the central formative influence of their peers or their exploitation of the opposite sex. Their life-chances have been largely determined by their parents' lack of wealth, their own lack of education, and the poverty of their environment."

The Wincroft workers insist that they were not merely concerned with

Window-Shopper

Aeromodeller

Leningrad Ice-Hockey Players

helping young people to adjust to their environment, but also with helping them to change it. "Indeed, the very existence of the project brought a radical change to their personal environment by introducing middle-class attitudes into their lives. One aim was to assist the participants to become more conscious of the factors, both personal and social, that shaped their lives and of the ways in which they could exercise more control over their own destinies. If they became dissatisfied with the poor range of jobs available in the neighbourhood they could be helped to apply for better jobs elsewhere; if they saw how the social pressures of their peers were forcing them into deliquency or maladjustment they could be helped to develop social ties elsewhere. It might be said, however, with some justification perhaps, that they were not confronted with the political choices that they might have to make to change their environment, and the concept of adjustment usually implied more effective relationships at the personal level rather than more active citizenship."

Non-teachers might very well have assumed that ten (now eleven) years of compulsory schooling would have given the Wincroft boys some awareness of the potentials for changing their own destinies. Teachers know that school is simply an episode in lives whose centre of gravity is somewhere else. It is very many years since William F. Whyte studied Street Corner Society and diagnosed not only the school but also the Settlement House as an "alien institution" requiring the acceptance of middle class standards, since its primary function was to stimulate social mobility amongst those who "are on their way out and up." All the studies of the deprived inner city child on either side of the Atlantic have shown how great are the odds against breaking out of the culture of poverty into the habit of using what the city offers. The issue is so intractable and so surrounded by social class assumptions, that some of the missionaries have understandably lost faith in their mission. In my own city those children with what middle-class sociologists sneer at as "middle-class" values, are set upon an escalator of experiences and activities which they travel up, at the public expense, so that the gap continually widens in the degree of urban competence and control over their own destinies which they enjoy, compared with that of the children who never set foot on this escalator.

12
Traffic and the Child

"For both children and teenagers, it is obvious that the local environment must be the focus of the planners' concern. Unless policies are directed towards providing local ease of movement and access, the curtailment of their independent activity might well be increased. Colin Buchanan has said that the freedom to walk around is a guide to the civilised quality of an urban area. But for these young people, the freedom to walk around defines the limits of their world."   MAYER HILLMAN

Traffic always was a hazard for the urban child. Old photographs of Victorian city streets show pedestrians wandering all over the road, standing in conversation in the middle of the street, ignoring the horsedrawn vehicles all around them. Nevertheless in 1865 in London 232 people were killed in traffic accidents. The 19th-century city child was familiar with iron-shod hooves and iron-tyred wheels, clattering and grinding with incessant noise over the granite setts of the street. He knew the names of the different kinds of carriage, and he knew horses from the delicate ponies pulling dog-carts and gigs to the huge shire horses of the brewers' drays, and the pairs pulling buses and trams and the splendid teams drawing the fire engine. The gutters he played in were lined with chaff and whisps of hay tossed out of the horses' nose-bags. The carriageway was continually manured with horse-dung, eagerly shovelled up before being ground into the road surface by the next set of hooves and wheels. When Arthur Newton was a boy in Hackney in the years before the First World War, children earned a ha'penny a bucket. When I was a boy in Ilford in the 'thirties, the milkman, the baker, the coalman, the old clothes man, the removal firm and the council's dustman still used horses, and the going rate was a penny. When Russell Miller grew up in the same suburb in the 'fifties, he used to hawk the manure from the milkman's horse from door to door at threepence a bucket. Today the only horses that pass our street are those of the brewery which still uses them for local deliveries, of the mounted policeman and the old iron man. No-one ventures into the street to collect the droppings, which just disappear into the oily road surface under the juggernauts from the other side of the continent.

A whole, lost, urban folklore grew up among the children of the 19th-century horse-propelled city, its principal element being the stories of the boys who were rewarded with a silver dollar or a gold half-sovereign for stopping a runaway horse. The risks were considerable. Another aspect of it is the vignette of the farrier, taking on a multitude of repair jobs for the locality, with an admiring child audience. One advantage of the horse-drawn city for the child was its pace. Most vehicles moved slowly enough for rides to be stolen. When my father was a child in the East India Dock Road, he proudly graduated one day to the status of the boys who chased the horse-trams and clung behind. He rushed home to tell his mother, "Mum, Mum, I run behind trams," and was mortified by a slap. E. M. Forster's Lucy Honeychurch, watching from her hotel window the life of the street in Florence, saw the tram conductor unaggressively spitting in the faces of the street boys to drive them off the back of the vehicle. In the Newcastle of Jack Common's boyhood "often there was a cry of 'Whip behind', and a couple of small boys would drop off the back and pick themselves up with bleeding knees and throwing sharp daring glances at any adults that might be about."

The ordinary residential street was free of fast-moving traffic. It was a safe place to play. Nor was it lined with parked vehicles. The horse-drawn city had a network of livery and "bait" stables, mews and coach-houses,

which, apart from ensuring that the streets held only moving traffic, provided work for the city boy in grooming, feeding and watering the horses. When a carriage was parked for, say, the doctor's visit, he would earn a tip for "holding the horse's head" in the same way that today, Latin American street children extort a fee for "looking after" parked cars. The child in the horse-drawn city was familiar with the lore of animal management, not only through the ever-present horses, but because herds of cows were kept in inner city dairies, pigs and goats as well as chickens in backyards, while sheep were driven to market in the inner city within living memory. In the nineteen-thirties, as well as in wartime, they grazed Hyde Park.

The poorer the street, the more absent were vehicles, and consequently the greater was the opportunity the street itself provided for children's games, and of course, because of overcrowding, the greater the need to use the street. It could be argued that the whole style of English football and cricket has been affected by the dimensions and constraints of working-class streets, especially since professional sport is one of the few avenues out of a lifetime of dreary and repetitive jobs for the poor boy. Consider the restrictive effect of neighbours' windows on those wide-sweeping master-strokes which bring glory to the game. West Indian cricketers and Brazilian footballers learn flamboyant play on beaches. Their British equivalents learn confined play in the streets and housing estates of provincial cities. In the handball, softball and baseball games played in the American city street, the ubiquitous parked cars are less of an inhibition than they are in Europe. In the USA the car is much more a utility than a status-confering object. It represents a smaller proportion of its owner's annual income, and less attention is paid to the hazards that street games present for it, or to the scratches and dents risked when children clamber over it.

But the modern city child is deprived not only because of the terrible casualty rate that traffic imposes, but also because of the restrictions on child activity that this implies. In Britain 800 children die and 40,000 are injured every year in traffic accidents and it is calculated that, if present trends continue, a child has a one-in-20 chance of being involved as a pedestrian before the age of 15. In 1972, 33 casualties to children under five occurred every day in Britain. The Royal Society for the Prevention of Accidents deduced from one city's statistics that "50 per cent of children were unaccompanied at the time they were involved in accidents," and it concluded that parents were "shirking their responsibilities by letting the children out alone." The head of the ROSPA road safety division said that a survey showed that one mother in eight of two-year-olds and half the mothers of five-year-olds believed their children capable of crossing a busy road unaccompanied, and that half the mothers of children between two and four are quite happy to let their children play in the street.

Many of these mothers of course, have no choice in the matter. Their children can either play in the street or not at all. In any case the other 50 per cent of children involved in accidents were actually accompanied by an adult or an older child at the time. In 40 per cent of the cases the child was obscured from the view of the driver by a parked car, and in 14 per cent of the accidents an ice cream van was involved in some way. However, to attribute the dreaful proportion of traffic accidents involving children to parental neglect is to ignore the people behind the wheel, and their responsibility. There is, commented Lucy and Michael Mulcay from York, "something very much amiss with the attitudes of motorists and the conditions with which parents and children are forced to contend." Over a third of the population of England and Wales have no access to the use of a car, and most of these are, needless to say, the inhabitants of the inner city. The children who are most at risk from the car in the city are those who have least access to its benefits. The Newsons in their survey of child-rearing in Nottingham, found that in the inner city, "children in these more dangerous streets are, if anything, kept under closer supervision, class for class, than children elsewhere."

The assumption that the car-driver has a natural right to take his vehicle anywhere in the city has, quite apart from the threat to life, gradually attenuated many of the aspects of the city that made it an exciting and useable environment for children. The street life of the city has been slowly whittled away to make more room for the motor car. There is scarcely a city in Britain where great swathes have not been cut through the pattern of streets to provide inner ring roads which leave the adult pedestrian, let alone the child, bewildered and directionless as he attempts to find his way through the city. Whole areas which were once at the disposal of the explorer on foot are now dedicated to the motorist. The city, which used to be

London

South Africa

The Corner of Tenth Street and Avenue B, New York

Chasing a car in Philadelphia

transparent to its young citizens who could follow the routes across it unerringly, is now opaque and impenetrable. Try to find your way on foot across Glasgow or Birmingham, or across inner London, just to see how impossible it would be for a child. In the American city such a walk has long been unthinkable.

In Britain the authors of the PEP report on personal mobility reach the conclusion that children and teenagers are now less mobile than they were in the past. Mayer Hillman and his colleagues find it symptomatic of the neglect of children's needs, that although in recent decades quantities of research and money have been invested in the study of planning and transportation, no comprehensive studies had been attempted until they undertook their work on mobility and accessibility. Of their own findings they write, "The main theme running through the surveys of both teenagers and children was that of independence. This was because, firstly, it would provide essential data for planning policy. If it can be seen that teenagers and children make the great majority of their trips with other members of the household, then one can assume that, in providing for adult needs, those of children will also be met. If, on the other hand, their trips are made independently, it would be possible to see how their special needs can be met in planning. Secondly, independence is a pre-condition of various aspects of growth and maturity. These aspects have been recognised for many years as important by educationists and psychologists in the planning of school curricula. It would be ironic if attempts to foster freedom and independence inside the school were matched by an increasingly inappropriate outside environment. Yet childhood memories of the freedom to walk and cycle anywhere, with few parental restrictions or cautions, point to this being the case. During the 1960s, traffic levels almost doubled, and while the rate for adult pedestrian fatalities or serious injuries increased by 9 per cent, the rate for those below 17 rose by 52 per cent."

Chasing a car in Shanghai

121

The present generation of adults, Hillman and his colleagues remark, took for granted when young the freedom of *independent* travel. "Were not many of the more memorable and instructive experiences of your childhood the ones which occurred when alone or with friends rather than with parents?" But they find that today's children are, so far as independent travel is concerned, placed in the role of second class citizens. Policy-makers used to talk glibly of "universal car ownership", ignoring the fact that it can never apply to the quarter of the population below driving age, while a "debased status" in transport planning is given to the methods of travel—walking, cycling and the bus—which *are* available to children. Most travel surveys, for example, ignore walking, yet the Hillman survey shows that walking is the most common method of travel that people, particularly children, mothers of young children, and the old, use daily. "Yet because of parental concern over road safety, we have found that the majority of children are not allowed to cross main roads on their own until they have reached the age of eight, and even at the age of nine, a third are subject to this restraint."

Public transport, cheap and easily available, was a great liberator of the city child in the form of the electric trams which appeared in British cities at the turn of the century. Gondolas of the people was Richard Hoggart's description of them, and Robert Roberts remarked that "for the first time in history the undermass enjoyed the benefits of cheap urban travel . . . In summer, loads of children were to be seen rattling along the rails *en route* for fields and parks, and innumerable families experienced the pleasure of day trips to attractions in far corners of the city, delights which previously time and expense had made impossible: now journeys were about half as dear and more than twice as fast as those made on the old horse trams." Asa Briggs, the historian of Victorian cities, told me that in his opinion, the tram was for the young traveller the most manipulable of all forms of public transport. "The circular routes meant that you didn't have to change buses," he explained, "but in the modern city, with its roads reconstructed in the 1960s, even our sense of direction has been lost."

On public transport children, like other bus users, are now the victims of steadily declining services. Bus routes are of course heavy traffic routes, and parents generally forbid unaccompanied bus travel up to the age of nine or 10. Secondary school children, the Hillman surveys found, also have serious problems, one of them being that although the minimum school leaving age is now 16, children have to pay adult fares from the age of 14. Another is of course that their journey to school is usually longer than that of primary school children. Hillman comments that in the policy of making secondary schools larger and fewer, little attention has been paid to the longer and less convenient journeys of many children, while local authorities bemoan the ever-increasing cost of free transport for the growing number of children who live beyond the statutory walking distance.

Transport planners and the police give priority to traffic flows. In March 1976, Peter Kavanagh, assistant commissioner for traffic in London was actually calling for higher speed limits. From the police point of view it is preferable that children should travel to school by public or private bus, while children themselves prefer the independence and flexibility of walking or cycling. (They are not incidentally, the favourite passengers of bus crews.) Thinking of the changes in policy needed to give justice to the urban child, Meyer Hillman's team give their first priority to reducing the need and incentive for motorised travel and to recognising cycling as a means of travel ideally suited to the needs of active children. Justice to the child implies, they say, "a drastic curtailment of the 'freedom of the road' currently enjoyed by the 23 per cent of the English population with a car of their own. But is that freedom so precious that more basic freedoms can be sacrificed for it?"

It is from West Germany that further important research comes on the particular vulnerability of the urban child. Professor Adolf Windorfer, chairman of the West German Pediatrics Association remarks that "It is intolerable that drivers should be acquitted in court following a road accident involving a child just because the child is held responsible from a legal point of view," and he cites the findings of psychologists in Munich on the understanding of traffic that can be expected from three- to six-year-olds. They conclude that children cannot discern from the sound from which direction a car is coming, and that they can recognise noise differences but not the direction of noise. Nor can they adequately estimate distances. "To a child a car 50 yards away seems to be 'miles' off. The child does not realise that at 30 mph it will only take the vehicle three seconds to reach him." Children also find it difficult to recognise the "shape of movement" "When a dog runs it constantly changes its shape, its appearance, but a car or a train at a rail crossing remains the same shape and only grows larger as it approaches nearer." Children have difficulty recognising left from right. Road signs have little or no meaning to small children. They also have difficulty in concentrating for a period greater than fifteen minutes.

The Munich findings are elementary wisdom for the Piaget-trained school teacher. In the light of them perhaps it is surprising that any child survives the experience of the modern city street. The effort to make children aware of the dangers of traffic are not new. British readers in their sixties and seventies will recall the "Danger Don'ts" printed on the backs of their school exercise books. Those in their forties will recall the kerb drill introduced in the early years of the war. The present generation of British school children were inititated into the Green Cross Code in 1971. But very serious doubts arise about the capacity of many children to learn and understand the concepts of the code.

The world's foremost authority on the behaviour of children in traffic is Dr Stina Sandels of the Institute for Child Development Research in Stockholm. The results of her years of study of children's capacity for coping with the modern city are profoundly disquieting. Her findings as to the peripheral vision and the capacity for sound location among children underline the Munich research. You can get children to learn kerb drill by rote, but you will find that they do not really understand it and cannot actually put it into practice. What is the point of urging them to look right, then left, then right again, if they cannot, or if the majority of an age group fail to, tell one from the other. "Considerable differences could be observed between the ability of children aged six to ten to grasp the meaning of words such as 'crossing', 'traffic regulation', 'vehicle', 'pedestrian', 'turning', 'main road', 'keep to the left', or questions like 'Why do ambulances have sirens on?' Some of the words were so easy that even the six-year-olds understood them. Examples are 'ambulance' and 'to get lost'. Others were so difficult that not even the ten year olds grasped them, and examples of these were 'communication', 'traffic island', and 'keep to the left'."

Adults may believe that children *ought* to be able to understand traffic signs and traffic terminology, but the fact is that very many do not. Dr Sandels argues that it is impossible to adapt small children to the traffic environment: "They are biologically incapable of managing its many demands". This does not lead to the conclusion that traffic education is a waste of time; on the contrary we must continually strive to make road safety education more effective and more comprehensible. But when some accident "was the child's fault" it was not. It was our fault for not having safeguarded him. But having said this, do we conclude that children should not be allowed out unprotected? This would be an impossible policy and in any case would delay the child's growth to traffic competence. But Dr Sandels quotes a Swedish insurance report that "among the most common errors made by vehicle drivers is the lack of caution shown when passing children," and she suggests that the reason for this lack of caution is probably that drivers have been given too little instruction about human behaviour.

If you think that a change in the attitudes of drivers is a forlorn hope, you are bound to wonder just what strategies of vehicle restriction are desirable to curtail city traffic in the interests of the survival of the city child.

When Pauline Pratt attempted to sum up current findings on child pedestrian casualties, she focussed attention on the findings of psychologists about "accident-prone" children:

"Many children are 'programmed for disaster' by their home environment. Parents are unwittingly sending them from unhappy, disturbed homes to death and injury in the street, and no amount of conventional road safety propaganda can keep them safe ... The most relentless losses occur between the ages of five and nine. Most vulnerable are town children—often struck down in the very street where they live. Among the most critical times is the late-afternoon period, after schools have closed, although more youngsters are killed or maimed on Saturdays or during school holiday periods than on schooldays ... Much of the well-meant propaganda effort has been misdirected and ineffective because nobody has understood the 'faulty mechanisms of childhood', or appreciated that, all too often, accidents in the street are triggered in the home."

She cites the findings of the paediatrician Dr Peter Husband, when he looked into the background of children in Fulham who were repeatedly involved in accidents. More than half of their families were badly housed, in more than half there was serious physical or psychiatric illness in other members of the family, and in more than a quarter of the cases the child came from a "broken" home. The children, who had an average of almost six accidents each, were described as unusually active, "daredevil, extroverted and rebellious."

Pauline Pratt concludes from a report of the European Ministers of Transport, that Britain has the worst child pedestrian casualty rate for all of Europe, but the same shameful statistic is claimed by Siegfried Bush-schluter for West Germany with its annual total of 68,898 children involved in road accidents, including 1,781 deaths. He observes that "It is not so much the lack of concern or understanding on the part of their parents, it is society's unwillingness to accept children as people with rights of their own. One has to appreciate the general attitude towards children in West German

Years ago Joe Benjamin devised this 2¼ acre Traffic Town off the Hampstead Road in London, with roads, traffic lights, a petrol station and pedestrian crossings

society if one wants to understand why so many of them are killed, maimed or injured on the roads. But it is not just this lack of regard for the young and weak members of society; one must add the general ruthlessness of the average West German motorist. Watching the behaviour of motorists in a big town like Frankfurt, one cannot help feeling that pedestrians are just 'traffic'—not people."

In Britain there is, as you will have seen, a sharp division among those who have pondered on the significance of child road accidents, and their implications in human terms, between ROSPA which condemns irresponsible parents and the authors of the PEP report who condemn social attitudes which assume that the vehicle has priority. In practice, those parents who have the luxury of being able to exercise a constant supervision of their children (and this does not include the parents of the "latchkey" children of the city) are in a hopeless dilemma. You cannot keep your children under house-arrest. If you attempt to do so, they will escape, and if they don't escape, they will undoubtedly have been deprived of vital environmental experiences. The day after Christmas in 1959 I met a man crying in the street. He was a clergyman and he had just come from visiting the home of a boy killed that very morning. The boy, who had not been allowed to have a bicycle himself, had been riding on a friend's cycle, a Christmas present from the previous day. He had swerved to avoid a motorist who opened the offside door of a parked car, and had been run over by a bus. The day after Christmas in 1974, a nine-year old boy from Brixton, was killed when he fell between an underground train and the platform at Victoria Station, while on a "fare-dodging" trip on the railway. His mother said at the inquest that she had not given him any money and that he had never to her knowledge been on a train, even though the family had lived in London for three years. Unfamiliarity with transport and its hazards can be as lethal as constant exposure to them. The architect Peter Shepheard told me for example the terrible and macabre story of the motorist who cheerfully drove over a cardboard carton in the road, only to find that there was a child inside.

Wheels in the Street

"One of the cyclists is in panoply, with a coonskin hat and totemic jacket, and on the handlebars foxtails and the flags of the United Nations, plus horn, mirror, speedometer, and other accessories. The other cyclist has the functional style; the wheels have no mudguards, the handlebars have no grips; he is barefoot and wearing a singlet and threadbare jeans; he would ride naked if it were allowed.

"Of the 3 kids at the red light, one keeps his seat, foot on the ground; the second stands on a straight leg, resting the other leg on the crossbar; the smallest stands, holding the bike . . ."

PAUL GOODMAN

The bicycle is so perfect a machine for the independent savouring of the city by the child, so healthy, so economical, so perfectly attuned, as Paul Goodman noted, to the personal skill and even the personal *style*, of its user, that it is one of the tragedies of the contemporary city that today cycling has become so increasingly hazardous and unpleasant that Meyer Hillman in the survey cited in the previous chapter, found that "total cycle mileage has

dropped sharply in recent years to about one sixth of what it was when today's parents were children." We have become so used to the idea of a bicycle revival, at least among adults, that we may be surprised, unless we are parents, to learn from Hillman and his colleagues that "mothers gave ten as the average age at which they will allow their child to cycle on main roads, (one in ten said they would never allow such a thing) although cycle ownership amongst seven-year-olds is 75 per cent and amongst ten-year-olds is over 60 per cent. Only half the cycle owners amongst junior school children ever use their cycle for getting to parks, playgrounds or friends' homes, and even fewer use them for getting to clubs, libraries and other less local facilities. For the journey to school only one in 100 junior school and only one in 10 secondary school children go by cycle."

In many United States cities the cyclist, and especially the child cyclist (for until the recent cycle boom, adult cyclists had become regarded as eccentrics) is given a privileged situation as a road user, at least by

comparison with British practice, (except in Stevenage with its comprehensive network of cycle paths) rather like the preferential treatment
awarded at sea to sail over steam. In some Eastern cities, though not in those
of the West Coast, the cyclist may ride on the "wrong" side of the road,
facing the oncoming traffic. He may also go against the flow of traffic in a
one-way street, as he can in Cambridge, England or Eindhoven, Holland.
This simple and desirable convention which treats the cyclist as though he
were a pedestrian (which by virtue of his pedals he is) is quite the opposite of
the treatment of the child cyclist in some European cities. In parts of
Germany even small children on miniature bicycles are not allowed to ride
them on the pavement, but have to take their chance with the ruthlessness of
the motorist. On the other hand some German cities like Hanover with 348
kilometres of cycle track or Bremen with 259, and some American cities like
Palo Alto, have in the last decade recognised the needs of cyclists in the
provision of networks of cycleways for their exclusive or semi-exclusive use.
In Finland and in other Scandinavian countries, child cyclists using the road
have a reflective pennant on a long stiff wire attached at right angles on the
off-side of their handlebar or saddle stems. Motorists have to keep a certain
distance from this pennant.

The kind of long-term vacant site in the inner city that used to be "won" by
young cyclists as a race-track is nowadays impenetrably fenced or is in use as
a car park. Suburban children can still find such sites, though the UNESCO
survey reports that "In Melbourne, the children were finally driven off the
mini-bike track, the one bit of ground in all that area which they had
changed to suit their own purposes. But the air photos show that previous
tracks have been made and abandoned on other vacant lots. This must have
been a continuing guerrilla war."

No city child today can perform such hair-raising tricks as "riding our
kid's bike between two trams" as Alan Brien remembers doing in
Sunderland, and in British and American cities children are unlikely any
longer to get free rides clinging to the backs of buses and lorries, though there
are plenty of cities where this is still a commonplace. In Glasgow there are
legends about the boys absent from school because they were "awa' for a
hurl on the midden cairt" and had to be rescued from the municipal refuse
tip. In summer, in those cities which still have water-carts washing down the
street in the daytime, children gratefully follow it, though few have the
experience of Sonia Keppel, an aristocratic child in Edwardian London: "A
water-cart rattled slowly towards me with plumes of water spraying out
behind like a peacock's tail. At the corner of the square, the cart stopped
beside me, and I noticed that it had a ledge across the back of it and a step up
behind the back wheel. I climbed up on the water-cart. And thereafter, I was
partially concealed behind a wall of spray. We forged across Portman Square
as though drawn by sea-horses. I felt rather sick but elated, and as wet as a
mermaid. So I was sorry when the cart hove-to in Wigmore Street. To my
alarm, a policeman approached the back of it, and lifted me off and put me on
my feet. The policeman asked my name. I answered 'Baby'. Fortunately he
discovered a label to give me identity: a small gold bangle with a pendant
diamond 'S'. Carefully he assessed it and my relative value to it. Then he
carried it and me to the police-station in Marylebone Lane."

Roller-skating is a pastime far less frequently met in the streets of
American and British cities than it was fifty years ago, though Sean Jennett

Following the water cart in Cotton Street, Poplar, London in 1919

*Roller-skating under the
Autobahn*

Skateboarding in London

notes that it is still to be found on the smooth surface of the Cour Carrée or in the Luxembourg Gardens, while "skaters are in season a frequent peril of the streets of Paris." But in the mid-seventies the place of roller skates has been taken over in America and Britain by the skateboard—the dry land equivalent of surfing, its manufacturers claim—in the form of a plastic board with four tiny wheels, which gives the experienced user the chance to perform the most graceful and exciting gyrations. When they first appeared in London, I wondered where on earth they could be used, since there is no room for them in the street. But slowly, in the crowded city, the skateboarders have sought out places smooth enough and sloping enough to develop the art. There is the Broad Walk in Kensington Gardens, the traffic island at the south of Wandsworth Bridge (known to the local children as "The Hills", since the landscape architect thoughtfully provided non-utilitarian slopes) and the arid concrete spaces under the Queen Elizabeth Hall on the South Bank (already in use by young cyclists for bronco-riding from steps to slopes). News of useable sites passes from mouth to mouth among the members of the skateboard cult. Junior members make adaptations of the roller skates they got last Christmas but could not use. Older experts save for the latest high-technology equipment. Fifteen-year-old Orlando works all day Saturday in a bakery for £5 to pay for the custom-built board he uses all day Sunday, standing on his hands in incredible acrobatic ingenuity.

In every African city, from Kano to the Cape, a different sort of ingenuity is displayed. "African children have few toys," John Gale remarked, "but

African boy's wire car

those they have they make from almost nothing." They make pull-along or push-along cars from any kind of bobbin, cotton-reel or cocoa-tin lid that turns up, mounted on bits of wire and wood. They collect the wire from the backyards of shops and from the municipal rubbish pit. Eleanor Laycock, watching the world of children in Lusaka, the capital of Zambia, reports that "Boys are most commonly seen running up and down with their cars, pushing them along from a standing position. A long heavy wire, bent into a circle at the driving end, is attached at the other end to the front axle of the car in such a fashion that the boy steers the car by turning the wheel in his hands. One of several steering mechanisms may be employed. After a boy decides which type of car or truck to build, he straightens and cuts lengths of heavy and light wire. The chassis is built first, and from this the proportions of the sides assessed. The model may be purely exterior, or finishing touches—a front seat, driver and steering wheel—may be added. No tools are used; none but hammerstones are available. Stove- or shoe-polish tins are usually used for wheels, enclosing wire circles stemming from the axles."

The African boy's wire car is built at every level of sophistication, from abstract skeletal outlines to sophisticated models which re-invent several engineering principles. "The cars I like very much to design", a nine-year-old told Eleanor Laycock, "are Fiats and Land Rovers." Norman Douglas remarked that if you want to know what children can do, you must stop giving them things, and the African children have shown how wise he was, but in the rich cities of Europe there is a hierarchy of shop-bought pavement toys, geared to the child's growing skill. First there is a little truck or trolley to pull or push, then a tricycle, then the scooter and the miniature cycle—what used to be called the fairy-cycle—and the pedal car. James Kenward remarks that pedal-motors "appeared on the pavements about ten years after grown-up motors had appeared on the roads" and lagged about ten years behind in body-style for a quarter of a century. He calls it the most fascinating but most unsatisfactory of pavement toys, "a knee-bumping, short-cranked, short-lived thing", too heavy for the toddler and too cramped for the older child.

The scooter, by contrast, is an economical toy of high utility but low prestige. But the prince of pavement toys is still a home-made four-wheeled vehicle, the soap-box or go-cart, or what Mr Kenward calls the urchin car:

"The urchin car, as you know, is perennial. It is time-honoured. Its layout has become traditional like that of the harvest waggon, the plough, the sailing yacht, the sewing machine, the bicycle and other satisfying functional things. It consists of a wooden box mounted on a stouter and longer board, at the front of which there is a swivelling cross-bars carrying the front wheels. Occasionally the driver sits in front of the box and steers directly with his feet. But traditionally, because the urchin car has descended to us from the days of the horse-drawn bus, he sits or kneels in the box and steers by reins of string attached to the cross-bar. He is a bit of a coachman in fact. Nowadays I have no doubt he pictures a motor bonnet in front of him; but I have no doubt that his predecessors saw that protruding board as a shaft, and the two front wheels representing a pair of horses in double harness. As a word can represent a different picture to different generations so can an affair of nails and wood."

In both Britain and the US, this kind of cart has been developed into a sophisticated competition racer by scout groups in Soap-box Derbies, but its great beauty is that the components for constructing it are to be won almost anywhere. Often its wheels are those from the perambulator or push-chair in which the builder was propelled as an infant. Sometimes they have been seized from abandoned push-along toys or from a wheeled shopping basket. Frequently today their chassis is recognisably part of one of those supermarket shopping trolleys which can be found abandoned in streets far from their origin. Ian Taylor and Paul Walton met in Bradford a group of ten and eleven-year-olds "utilising the technological spin-off from consumer society. They had stripped down several supermarket trolley baskets and had perfected their own roller coaster gliding down the car-park slope at hair-raising speed, all the time spinning round in circles . . ." In Lusaka a ten-year-old explained to Eleanor Laycock, "It is difficult to obtain the wheels, because sometimes it is risky. I went to a construction site to look for wheelbarrows to take the wheels out. After I collected the wheels, I got a wide plank and two iron bars, to which I fixed the four wheels. I tied the axles to the plank with wires, and made a steering wheel. Friends pushed me, and one day we went to Lilanda where the traffic policeman caught us and took the car away from us."

A slope is the essential terrain for the go-cart, and James Kenward, growing up in South London at the time of the first world war, was fortunate in living on a hill, and in having as a neighbour the unforgettable Mervyn: "He lived a few houses further up the hill, he was thirteen years old, and he built himself an elaborate motor-car . . . for going downhill. But while the other pavement toys, pedal motors included, rattled over the knobbly patches, Mervyn's car rumbled. You might say it thundered. It had a pair of grown-up tricycle wheels in front and a pair of thick trolley wheels—I imagine they came from a porter's trolley—at the back, and its weight was the secret of its speed. Owing to its weight it had to be towed up the hill in stages. . . .

"The elaborate features of the car were its steering and its brakes. Both were made up of Meccano parts. As for the brakes, a variety of hand-levers situated at intervals along the right-hand side of the car, so that passengers could assist if and when the driver ordered, worked upon a variety of interconnected Meccano strips that ended at a wooden block; and as for the steering, that was an equally complicated arrangement of Meccano parts underneath. How these were connected with the steering wheel—a small child's hoop with a cross of Meccano strips, possibly the earliest example of 'spring spoke' steering in the world—I cannot imagine. But they were. Moreover the car could be steered by one hand. Under the bonnet, which was lifted from the front and supported by a rod in the present-day fashion, Mervyn kept oil, rags, ointment, tools and all the rest of his Meccano parts. After each adventure he would sit down in the lane at the bottom of the hill and go over all the nuts, surrounded by a little circle of admirers anxious to pass him down any extra tools or parts required. Yet he never dominated. He had a soft, almost singing voice, and a protective attitude towards the smaller children. Only once, so far as I can remember, did he give me a ride. We crashed. Almost at the bottom of the hill something went wrong with the steering, and we slewed off the pavement into the road and overturned. I remember standing and looking at the bent brake-levers through my tears. But Mervyn paid no attention to them. He mopped my face with his roll of bandage, led me up the hill, over the railway bridge, and into the little shop on the opposite corner, where he bought me two half-penny Easter eggs. Then he led me home."

In the contemporary city, boys of Mervyn's age have often graduated to a

the Go Cart

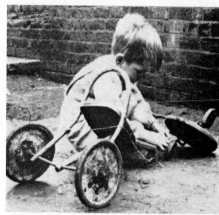

different kind of joy-riding: the offence known to both boys and police as TD—taking and driving away. In London, where half the people arrested for indictable offences are under 21, twenty-nine per cent were in 1975 aged between ten and 16. The assistant Crime Commissioner remarks that "Fourteen years of age is a popular age for auto thefts. They've got bundles of keys on them—you'd be amazed." Howard Parker in his study of the activities of boys in inner Liverpool, reports on joy-riding as a common practice among the ten to twelve-year-olds:

"The Tiddlers have shown considerable initiative and ability in learning car-key codes, makes of cars, types of gear change and various methods of starting cars such as making a circuit with a pair of scissors. Chalkie and Tiddler are now in fact fairly safe drivers, with gear changing and improved cornering part of their repertoire. Further, it is no longer enough to take any old car; the status of the car has become relevant, with Cortinas and Marinas (which the police also drive) being highly favoured. In lots of ways these youngsters are showing a desire for the straightforward respectable status of being a car owner. They talk at length about the merits and drawbacks of various cars, the only big difference from the talk of the ordinary car owner being their addition of status matters important to their image amongst the conversation culture. Hence talk is often centred on how fast you've been, have you had a chase off a police car, have you had a crash, a lucky escape and so on." Mr Parker says that the older boys look at these escapades with a certain amazement. "They're doing things now we never dared to do when we were kids, they're much worse than we ever were."

It is not a new story. In the summer of 1890 in New York City, Michael Givigia, aged seven and William Naegee, aged ten, were arrested, locked in jail and charged with horse-stealing. "Naegee was already familiar with the craft of horse-stealing. Earlier he had stolen a wagon and its team, a goat-cart, and a horse. Naegee and Givigia found a horse and wagon at Pier 29, and took off on a joy ride." Their modern equivalents have formidable technical expertise. A London magistrate told me that there had appeared before her a boy whom no-one would believe was nine years old, who admitted to 56 offences of taking and driving away, and knew all about the gear-changing characteristics of many types of cars. An eleven-year-old, who succeeded in driving and safely bringing to a halt a heavy lorry, was so small that the police thought there was nobody in the vehicle.

The motorised city provides other opportunities for the urban young to exploit its technology. Scrumping in the meter orchard is one. Inspector Jane Foley of the Metropolitan Police told the Howard League that many city children see the coins in parking meters in the same way as rural children regard apples on the tree: it's all right to take one or two. The city children had the advantage of course, that their trees always had fruit.

14
Filling the Shelves of the Supermarket

"I am on Bombay railway station, bag in hand. An urchin of about five years of age, carrying a child of about two, a smouldering *bidi* tucked in his mouth, approaches me and says 'can I haul your luggage, chief?' 'You seem to be having a tough time hauling yourself, child, I say. He throws his cigarette with a touch of film-starism to the ground, as though accepting a challenge. 'Who are you calling child'? he demands indignantly. 'I've got kids as old as you pulling rickshaws in Singapore.' "

FARRUKH DHONDY

North Europeans, visiting the cities of the Mediterranean, or North Americans visiting the cities of Latin America, sit in cafes in sunlit streets, noticing with what sweet gravity Yusef or Pedro takes their order, and with what a flourish of napkin over skinny arm he whisks away the dishes. "Why, he can't be more than eleven" whispers one tourist to another, as they watch the boy in the bazaar, sitting cross-legged, stitching together the tooled leather purses they are about to buy.

The reflective traveller thinks about the long hours these children must work, but secretly contrasts the demeanour of the bored visiting children and the busy indigenous ones. Thoughts cross his mind that contradict the conventional wisdom about children and work. But he knows that the industrial revolution in Britain reached its take-off point through the systematic exploitation of the labour of children, and that, decades later, the same was true of the period of maximum capital accumulation in United States industry, and that in consequence generations of humane people dedicated themselves to eradicating child labour. He would certainly find it difficult to name an instance where juvenile labour had an institutionalised place in the economy and was not associated with unconcealed exploitation.

There is of course a fundamental difference between the situation of the child who must work, to support or help support the family, and the child who works to provide himself with those non-necessities which he would otherwise go without, or for which he would otherwise be dependent on others. This is the difference between child labour in the cities of the poor world, or in the poor districts of the rich world's cities, and the work performed by children in the rich world, where it is frowned upon but provides a different kind of experience: that of independence, rather than of servitude. Even when child labour is an economic necessity, there have always been those children right at the bottom of the social heap, who saw the opportunity to work as an aspect of personal freedom. Mike Francis told me about ten-year-old Nizamuddin, who sells cigarettes for from 12 to 18 hours a day outside the Intercontinental Hotel in Dacca. Like the other street boys of the city, he is fiercely independent, accepting help on his own terms. Nizamuddin is incredibly tenacious: he has to be to retain that pitch against all comers. He speaks three languages and talked to Mike Francis about his desire to go to school. But in the background there is a family of eight people dependent on his earnings.

Who is, and who is not, a child from the point of view of the labour market, differs from place to place and from one legislature to another. In Britain, when the proposal to raise the minimum school leaving age from 14 to 15 was being debated in Parliament in 1936, Lord Halifax declared that manufacturers assured him that there was work for nimble little fingers in the mills of Lancashire. It was not until 1947 that the age was actually raised. Similarly the next stage: that of raising the age from 15 to 16, envisaged in

School attendance officer questioning the boy who is helping the milkman

Selling fruit to travellers in an African city

Newsboy, Johannesburg

Newsboys playing cards

the 1944 Education Act, was actually accomplished in 1974. No-one has yet suggested the next redefinition of the child's right not to work, though as Farrukh Dhondy says, "if schoolchildren are indeed children because they are forced by law to exist as dependents, then the raising of the school leaving age gave us a new generation of them. Through the immaculate conception of law, a whole new stratum of school children was brought into being. Waged adults or unemployed workers of 15+ were at a stroke cut off from this potential wage or from the right to unemployment payment."

In developed countries the legitimate ways in which children can earn money for themselves outside school hours have dwindled to the consumer end of the distributive trades: filling the shelves in the supermarket, helping the milkman, delivering papers, and similar activities which depend on putting items with a low unit price into the hands of customers, at a delivery cost below the normal cost of labour. The obvious instance, sanctified in American folklore, is the paperboy. From the newsboy to editor, tycoon, mogul, president, is the stereotype celebrated in the nineteenth century by Horatio Alger and exemplified by all those magnates who had the foresight and self-confidence to get photographed in the act of selling a newspaper when young.

Their contemporary equivalent in British and American cities does not sell papers at the city street-corner, but delivers them before school in the morning or after it in the afternoon. His earnings hardly expand the family budget, but they do give the boy or girl a precious degree of independence from parental pocket money. The job also induces habits of early rising—yet another aspect that endears it to the puritan conscience. The biggest English wholesale and retail newsagents, W. H. Smith and Sons, published in the 1930s an account of the virtues of the task:

"The Newsboy—the term includes the Newsgirl as well—when he starts out on his first round, is setting his foot on the lowest rung of a ladder which reaches up step by step to the highest positions in the Firm. How far he climbs and how fast he climbs depends almost entirely upon the boy himself . . . As for the healthiness of the jog— ask the parents of any W.H.S. boy; the regular early hours, the fresh air, the exercise, have made it a perfect health cure to many a weakling, and there are plenty of men today who could tell you that they owe there vitality to their early days on 'rounds' . . . It would provide a wonderful record if all the friendships which have sprung up between customers and W.H.S. boys in the course of their work could be told; there is hardly a boy who could not tell of some customer from whom he will be sorry to part one day . . ."

Notwithstanding the unctuousness of W. H. Smith and Sons, the paper round *is* a very satisfactory task for a child. It gives a functional justification for the desire for a bicycle, it may enable him to pay for it, and it encourages him to maintain it. It gives him an intimate knowledge of the local townscape: the quickest route, the sheltered or windy roads. It gives some insight into the class structure of readership—what kinds of papers are read by what type of households. It opens his eyes to the immense variety of periodicals catering for specialist and minority interests: the task is propaganda for the rewards of literacy. Back in the newsagents, his round complete, the newsboy sips his mug of tea—leaving a tidemark of printers' ink round his mouth—while flitting through the pages of the handicraft

Shanghai

journals or the latest delivery of soft porn. In Britain the legal minimum age for this kind of part-time employment is thirteen. This is often the age at which the oldest in a family takes the job, but younger members usually start below the legal age, under his tutilage. The job is passed down as it is in Thornton Wilder's Crowell family. Like Joe Crowell, the American boy on his paper route today hurls the papers from a standing position on his bicycle into the customer's porch. The British boy on his paper round delivers through the letter box. (W. H. Smith deplored those who were content to throw papers on the doorstep or over the garden gate). One minor irony of the paper delivery industry in both countries today is that in many neighbourhoods it tends to be monopolised by middle-class children.

It brings interesting encounters. Clay, a thirteen-year-old, found a camaraderie (membership of the fraternity of early-rising workers) with the refuse collectors, who gave him a tv set, discarded because one component was faulty. In vain he combed the shops for the requisite but obsolete part. He told the dustman, who next week brought him a set of the same make, the necessary part intact, so that he was able to cannibalise the two. Another family I know live in the West End of the city where it is hard to find children willing to deliver papers, with the result that the four teenage children have a virtual monopoly, command their own price, and bring £20 a week from their paper rounds. In the 1970s the newspaper trade instituted a competition for the newsboy of the year. The winner is able to take his parents for a holiday in North Africa (where boys half his age work for twelve hours a day).

Children Working

Before the second world war it was the practice in British cities to have two milk deliveries a day, the milkman being aided by a fulltime fourteen-year-old. Nowadays, with only one delivery, boys, other than truants, are only able to "help the milkman" in school holidays or at week-ends. The pre-war butcher's boy, baker's boy or grocery boy, who hoped to get a job in the shop after serving his time on deliveries, but usually simply joined the unemployed when he graduated from a boy's wage, is now in full-time schooling. His present equivalents are the boys and girls who work in the supermarket after school and at weekends, stocking the shelves, or working on the check-outs, or more humbly collecting the trolleys. A fifteen-year-old told me that he worked in the supermarket for two and a half hours after school each weekday and for eight and a half hours on Saturdays at 50 p an hour. Interesting work? Friendly people? No, he said, nobody knows anybody, nobody trusts anybody, and they search you coming in and going out. "And they creep up behind you to see what you're doing." Many children earn the same money less onerously by baby-sitting.

More attractive for the child who enjoys human contacts, and easier to penetrate, is the street-market. Something of the glamour of the fairground still clings to it, and the street trader often belongs to a family which has years of association with a particular pitch. There is an extravagant bonhomie which envelops the child helper, who is flattered by his easy acceptance and feels that he is absorbing something of the magic of the market. Which of course he is. Mayhew remarked that "Among the costers the term education is merely understood as meaning a complete knowledge of the art of buying in the cheapest market and selling in the dearest," while a century later Elbert Hubbard asked, "What boy, well raised, can compare with your street gamin who has the knowledge and the shrewdness of a

grown-up broker?" It is this precocious entrepreneurial insight that the education industry finds it hardest to forgive among the lessons learned in the street, though I would worry more about the much greater proportion of city children who readily discover that you can make more money easily from sporadic petty theft than from any kind of employment.

Les, aged thirteen, is a third year pupil in a remedial class in a London comprehensive secondary school. His "reading age" is about six or seven. His father is in and out of prison and his mother has gone off with another man. He is very knowing about the current marital situation in the other homes in the block of flats where he lives, although most of his time is spent not in the home, but in the nearby street market, where he usually works on a vegetable stall, though he sometimes helps the fishmonger, and knows how to keep the fish looking attractive on the slab, and how herrings are kippered. He made £50 in three weeks in December, selling Christmas trees. His record of truancy is not particularly bad. His absences seem to relate not so much to his business commitments as to whether he likes or dislikes the teachers he will be encountering on that particular day. His arithmetical ability is high, as you might expect, and he has the market trader's habit of thinking

simultaneously in both "old" and decimal money. Why is his grasp of written English so poor? Well, his teacher told me, "he has gathered all he thinks he needs. After all, the street trader uses only the oral language."

Around the street market, the scrap metal merchant and the tarmac site, you can find some of the city's invisible children, the travellers or gypsies. We think of them as rural people, but since the changing character of rural life has taken away their traditional means of livelihood, they are more likely to be found in the urban fringe and on derelict sites in the inner city in the metal-recovering and tarmac-laying industries. Most local authorities have failed to comply with their statutory obligation to provide sites, so travellers find themselves as harried as they ever were. Their foraging children are bold and timid according to circumstance. The invisible children of European cities are usually the sons and daughters of migrant workers. In 1971 it was estimated that there were ten thousand of these children living clandestinely in Switzerland, none of them attending school for fear of being deported, picking up what they could in the rich cities. In 1970, after the death of two ten-year-olds working in a West German coal mine, the authorities found 97,800 children of foreign workers illegally employed.

Perhaps the saddest group of invisible children in Britain are the Chinese, the offspring of elusive parents who work long hours in the restaurant trade. Unlike the gypsy children, they attend school, sitting quietly and uncomprehendingly in the classroom, but then their working day begins. Brian Jackson and Anne Garvey, through patient enquiry built up a patchwork picture of the life of the Chinese immigrant child:

"Four o'clock is not the end of the day for many Chinese children. It is the beginning. Su-su goes straight to bed when she comes in. She sleeps until 9 o'clock and then her brother gets her up to serve in the chippy until 1 o'clock in the morning. Su-su is not yet ten.

"Kwok Wai is eleven. He came to England from Hongkong four months ago to join his parents. They work as cook and washer-up in the restaurant, so Kwok Wai sees them on Sundays. He speaks no English and has no friends at school. At night he lies on his bed in the boxroom above the restaurant and cries himself to sleep.

"Eng Tei is fifteen. Her uncle employs her in his fish and chip shop after school every day. She serves until 12.30. There is little time for homework and no time at all for going out. But then that doesn't really matter so much because Eng Tei has nowhere to go anyway—her ambition is to have one English friend."

The city child of a century ago was familiar with the workplace of the family breadwinner, but this is scarcely true today. It is only above a certain status level that the modern city child is acceptable as a visitor to "Dad's office". The exceptions are the children of small shop-keepers who are expected to help out in the shop, or the children of the self-employed, the children of drivers who are permitted to sit in the cab with Dad and eat with him in the bonhomie of the transport cafe, or the children of women employed in small firms, often part-time, where in the school holidays Mum can bring them into help in the tasks of labelling the bottles, packing the sweets or stuffing the envelopes. Indeed it is one of the tragedies of "women's work" in the British economy, that her children can do it just as well as she can, without feeling the stifling boredom of the task.

Children's contacts with manufacturing industry in the cities of the rich

world are nowadays usually confined to those businesses which are small and informal enough to countenance the employment of casual labour without involving employment cards, tax deductions, unionisation and so on: principally the ramifications of the garment and novelty industries and similar small-scale, close-to-the-market trades. Every now and then a small employer is prosecuted for employing children, or is quietly warned off by the Inspector. The press picks up the story with headlines like "The Child Slaves of Streatham", but the slaves themselves, when consulted, tell a different story, talking bitterly of what they had proposed to do with the earnings they had been denied during the long summer holiday. Just like their parents they would willingly forgo leisure for the sake of purchasing power.

Modern urban life in fact exposes the young to the cornucopia of consumer desires while progressively denying them the means of gratifying these expensive wants except through the munificence of parents. The truant child quite often is a child who has found a means of making money, and who regards this as more pressing and more alluring than sitting in school for a lesson on coming to terms with the world of work. The American ethos of self-help and independence, or of working your way through college, means that at least as far as high school and college students are concerned, it is taken for granted that they will augment their incomes by their own efforts, and that society will provide the opportunities. In Britain no such assumption is made, and the whole trend of social legislation and of enlightened opinion has been progressively to postpone the entrance of the young into the labour market while at the same time reducing the legal age of majority. We consequently have the comedy of students in their twenties who have never been gainfully employed, acting out a kind of parody of the militancy of organised labour. Meanwhile children ten years younger scour the city for a chance to be exploited.

And exploited they very often are. The Nottingham branch of the National Union of Teachers, in the course of preparing a document on behavioural and disciplinary problems in secondary schools, made a spot check in four schools in one week of 1976. In one school they found 12 children under the age of 13 who admitted to having jobs. In all they found what they regarded as the problem of 15-year-olds truanting from school to work with the connivance of parents, and among the 13 and 14 year olds, they cited the examples of the boy who worked for a greengrocer and was encouraged to get up at 3 am to go to the wholesale market; the boy who spent twelve hours on Saturday and ten on Sunday selling clothes in a market; the boy who thought he was doing very well working long hours for $11\frac{1}{2}$ p an hour; and the girl who did eight hours on Saturday and four on Sunday in a newsagents, for £3. The cry is for more stringent legislation, although we already have a bewildering confusion of laws and local bylaws regulating the employment of children. In 1973 the Employment of Children Act was passed to allow the Department of Health and Social Security to introduce standard regulations. In spite of pressure from the Trade Union Congress and the National Union of Teachers these regulations have not yet been introduced, partly because of the lack of resources for making them enforcible and partly because there is an unadmitted difference of opinion among the professions concerned with the welfare of the child.

The believers in enforcement always cite the report by Dr W. Emrys Davies, sponsored in 1972 by the Department of Health and Social Security, which cites many similar instances of exploitation and also draws a "general inference" that "pupils who spend more of their out of school time in employment tend to be less able, less industrious and less well-behaved; they attend less regularly, play truant more frequently, are less punctual and wish to leave school at an earlier age than those who work for fewer hours or not at all." Dr Davies deprecates "the not uncommon assumption among educators and others that part-time employment develops desirable qualities in the young." He is right to see this assumption as one reason why there is not greater pressure for tighter regulation of child labour. Another is the sheer impossibility of inspecting the thousands of tiny factories, workshops and market stalls involved. One of ten or eleven under-age boys working in a small plastics factory explained how, when two policemen called one day, "the boy ran upstairs to the workshop and told us to go down the back stairs till the police had left."

The tradition of the clothing trades in Spitalfields in the inner East End of London provides one example to explain why many well-intentioned and socially conscious citizens feel unable to join a crusade against child labour. This area has always been the zone of transition, the place where new arrivals gain a foothold in the urban economy. The Huguenot silk-weavers were followed by the Irish, who apart from manning the docks, were used to undercut them in the weaving trade. Then came the Jews, who made good in the clothing trade, just as they did on the Lower East Side in New York. Today it is the Bengalis who in the very same houses in the same streets are working at the same trades, subcontracting in the garment industry. This industry is a byword for sweatshops, home work, poor working conditions, long hours on piece work, the exploitation of children, and so on. Yet there is another way of looking at it. The Runnymede Trust published a report by Samir Shah on *Immigrants and Employment in the Clothing Industry*. Mr Shah is not an apologist for capitalism, but he can see that well-intentioned legislation can create more misery than it dispels and can deprive the underprivileged young from the chance to pick up a skilled trade. In his preface to this report Tom Rees remarks that the rag trade "provides an economic life-line for families who would otherwise be in poverty; its informality suits those whose main social and economic networks have in the past been based on kith and kin." The publication in the British papers of photographs of young children from Bangladesh working at sewing machines in East London, was thought by members of the Bengali community to be motivated by hostility. But the thoughtful reader would be more inclined to see it as a tribute to the tenacity with which, unaided by the official economy and the official education system, people who a year or two earlier had been poverty-stricken peasants in a doomed village economy, had made for themselves a minute niche in an alien society and had found a more hopeful means to security and a livelihood for their children than the host culture was able to provide.

The other, equally paradoxical, reason why many teachers and more social workers feel unable to support the further curtailment of child labour is that they are conscious that very many children at school are totally alienated from the world of work. They feel obliged in order to give "relevance" to the last year of schooling, to provide work experience courses

Look-out boy for unlicensed street

aimed at acclimatising the young to the shock of going to work, or to provide courses in further education colleges with such titles as "Adjustment to Work" for the benefit of those unable or unwilling to hold down a job. Candidates for such courses are less likely to come from those who have given themselves some foretaste of the working world in which the rest of us live, and this is why teachers interviewed by Barbara Fletcher disagreed with Dr Davies and shared the view that part-time work "tempers the cosy world of school with the world of work outside, whatever the social background of the child, and develops a sense of responsibility the school cannot give." The idea of "productive work" in the schools of the communist countries has a similar aim, with the additional intention of inculcating some sense of our mutual social obligations.

Young people from the cities of Eastern Europe have told me of the cynical ingenuity with which they evaded their quotas of productive work, but there is little reason for the British to feel superior to the idea that the ethos of work should be instilled in school, since in 1976 a report to the prime minister from the Department of Education and Science made the schools the latest scapegoat for the decline of British manufacturing industry, and a consequent speech by the prime minister lamented the unwillingness of the young to take up industrial jobs, while the national body for curriculum development, the Schools Council, with the backing of the Trade Union Congress and the Confederation of British Industries, launched a project for informing school-children about industry. It is ironical that, having discovered that the young don't like the idea of working in industry, the first thing that occurs to the politicians is that children should be acclimatised to industry rather than that industrial work should be changed to make it attractive to the young.

Arthur Young, the headmaster of Northcliffe Community High School in Yorkshire, has for many years been trying to find the right equation between earning and learning. He values the efforts of his pupils to earn money for themselves and has sought, within the narrowly prescribed limits of the law, to provide such opportunities in and out of school. He remarks of work experience projects that they "have never really got off the ground because of the legal, insurance and trade union problems that hedge them around. I have always thought that the schemes proposed were phoney—the most important aspect of work experience being neglected completely—the wage at the end of the week." Describing the efforts made to provide actual cash-earning experiences for the most unlikely lads at his school, and the effect it has had on their attitudes to running their own lives, taking decisions, budgeting, fulfilling obligations, dealing with strangers, as well as such mundane things as using the telephone, Mr Young remarks, "We have to overcome the ridiculous idea that giving children the chance to earn money in school is somehow immoral . . . In the changing situation in education, pupil-teacher relationships and roles are the essence of much heart-searching and debate. We might do well to compare the differences in an earning-learning situation between master and apprentice and in the traditional school situation, captive scholars facing chalk and talk across the barrier of the teacher's desk. The comparison of relationships between newsagent and paperboy and between paperboy and schoolmaster might also be revealing." There is certainly more wisdom here than in trying to deprive children of the dignity and independence that goes with doing a job.

15
The Girl in the Background

"In Lucania, when a boy is born, a pitcher of water is poured into the road to symbolise that the newborn baby's destiny is to travel the roads of the world. When a girl is born, water is thrown on the hearth to show that she will lead her life within the walls of the home. Elsewhere such symbolic gestures are not made. But the reality remains the same."   ELENA GIANINI BELOTTI: *Little Girls*

In the decade of the first world war a whole shelf of books was written about the life of the city boy in Britain. They were concerned with the working-class boy who on leaving school got a "dead-end" job as errand boy, street vendor, living-out domestic servant, porter or carter's assistant, golf caddie or page-boy, which he lost as soon as he would have to be paid something approaching a man's wage. Never before or since has he been shown such attention. But there was no similar concern either in Britain or America about the girl in the city. The nearest thing to such a study is the aptly titled chapter "The Girl in the Background" in E. J. Urwick's *Studies of Boy Life in Our Cities*. Peter Laslett in commenting on the swarms of children surrounding our ancestors, as well as on their pitifully low expectation of life, remarks that these crowds of children are strangely absent from the written record. "There is something mysterious about the silence of all these multitudes of babies in arms, toddlers and adolescents in the statements men made at the time about their own experience." When this silence is broken, it is the boys that we hear about. The girls are only brought to our attention when they are in trouble.

Much more recently compilations about contemporary youth cultures have the same overwhelming concentration on the activities of boys. The editors of *Working Class Youth Culture* remark with some embarrassment that "there is an appalling neglect in the considerable literature on adolescence of young women and girls. Youth culture is held to be synonymous with male youth culture, so that girls—when they do appear—appear only as something which boys sometimes fight over, or merely as objects in the gaze of men." In their contribution on *Girls and Subcultures* to another similar symposium, Angela McRobbie and Jenny Garber discuss the invisibility of girls in youth sub-cultures. "Girl culture", they remark, "from our preliminary investigations, is so well insulated as to operate to effectively exclude not only other 'undesirable' girls—but also boys, adults, teachers and researchers." They note that unlike the various subcultures of city boys, the Teeny Bopper culture "can easily be accommodated, for ten to fifteen-year-old girls, in the home, requiring only a bedroom and a record player and permission to invite friends; but in this capacity it might offer an opportunity for girls to take part in a quasi-sexual ritual (it is important to remember that girls have no access to the masturbatory rituals common amongst boys)."

Certainly, whenever we discuss the part the city environment plays in the lives of children, we are really talking about boys. As a stereotype the child in the city is a boy. Girls *are* far less visible. The reader can verify this by standing in a city street at any time of day, in school time or holiday time, and counting the children seen. Unless you happen to be in the vicinity of a girls-only school or a pop-concert, the majority of the children you observe will be boys.

It is customary to relate this relative invisibility of girls in the city scene to the tests indicating greater visuo-spatial ability in boys and to the evidence

that this ability is partly determined by a sex-linked recessive gene. But is the ability to manipulate the city the same skill that is measured in the tests? Eileen Byrne of the Equal Opportunities Commission in Britain says, "I'm a sceptic when we come to the so-called innate differences between boys and girls. I believe 98 per cent of it is social conditioning. I may be wrong but if there is so much difference between their verbal and spatial skills why do teachers reinforce it?"

Obviously in any random sample there are girls with higher than average spatial ability for their age and boys with a lower than average ability. But in the traditional upbringing of the two sexes in our culture, everything about the experience of childhood is likely to depress that ability for the girl and to develop it for the boy. The kind of play and playthings thought appropriate for boys tend to enhance the exploration and manipulation of the environment. Those considered suitable for girls probably do the same. It is easy to exaggerate these differences in play. Most young children of either sex alternate between active physical occupations and contemplative or make-believe ones, and most students of the games children play usually categorise them as boys' games or girls' games. Norman Douglas remarked sixty years ago that "you'll find the girls far less shy about their games than the boys are. And you'll also notice that they're just as good at inventing sports . . ." I am sure that if some pedant were to apply an analysis of the environmental experiences to be gained from the games which Iona and Peter Opie ascribe to one or the other sex, it would be found that in terms of the skills imparted there is little to choose between them.

The differences are not in the quality of environmental learning so much as in the quantity of environmental experience. If you were to bribe a class of children of the same age to keep diaries for a week, recording their movements and the amount of time spent inside and outside the home, they would confirm your impression that boys are out longer and go further than girls. It depends of course on factors like social class, age and position in the family. And it depends too, on the ethnic and religious background of the family. Some immigrants to Britain from countries where tradition places severe limitations on the personal liberty of women and girls, and who are profoundly shocked by the laxer standards of the host community, deprive their daughters of all but the most minimal contact with the environment.

Change will come as a result of internal rebellion rather than external propaganda, but if you go back far enough the same is true of most cultures because of the sexual division of labour. In simpler societies where the activities of children were more directly a rehearsal of adult roles, it is clear that the boys gathered more environmental experience herding or hunting with their fathers than the girls did in cooking or weaving with their mothers. In households all over the world domestic tasks are alloted to the women and girls rather than to the men and boys, and this applies even when the mother is a breadwinner too. This is still true of urban America for example, where Mary Lynch of Cornell University found that "Children between ages nine and eleven already showed traditional sex-role differences, with the girls taking on eight minutes of work for every five minutes the boys contributed." The differential increases with age. Twice as much of the time of girls between twelve and eighteen as that of boys is spent on household chores. Four girls in five among sixteen year olds help clear up after meals, less than one boy in five does so.

At the jumble sale

In their use of the city streets girls have always been constrained by being entrusted with the younger children, as so many reminiscences of childhood show. Molly Weir remembers Springburn, Glasgow and going to the pictures: "When the cinemas emptied after the matinees, the boys, like the innocent, unconscious animals they were, immediately relieved themselves. Now that was a bad habit, I quite agreed. We girls turned our faces away delicately, and pretended we were unaware of the fierce jets battering the corrugated fence which lined the side exits. When boys were very small they were looked after by older sister or bigger girls, but the moment they realised that boys had far more exciting games like 'buckety-buck-buck-buck' played with a tin can, and involving faster races through the closes and back courts, and that boys had far higher jumps from the dykes than mere girls, they were off. They would have been regarded as Jessies if they had behaved otherwise, and even mothers and sisters accepted this, though sometimes with sighs of misgiving when the toddlers were very wee. We hated having to take any of the wee boys with us to the matinees, for they often became frightened, and started to yell, and an attendant would race down the passage, jerk a thumb in the direction of the screaming boy and shout, 'Who's wi' this wean? You? Right, oot wi' him.' "

One aspect of childhood which remains in everyone's mind, however dulled by resignation or compromised with reality, is the sense of fairness, of equity. How many thosands of millions of girls must have felt outraged by the unfairness of the conventions of domestic life. Was it *fair* that the boys could go untrammelled to play, while *they* had to stay home to help in the house? Was it fair that, when *they* went out, they could not follow their own inclinations like the boys, but had to be a "little mother" for the younger members of the family? Certainly a girl might be proud to be entrusted with the next-door baby as she pushes the pram to the park, but mustn't she feel resentful that her goodhearted gesture should be taken for granted as "only natural", just as it was only natural that the boys should climb trees, get muddy in the pond and return home with their clothes torn, while *she* is expected to return immaculate?

Boys can stay out longer and later. They, it is assumed, are more capable of looking after themselves. Parents fear for their girls, by no means without reason since in most parts of the world the unaccompanied girl in the street is regarded as fair game for minor molestations. Thus Gwenda Linda Blair bitterly comments, "The street in this and most other societies, belong to men, the home to women (subservient to men, to be sure, but at least women don't have to prove their right to be there). In our society, of course, women are allowed to use the street, but only by permission—men retain domination and the Damocletian sword of repossession is always present. Being with a man gives you a passkey; otherwise you're fair game for eviction." An exaggeration? Well, ask any city girl about her experiences in the street.

The winds of change in our assumptions about sex roles have penetrated to youth organisations. In Britain the largest of these are the Guides, with their 834,660 girls, and the Scouts, with their 596,934 boys (the equivalents of the Girl Scouts and Boy Scouts of America). But girls in London have begun to penetrate the Scout movement. Anna Coote found that this was tolerated at a local level, while disapproved of by the headquarters of the two organisations. She writes, "The main emphasis of the Scout programme is on

Practising for the Girls' Band, Newcastle

developing independence and a sense of adventure. Scouts can go to camp, or set off on a cross-country hike, unaccompanied by adults. Guides have less opportunity to camp and they must be accompanied by specially trained adults. 'We owe it to the parents,' explained the Chief Commissioner, 'when we take away their very precious teenage daughters. After all a boy can get lost on a hike, but a girl can get lost *and* raped.' " Janice and Marie have joined the Thirty-first Battersea Scout Group. We do not hear of any boys anxious to join the Guides. There have always been bold spirits among the girls who yearned for the excitement of the street that the boys took as their right. The celebrated Dottoressa Moor, when a girl in the nineties in the Fifth District of Vienna, used to run out to play with the *Strizibuben*, the guttersnipes, and would be punished when she got home:

"So I climbed down the fire-escape to the street to escape the beating. I can still remember that. I wanted now to go and live among the *Strizibuben*. They were rough and I too was rough and no more would I live that lonely and respectable life in which I was beaten."

Girls seize fewer of the opportunities the city offers, they also succumb to fewer of its dangers and temptations. Of the runaways wandering the American city during the depression, only one in twenty was a girl, and as we have seen, when the boys were moved on, the girls were locked up. Years ago Barbara Wootton drew attention to the way in which criminologists examined every aspect of the epidemiology of offenders except the amazing sex differential. In the 1960s ninety per cent of convictions in Britain and 95 per cent of conviction for crimes of violence were of male offenders.

As girls penetrate the approved or tolerated activities of boys, they are also engaging more in those which we desperately try to restrain in boys. Professor Joseph Sorrentino, a juvenile court judge in Los Angeles says, "Ten years ago, young girls might get into trouble over sex, or play truant from school. Today they are heads of burglary rings, accessories to gun robberies and principals in homicides. We are seeing a new genre of women gangsters emerging as the heroines of our time." In the milder atmosphere of Britain the pattern of female criminality is changing in the same way. Magistrates and probation officers are convinced of this, and the superintendents of remand homes for girls in several British cities (London, Bristol and Sheffield) confirmed to Peter Watson in 1973 that they now encounter far more girls with histories of violence. "Many of the girls, they say, show no signs of aggressiveness until they are in their low teens—and the Home Office figures show how true this is. It is particularly among the 14 to 17 age group that the recent increase has been so pronounced." (In fact the statistics of crime in Britain are notoriously misleading, but no-one in the law-enforcement industry doubts this trend).

Carol Smart, who argues that the "science" of criminology has, all through its history, been riddled with anti-feminist assumptions, remarks that "the perceived changes in female delinquency and criminality may be based on statistical fallacy, a changing consciousness on the part of researchers and social workers or on actual changes in the frequency and character of the behaviour concerned, but whatever the basis it would seem that the Women's Movement has been influential in some way," and she fears some crude causal assumption that will oppose emancipation of this ground. She stresses that "emancipation is not synonymous with the 'freedom' to be like a man, it refers to the ability to resist stereotyped sex roles and to reject limiting pre-conceptions about the inherent capabilities of the sexes."

The preconceptions affect every aspect of the lives of urban children described in this book. We know whose play is likely to be exploratory and adventurous, who has the freedom of the streets, who is likely to be adept at using the transport system or at devising and building exciting wheeled playthings. We know who is likely to gain some insight into the world of work in a part-time job, and we know that the part-time jobs available to schoolgirls are most likely to be domestic ones like babysitting and housework.

Behind all our anxiety to explain the observed differences between the sexes in their contact with the street and the city is the assumption that interaction with the environment is a good thing, that this is what the city is for, and that this is the way people become citizens. We put a high valuation on environmental involvement. But if our prime concern were the prevention of crime or the prevention of accidents, we would be bound to conclude that the environmental deprivations tacitly taken for granted for girls are one guarantee of survival, and should be extended to boys. Far from wanting girls to be liberated into the environmental freedom of city boys, shouldn't we want the reverse to happen? When I was young, billiard tables for domestic use were advertised with the slogan "Keep Your Boys at Home."

The problem of the girl in the city is a male problem. If she is deprived of her fair share of environmental contact because she has household tasks which her brothers are able to evade, the answer is a more equitable sharing of these tasks in the family, especially since her mother too probably feels oppressed by the same assumptions. If it is because of a patriarchal religious tradition, the patriarchs have to change. If it's for fear of sexual exploitation, it is the exploiters rather than the girls who have to change their ways. And if the liberation of girls brings in its train an explosion of female crime, it is the equation between anti-social acts and bravery which has to be broken. The environmental liberation of girls, far from implying that the girl in the city should become hard and tough in the way that the city boy aims to be, demands that the boy too should pride himself on those allegedly feminine qualities of care and tenderness. One of the discoveries that Urie Bronfenbrenner made in Moscow, was that the taboo on tenderness had not infected the children of that city:

"Older children of both sexes show a lively interest in the very young and are competent and comfortable in dealing with them to a degree almost shocking to a Western observer. I recall an incident which occurred in a Moscow street. Our youngest son—then four—was walking briskly a pace or two ahead of us when from the opposite direction there came a company of teenage boys. The first one no sooner spied Stevie than he opened his arms wide and, calling '*Ai malysh*!' (Hey little one!), scooped him up, hugged him, kissed him resoundingly, and passed him on to the rest of the company who did likewise, and they began a merry children's dance, as they caressed him with words and gestures. Similar behaviour on the part of any American adolescent male would surely prompt his parents to consult a psychiatrist."

Girls making wiring circuits for cars in a Peking Middle School

*"Productive work" at the
Middle School in Shanghai*

It was, interestingly enough, a Russian exile, who saw the protective behaviour of slum children in Victorian London as exemplifying the principal of mutual aid. Peter Kropotkin noted that "As soon as a mite bends inquisitively over the opening of a drain—'Don't stop there,' another mite shouts out, 'fever sits in the hole!' Don't climb over that wall, the train will kill you if you tumble down! Don't come near to the ditch! Don't eat those berries—poison! you will die!' Such are the first teachings imparted to the urchin when he joins his mates outdoors. How many of the children whose playgrounds are the pavement around 'model workers' dwellings', or the quays and bridges of the canals, would be crushed to death by the carts or drowned in the muddy waters, were it not for that sort of mutual support. And when a fair Jack has made a slip into the unprotected ditch at the back of the milkman's yard, or a cherry-cheeked Lizzie has, after all, tumbled down into the canal, the young brood raises such cries that all the neighbourhood is on the alert and rushes to the rescue."

His fair Jack and cherry-cheeked Lizzie are still protected by their peers, though the separation of the children's habitat from the working world in the modern city, makes it less likely that there are any neighbours in the neighbourhood. At the same time, the element of "feminine" protectiveness in the life of the city child passes unnoticed and certainly undervalued. What we do notice and tacitly value are the "masculine" qualities of callousness and daring. When a nine-year-old girl stabbed a neighbouring child with a bread knife, the press descended on the neglected and forlorn Glasgow estate where she lived and found that "you could guess at the true nature of the girl's world just by watching the tiny rituals of violence of the children playing on a scruffy path of ground below." To another visitor the estate "resounds to the sounds of thumps and curses and imprecations, both juvenile and adult."

Similarly the modern train driver does not notice the protective care exercised by one child over another in avoiding the perils of the railway track. He reports in fact that *he* is scared out of his wits by the games of daring of young trespassers. "In 'legs eleven' a child hangs from a bridge over the line and swings his legs up at the last second as an express train goes underneath. In 'chicken' children vie with each other to see who is last across the line in front of an express."

The fact that girls as well as boys are now seen in such activities cannot be interpreted as a triumph of sexual equality: it represents instead the triumph of aggressive masculinity as the quality the child's peers most admire, and which juvenile subcultures reward most highly. The liberation of the city girl from the expected norms of passivity and docility implies also the liberation of the city boy from the pressure to be a predator.

At the water pump, Blantyre, Malawi

16
At School in the Alien City

"For many poor children, school is orderly and has food, compared to chaotic and hungry homes, and it might even be interesting compared to total deprivation of toys and books. Besides, the wish to improve a child's lot, which on the part of a middle-class parent might be frantic status-seeking and pressuring, on the part of a poor parent is a loving aspiration. There is here a gloomy irony. The school that for a poor Negro child might be a great joy and opportunity is likely to be dreadful; whereas the middle-class child might be better off *not* in the 'good' suburban school he has. Other poor youth, herded into a situation that does not fit their disposition, for which they are unprepared by their background, and which does not interest them, simply develop a reactive stupidity very different from their behaviour on the street or ball field. They fall behind, play truant, and as soon as possible drop out. If the school situation is immediately useless and damaging to them, their response must be said to be life-preservative. They thereby somewhat diminish their chances of a decent living, but we shall see that the usual propaganda—that schooling is a road to high salaries—is for most poor youth a lie; and the increase in security is arguably not worth the torture involved."

PAUL GOODMAN

Paul Goodman, who expressed so cogently the dilemma of urban education, was himself an orphaned Jewish boy reared in a dreary apartment on the Upper East Side of Manhatten. He attended a highly selective school, Townsend Harris High, which used to be part of the New York public school system, and left at 16, top of his year, to enter the College of the City of New York. He was, as he told me, "a poor boy who made out within the system." In London his school's equivalent, the Jews' Free School, cradle of many an immigrant child of genius, has long since moved to the suburbs as the JFS Comprehensive School, while all the other selective schools have been obliged to decide either to become non-selective comprehensive schools or to become private fee-charging establishments without grant aid. The expression "urban education" in America and in Britain today is simply a euphemism for the education of children with problems, or for the education of children who are doomed to failure, or simply for the education of black children or of immigrant children.

On a world scale there is an immense paradox in the way the city is viewed as a provider of education. In the poor world one of the motives for a family's migration to the city is the hope of providing better educational opportunities for its children. In the rich world one of the motives for a family's emigration out of the city is precisely the same. The custom was widespread in the Middle Ages of placing one's child in someone else's household, whether as boarder, servant or apprentice, since "being in service" had not acquired any perjorative undertones, and occasionally it was specifically included in the agreement that the master must "teach" the child and "show him the details of his merchandise" or that he must "send him to school". Similarly in African cities today, "people in the villages sometimes send their sons and daughters to be taught a trade or 'minded' while at school." And in many parts of Latin America it is common for rural migrants to urban centres "to send their children to work in a home in the city to work as servants without pay with the understanding that the family accepting the child will send him or her to school."

Douglas Butterworth studied Mixtec Indian migrants in Mexico City and learned that the desire to educate oneself or one's children was one of the primary reasons for the emigration to the city. "Sacrifices of some financial

magnitude are frequently undergone by migrants in order to keep the children in the home and send them to school, even though the children are of an age when they could be making important economic contributions to the household." It is quite certain that the poor immigrants to the cities of Latin America, Africa or Asia are going to be disappointed in their faith in the education system. Often it is geared to archaic ends and in any case the pace of urbanisation is more than the system can possibly contain. All the more impressive are the expedients to which parents will resort: providing their own labour for building schools for their communities on the fringe of the city, hiring their own teachers, taking every conceivable step to procure an education for their children.

This hunger for schooling contrasts poignantly with the crisis of education in the cities of the rich world. There was certainly a time in this century when the public education systems of New York and London were regarded as the best in the world. As recently as the 1950s some middle-class parents outside inner London would move house in order to make their children eligible to attend an inner London school. By the 1970s the move is much more likely to be in the opposite direction. The answer of Sir Ashley Bramall, as leader of the Inner London Education Authority is this: "The old County of London, with a population in 1939 of four millions (compared with the present $2\frac{1}{2}$ millions) was mainly a city of small houses. Not only did the war scatter the population and destroy the homes, but it led to the rebuilding of London as a city of blocks of flats, of increasing height. This change has never been fully accepted by the population and there has been an increasing urge for movement to outer London and to the counties beyond, where the old pattern of street and house and garden could be recaptured. Those who have been able to make this move have mainly been the prosperous, the intelligent, the fortunate and the stable. The poor, the limited, the unstable and the unlucky have stayed behind ... London schools, progressively deprived of their most teachable and tractable children from stable home backgrounds, have had to retain an increasing proportion of pupils from broken homes, one-parent families and other unsatisfactory social conditions. To them have been added succeeding waves of immigrants, each with their own complex of problems. Inner London has 25 per cent of the West Indian population of the whole country; in Spitalfields 40 per cent of the population is Bengali and of 28 children taken into one primary school in the area in September 1976, 23 knew no English at all; in one Church of England school in Soho 50 per cent of the children are Chinese; in North Kensington and Paddington hotel owners are recruiting ever-increasing numbers of rural Moroccans, whose children arrive in schools without even the most rudimentary knowledge of European urban life."

This is his explanation as to why, in spite of a statistically dwindling child population, in spite of an enormously enlarged administrative staff and in spite of a much improved pupil to teacher ratio, there is, as Sir Ashley Bramall says "no diminution in the stresses under which London schools operate." Whole libraries have been devoted to the dilemma of the school systems in American cities, but the ultimate implication of the argument is not that the schools have let the children down, but that the children, *by not being the kind of children the system was designed to educate*, have let the system down.

Yet seventy years ago, the schools of London and New York had huge immigrant populations, and felt able to cope with the educational problems they presented. Perhaps the difference is that in those days the problems were contained or ignored or supressed from sight because they were confined to one sector of the city, the zone of transition, while today the whole residential part of the inner city has become a zone of transition. How does the actual process of transition appear to the child? There is something in common of course in the experience of the black child from the South who finds himself in a northern city, the Sicilian child coming to Milan, the West Indian child sent to join relatives in Brixton and the child from a Bengali village who after an incredible journey sets eyes on Hounslow. The

Truants playing pinball

transition is one of bewildering excitement and shock, and individual differences of temperament and previous experience determine whether it is accomplished as an adventure or a nightmare. How precious must be those familiar faces, idioms, meals and rituals in this strange land, and how menacing must seem those strange wild children down the street. If we can empathise with the shock to the children, we can measure the anxieties of their parents seeking to shield them from the overwhelming contact with the unfamiliar which they themselves are experiencing.

It is an awe-inspiring testimony to the resilience of children that so many go through the experience unscathed. But how many do? And how many carry the scars of transition? A Puerto Rican girl writes of her first experience of school in New York: "Sitting in a classroom and staring at words on a blackboard that were to me as foreign as Egyptian hieroglyphics is one of my early recollections of school. The teacher had come up to my desk and bent over, putting her face close to mine. My name is Mrs Newman,' she said, as if the exaggerated mouthing of the words would make me understand their meaning. I nodded 'yes' because I felt that was what she wanted me to do. But she just threw up her hands in despair and touched her fingers to her head to signify to the class I was dense. From that day on school became an ordeal I was forced to endure."

The saga of immigrant communities in the United States is that of the self-sufficiency and consolation engendered by the transplantation of social, religious and dietary customs. The first generation is nourished by them, the second generation rejects them and the third generation, from the strength of being established in society, looks back on them with an indulgent nostalgia. As a Yiddish saying goes, "What the children want to forget, the grandchildren want to remember." In the milder climate of immigration in

Britain, the same truth is evident. Hindu or Muslim children from India, Pakistan or Bangladesh, or from the West Indies or East Africa, are sheltered from the cultural shock of absorption into the community of the British poor by a network of affiliations which affirm an identity of their own. It is only when the young begin to rebel at the constricting attitudes and customs of the traditional culture that the heartaches of conflict between parents and children are felt. But by this time the zone of transition has fulfilled its purpose. It has initiated the immigrant family into the social economy of the city. And, set against a secure family background, the education system has usually worked for such children.

Every survey of the housing situation of immigrant families in British cities has shown that in the publicly rented sector, the invisible hand of housing allocation steers them, without any overt discrimination, into the least attractive housing. But surveys of the housing situation of Asian families show a much higher proportion of owner-occupation among them than in the population as a whole. This could be seen as a realistic assessment of their chances in the public rental market or it could be seen as an equally realistic assessment of the function of the zone of transition. An Asian family may buy a sub-standard house by borrowing at exorbitant interest rates. It may then cram in as many relations as possible to share this burden and hasten the repayment of the loan, and will deny itself the consumer luxuries its neighbours take for granted. In time the need to fill the house diminishes, money becomes available for improving it, and after a relatively short time it becomes a single-family house acceptable to the public health inspector, or it is sold again as the family moves up the housing market. For the children of the family, as for their elders, future security has been bought with present discomfort, sustained by family solidarity. Psychologically this is infinitely more tolerable than the situation in families who may be in superior or less crowded housing but for whom the inner city is not a zone of transition but a ghetto.

I mentioned in the second chapter of this book the tests applied by Michael Rutter which indicated a far greater proportion of maladjusted children in London than in a rural area. The same tests were applied by Professor Rutter and his colleagues to the children of West Indian immigrants in London and by A. M. Kallarackai and Martin Herbert to Indian immigrant children and to a matched group of English children in inner Leicester. The Indian parents were mostly poor peasants from Gujerat and the Punjab, with a poor command of English. A very much smaller percentage of the Indian children were rated as maladjusted than of the English children. "Why," the researchers asked, "should environmental factors, such as living in twilight areas, have an unfavourable impact on the English families and their children?" They concluded that the low level of maladjustment could be attributed to "the affectionate but strong and protective nature of the Indian family life, effective discipline and close supervision of children, and relative economic success."

But among *West* Indians in London, the same insistence on parental discipline and close supervision adds the miseries of family conflict to those of educational frustration. The 1974 report of the Community Relations Commission said that about 3,000 black Londoners between the ages of 12 and 20, a quarter of them girls, were roaming homeless in the streets of the city. Bert Luthers, a Wandsworth councillor who comes from Guyana says,

"In my opinion some of the West Indian parents are Victorian in their outlook. They are very strict with their children and many youths are finding it very difficult to get any dialogue with their parents, so much so that quite a lot of them have to leave home." Cecil Ross, the youth worker for the Wandsworth Council for Community Relations underlines his view, "Some youths are not being allowed out. If they are, they are finding the most severe restrictions placed on them. Then when they start work, many find that they have to give up nearly all their wages to their parents. Not surprisingly, they feel if they are contributing to the home they should be allowed a voice of their own but instead they find that they are restricted. When they challenge their parents, or ask to be allowed to stay out later, the resulting family dispute often leads to the father telling the children who refuse to toe the line to leave." Black girls in London feel conscious that they are even more constrained than the boys.

Farrukh Dhondy believes that the economic plight of young black Londoners is worse than the statistics show, "because a large number of black unemployed youth refuse to register with state agencies and support themselves by drawing sustenance and strength from the life of the community. They refuse the work that society allocates them ... The rejection of work is a rejection of the level to which schools have skilled them as labour power, and when the community feeds that rejection back into the school system, it becomes a rejection of the functions of schooling."

The generation of young black British, who feel themselves to be the scapegoats of their parents, of the police and of the diminishing job market, are also the scapegoats of the education system. And one of the tragic ironies of their situation is that when West Indians were first recruited for humble, ill-paid but essential jobs in the transport system or the hospitals, one of their motives in coming was the age-old lure of a better education and better job prospects for their children. A generation of London-born black children has now passed through the schools and it cannot be said that their parents' hopes have been fulfilled. Indeed one London teacher told me of a family of teen-age children "straight off the boat" whose basic literacy and whose attitude to learning, made them far more receptive to school than other black children in the class with, in spite of their parents' aspirations, a lifetime of attunement to failure. When I told this story to a black teacher from an American city, she nodded in understanding, for she had a similar experience with newly-arrived children from the South.

How general this experience is I do not know, but its implications are devastating. The longer a black child's residence in a British city, the more certainly he is programmed for educational failure, and to occupational failure too. This is not related to the situation of being an immigrant or the child of immigrants, because Asian children, far less attuned to British tribal mores, and without the benefit of a shared mother tongue, do well in British schools. They are certainly successful academically (and are sometimes resented for their success).

Of the many explanations that have been offered for the failure of the black child in the white city, the most convincing and the most disturbing is that of *self-contempt*. A famous American study, repeated much more recently in Britain, showed that black children identified with pictures or dolls representing white children and rejected images of black children. Bernard Coard, in his pamphlet *How the West Indian Child is Made*

Educationally Sub-Normal in the British School System, comments that "Not a single black child has ever drawn me a picture of a black man. Of hundreds of drawings done for me over the years by black children, every one is of a white man." The brown child from an Asian community, whether Hindu or Muslim and whatever the country of his family's origins, identifies with them in psychological tests. He does not wish he was something else.

The black child wishes he was white. The damage that this imposes on the self-perception of the child can scarcely be over-estimated. It was spelt out years ago in the context of New York by Claude Brown in his account of his boyhood in Harlem. Charles Silberman, writing in the 1960s remarked that "Black children are not the only ones who are harmed in these ways. In California and the Southwest, prejudice against Mexican Americans is almost as great; teachers, administrators, school boards, and even state legislature and boards of education convey their contempt for these youngsters and their parents by forbidding the use of Spanish anywhere in the schools." However, Ernesto Galarza, a Mexican American, discussing "the experiences of a multitude of boys like me" in the slums of an American city, comments that "Psychologists, psychiatrists, social anthropologists, and other manner of shrinks have spread the rumour that these Mexican immigrants and their offspring have lost their 'self-image.' By this, of course, they mean that a Mexican doesn't know what he is; and if by chance he is something, it isn't any good. I, for one Mexican, never had any doubts on this score. I can't remember a time I didn't know who I was; and I have heard much testimony from my friends and other more detached persons to the effect that I thought too highly of what I thought I was. It seems to me unlikely that out of six or seven million Mexicans in the United States, I was the only one who felt this way."

But Mr Galarza himself makes the point of the "shrinks" he derides. How many of those other Mexican Americans made it from the Sacramento barrio to high school, let along to Stanford for an MA and Columbia for a PhD, as he did? Puerto Ricans too have succeeded in the American school system, but the Task Force on Children Out of School found that half of Boston's 10,000 Spanish-speaking school children were not in school and that "between 1965 and 1969 only four Puerto Rican students graduated from Boston high schools."

Similarly for every success story that contradicts the stereotype of the black child doomed to failure by the standards of the school and subsequently rejected by the job market in the city, there are a thousand that confirm the gloomy prophesy. There are also, both in Britain and in the United States, a thousand prescriptions for changing the situation. If the root of the problem is the derogatory self-image, the whole campaign to assert black pride is the best strategy. But the immediate result of this is simply to make the black child in Britain despise his parents, working uncomplainingly at menial jobs. Graham Lomas notes that "Their fathers came over to this country inspired with the work ethic and they have followed jobs great distances. The young West Indians have seen the stress of the mother out working and the father leaving early and coming home late at night, and they do not want it. Sons often show all the frustrations of an educational system which has not coped with their problems and has left them underqualified but with high aspirations."

The small West Indian child in Britain spends much of his time "doing

Asian pupils replanning Englis

Sikh family, London

nothing". Traditionally he would be sitting dreaming on the step under the eye of grandmother in her rocking chair. In England his working mother has to pay a baby minder to watch over him. Pauline Crabbe remarked to me what a boon television was to the West Indian family in this respect, and this in turn is a reminder of the need for more children's programmes of the Sesame Street kind. A South London doctor told me that the effect of the absence of play in West Indian culture was noticeable as early as the age of eighteen months. In her view the neglect of nursery education and the absence of access to it in districts where it was most needed was our worst disservice to the black child in Britain. "Worse than the lack of jobs for unskilled teenagers?" I asked. "It's the ultimate reason for it," she replied. And Joe Benjamin remarks, "To establish an adventure playground, for instance, in a predominantly West Indian neighbourhood pre-supposes that West Indian children do play, whereas in fact they do not; nor is play part of their culture, upbringing or education. If, on the other hand, their culture, upbringing and education is designed to produce the working adult, then it can be argued that the adventure playground could offer opportunities as relevant to this as it can and should to the growth and development of the indigenous child. Both go through a period we describe as adolescence, but the West Indian youngster reaches out for and is given increasing contact with the workaday world, while his host cousin is fobbed off with spurious coffee bars and ineffective counselling."

But now, trapped as they are between two cultures, rejecting the values of their parents, and shut out by invisible and baffling barriers from the affluent city, many young black Britons feel bitterly alienated from both. In Manchester Colin MacGlashan watched "the kids walking slowly back from the Medway shebeen into a grubby urban dawn, small, lost and bedraggled like peacocks left out in the rain. Down Great Western Street, twos and threes of black men in their forties wait for the 53 bus to take them to the early shift. They look tired and defeated. Both groups avert their gazes, as though they find looking at each other painful."

Perhaps we always demand more of the education system than it can possibly give. It is one thing to hire someone to instill literacy and numeracy, and another to expect the teacher to act as society's conscience or to expect the school to be a remedy for social and economic injustice and prejudice. In Britain the advocates of positive discrimination have yet to grapple with the paradox that there are more educationally deprived children outside the schools given special attention as Social Priority Schools than in them, while the children who benefit most are the non-deprived children who happen to attend those schools.

British teachers watch from a distance the drama of bussing in American cities. Their own experience of such policies is confined to rural schools and to the efforts of education authorities to cope with a flood of non-English-speaking Asians. In the London Borough of Ealing, where bussing is still adopted, but is likely to be challenged in the courts on the grounds that it constitutes racial discrimination, Amrit Wilson concludes that ten years of experience show that it places children "seemingly deliberately, at a disadvantage." For, "to a child of five, bussing can mean leaving home at 7.30 a.m. and returning to a collecting point at 4.30 having completed a working day as long as an adult's, waiting for long periods for coaches, often at uncovered stops, facing long tedious journeys every day of their school life and always being tired. For parents bussing means no contact with their children's school or teachers and constant worry, since a child who misses the coach to school has literally nowhere to go if both parents are at work. In addition bussing denies parents the legal right to send their children to schools of their own choice." The environmental psychologist Terence Lee concluded from his study of the bussing of rural primary school children that "it is the perceived *accessibility* of the home territory and the mother that is so very different for walking and bus children. In the former case, the child walks of his own volition over what very soon becomes familiar territory. He forms a schema of the route which unites the home schema with the school schema and he knows that, although the walk constitutes a psychological barrier greater as a function of its length, he can cross at any time during the day. On the other hand, the bus child builds little in the way of a connecting schema. The journey itself is not articulated by action of any form of decision-making on the part of the child nor recorded in his cognitive structure. At best he may register a disconnected set of images but, more important, once the child has been deposited at the gate of the school, the bus disappears for six and a half hours and the main means of home access is removed as surely as the kicking of a gangplank." Roger Hart reports the same cognitive loss in "bussed" children in a New England town.

No-one in either Britain or America has presented any evidence of the educational gains from bussing as a city policy. In the United States the issue is complicated by city politics which have nothing at all to do with the redressing of educational disadvantage. What may have appeared to be a progressive policy of social engineering a decade ago, has become an alternative, as in Boston, to a reallocation of resources in favour of the underprivileged child.

But this kind of reallocation is the very last thing that the world's education authorities would ever dream of undertaking. A decade ago Everett Reimer found that the children of the poorest one-tenth of the population of the United States cost the public in schooling $2,500 each over a liftime, while the children of the richest one-tenth cost about $35,000. "Assuming that one-third of this is private expenditure, the richest one-tenth still gets ten times as much of public funds for education as the poorest one-tenth." In Britain we spend twice as much on the secondary school life of a grammar-school sixth former as on a secondary modern school leaver, while if we include university expenditure, we spend as much on an undergraduate in one year as on a normal school child throughout his life. The Fabian Tract on *Labour and Inequality* calculates that "While the highest social group benefit seventeen times as much as the lowest group from the expenditure on universities, they only contribute five times as much revenue." No wonder Everett Reimer calls schools an almost perfectly regressive form of taxation.

If we ignore the major inequalities and simply demand more spending on the education of the inner city child, what would we actually spend the money on? It is sad to think that so great is the hold of the administrative machine at all levels of the school system that most of it would feed the machine and not the individual teachers and children. How much of it would become actual disposable spending money in the bestowal and at the discretion of the teacher or the class? More than one teacher has told me that it was easier to get the school to buy an illuminated terrestrial globe to hang

Child minder

from the classroom ceiling than to buy a set of street maps of the city to put in the hands of the children.

Several acute educational thinkers, from Paul Goodman to Mario D. Fantini (the former in *Compulsory Miseducation* in 1963 and the latter in *Public Schools of Choice* a decade later) have insisted that it is not bigger budgets but a wider range of alternative choices that are needed, and have given specific lists of possibilities. The characteristics of both are that they emphasise a plurality of approaches, since they do not believe that there is any one "solution" to the "problem" of urban education; they insist on local control and involvement, since they believe that self-government is more essential in education than good government; they seek the availability of academic excellence as well as of a completely non-academic approach, since they actually recognise that schools create two kinds of student: those who can work the academic treadmill and those who cannot; they want a system that is flexible enough to teach students of any age when they are motivated to learn.

My own priorities in inner city education are in nursery education and the infant and junior schools. When the "scandal" of unregistered and consequently illegal child-minding became a public issue, it was left to an outsider, Brian Jackson, to formulate a scheme for giving the child-minders training in nursery nursing, and it is notorious in British cities that where there is the most pressing need for pre-school education, it is least available. John Bird, chairman of Wolverhampton Education Committee, wisely notes that whatever criticism we may make of the variety of government-sponsored urban programmes, they have at least enabled some authorities like his "to open a very significant and extremely important salient into the provision of nursery places which would not otherwise have been possible. On practically every ground one can think of—early introduction to the tool of language being not the least important—nursery education is vitally urgent . . . It represent furthermore the early involvement of the family in general society. It opens up, at the point where it is most telling and most rewarding, the concept of the community school . . ."

In England and Wales in 1972 there was pre-school provision, including play groups for 29 per cent of four-year-olds, 2 per cent of three-year-olds, and 0.3 per cent of two-year-olds. If it is true, as most observers believe it to be true, that large numbers of inner city children suffer from their earliest years from the results of isolation and lack of stimulation, and if an increasing proportion of them are being reared in single-parent families or in families where both parents are working, the need for more provision for the pre-school child is increasingly obvious. The world of pre-school education is split by ideological differences between those who believe on principle in professionalism—in day nurseries and in nursery schools, and those who believe in play-groups or in child-minders. The harassed mother has to make use of what is available to her, and cannot afford to have principles. Nor in fact can society. In spite of years of pressure and recommendation it was not until the British government's Urban Air Programme was initiated in 1968, that local authorities were urged to make proposals for nursery projects in their most deprived areas, resulting in the provision of 24,000 more full-time nursery places. A government policy statement in 1972 proposed that by 1982 there should be places for 50 per cent of three-year-olds and 90 per cent of four-year-olds, with 15 per cent of each of these age groups attending full-time and the rest part-time. Subsequent cuts in public spending have ensured that if these aims are to be achieved, it will not be through the official machinery.

Yet if we want to break into the lives of those children who seem doomed to failure and frustration, this is the area of education where the likelihood of improving their chances is greatest.

17
The City as Resource

"The aim of education is to help people learn how to understand, control and, ultimately, change their environment. But the education system in this, and in most other advanced industrial societies, is geared to precisely the opposite end: i.e. pupils are taught that the world is extremely difficult to understand; that only a privileged few can reach such an understanding; that these few have the right to control the activities of all the rest; and that, far from trying to change their environment, the vast majority of people should try and fit happily with the situation as it is."

ALBERT HUNT

If there is an urban education crisis because so many city children do not fit the style and method of the city's education system, if as Mario Fantini and Gerald Weinstein put it, "the urban context is one in which there is persistent stress imposed by intensely concentrated social realities", it is also a context which can provide, in Edgar Gumpert's words, "education networks of fantastic richness and variety." The city is in itself an environmental education, and can be used to provide one, whether we are thinking of learning *through* the city, learning *about* the city, learning to *use* the city, to *control* the city or to *change* the city.

It was Paul Goodman once again, who (as well as anticipating the dilemma of the urban school, and as well having shown more clearly than any other observer in *Growing Up Absurd* how hard we have made it to grow into responsible adulthood) casually enunciated many years ago the philosophy of urban environmental education which the city teacher of today is painfully evolving. How do we rear citizens who will make the city their own? Goodman's answer, written in 1942, took the form of a conversation between a professor of education and a street urchin, Horace (Horatio Alger) who is a kind of urban Huckleberry Finn, and had the foresight to tear up his registration card on the first day of school so that he had no official existence and used the streets for his education like Horatio Alger Jr's 19th-century rags-to-riches heroes. The professor begins:

"It seems to me prima facie to use the Empire City itself as our school. Instead of bringing imitation bits of the city into a school building, let's go at our own pace and get out among the real things. What I envisage is gangs of half a dozen, starting at nine or ten years old, roving the Empire City with a shepherd empowered to protect them, and accumulating experiences tempered to their powers. Questions?'

'Holy cats!' cried Horace, goggle eyed to think of others carrying on the way he did. 'Would they ever make trouble and stop the traffic!'

'So much the worse for the traffic', said the professor flatly. 'I'm talking about the primary function of social life, to educate a better generation, and people tell me that tradesmen mustn't be inconvenienced. I proceed. Fundamentally, our kids must learn two things: skills and sabotage. Let me explain. We have here a great city and a vast culture. It must be maintained as a whole: it can and must be improved piecemeal. It is relatively permanent. At the same time, it is a vast corporate organisation: its enterprise is bureaucratised, its arts are institutionalised, its mores are far from spontaneity. Therefore, in order to prevent being swallowed by it or stamped by it, a kid must learn to circumvent it and sabotage it at any needful point as occasion arises.'

'Wait up! Wait up!' said Horace. 'Ain't this a contradiction? You say we got to learn to be easy at home here, then you say we got to sabotage at every point. On the one hand, you gotta love an' serve 'em: on the other hand, you gotta kick 'em in the shins. Does it make sense to you?'

'There's nothing in what you say, young man. In the Empire City, these two attitudes come to the same thing: if you persist in honest service, you will soon be engaging in sabotage. Do you follow that?'

'Yes, I think we follow that', said Eliphaz quietly. 'But I doubt that other people do.' "

The vernacular is unconvincing, but all the characteristics of an urban education to make the child the master of his environment are in this dialogue, as well as the dilemmas of attempting to put it into practice: the questions of the dangers of the street, the size of the group, the role of the shepherd or teacher, and the fact that if we teach the skills to manipulate the environment we are also teaching the skills to sabotage the activities of its destroyers. Much later in his life Goodman wrote that the model for the kind of incidental education that he recommended was that of the Athenian pedagogue touring the city with his charges, "but for this the streets and working places of the city must be made safer and more available. The idea of city planning is for the children to be able to use the city, for no city is governable if it does not grow citizens who feel it is theirs."

He had to wait many years for the climate of educational experiment to change sufficiently to try out a "school without walls" *using* the city. The best known such experiment is the Parkway Education Program in Philadelphia initiated in 1969 and run by the School Districts there. Students were not handpicked, but were chosen by lottery amongst applicants from the eight geographically-determined school board districts of the city, in grades 9 to 12 (ages 14 to 18) regardless of academic or behavioural background. There was no school building. Each of the eight units (which operated independently) had a headquarters with office space for staff and lockers for students. All teaching took place within the community: the search for facilities was considered to be part of the process of education. "The city offers an incredible variety of learning labs: art students study at the Art Museum, biology students meet at the zoo; business and vocational courses meet at on-the-job sites such as journalism at a newspaper, or mechanics at a garage . . ." The Parkway Program claimed that "although schools are supposed to prepare for life in the community, most schools so isolate students from the community that a functional understanding of how it works is impossible . . . Since society suffers as much as the students from the failures of the educational system, it did not seem unreasonable to ask the community to assume some responsibility for the education of its children."

No British local education authority has instituted a Parkway Program. Some of the "free schools" set up to provide educational alternatives have sought to use the resources of the community, and now and again one hears of a child who has conducted his own education like Goodman's Horace. Keith Kennedy, for example, describes "an exemplary truant" a 13-year-old called Barker: "He absented himself for three weeks was eventually caught, tried and punished (caned and placed on 'daily report'). Afterwards he told me that he had usually taken buses to those places he had never visited before—museums, art galleries and buildings of historical interest in the centre of London. The school had never offered him such opportunities to see and learn. A year later Barker would join a fourth-year 'adventure'

Exploring the transport system, London

Exploring the street in Tirana

Carnival

ing a town trail, Bath

Barbecue

class in which he would make canoes, tinker with motor car engines, paint pictures throughout extra art lessons; and continue the formal motions of Mathematics and English. He might well have been asked to continue his own course of self-education. But he wasn't." Another British teacher, Gerald Haigh, who has had considerable experience with "difficult" children, proposes a "City College" modelled on Parkway, but with significant differences. He wants to start with one unit of a hundred children and ten teachers, and he wants specifically to cater for reluctant students recommended by the heads of other city schools and spread over the eleven to sixteen age range. "No child will be admitted unless his parents visit us and understand what we are about." The good pupil:teacher ratio is financed by the absence of a school building, though he needs a unit office and nine tutor bases, spread around among the buildings of the city—the Library, the Fire Station, the University and so on. Basic skills in literacy and mathematics will be covered in the formal tutor group meetings, and the rest of the day in using the city's resources. "City College" claims Mr Haigh "is a *real* community school. It is *in* the community, making what use of it the teachers choose. It can still insulate itself as a community of scholars; it is not *controlled* by the community. It is the exact opposite of the kind of community school which is so named because it has to open its doors to the public and share its facilities. City College has no facilities of its own; it goes into the community and uses theirs instead. Any it does not like it will leave alone."

Street encounters

He is convinced that one of the gains will be that "the children will find it easier to work and cooperate because they have been removed from the school environment. No more dismal furniture, no more rules about running in corridors, no more general feeling of oppression and confinement. They will still have to conform to a high standard, but the reasons will be that much more apparent, and the example will be set by the adult community about them, provided that we choose where to contact that community. There are many advantages to be gained from decentralisation, too. The small groups of children and teachers will be much more easily handled, and there will be no such thing as an anonymous bunch of ruffians terrorising everyone else."

He emphasises that the City College he envisages cannot be a complete answer. How many such institutions could a city support? "Beyond a certain limit, the town would be overrun by pupils, and we would be in danger of producing a sort of educational dustbowl." There are in any case many other ways of using the city as an educational resource. For as well as the hard city of buildings, places and artefacts, there is the soft city of human contacts and activities.

The city, before the motor age drove them off the streets, was full of street characters, who provided the young with incidental amusement and instruction. Peter Mackenzie recalled from 18th-century Glasgow the famous city porter James Dall. "When the coach was away and time hung rather heavy on his hands, he might be seen with the Grammar School boys, or other urchins of the city, trying his powers at leap frog, over the well known row of old twenty-four pounder cannons that stood on end along the edge of the plainstanes opposite the Tontine—a feat that required great agility. When successful in jumping over them all, our hero grinned horribly a ghastly smile, which made the youngest to look upon him with awe and

Pentecostal service

amazement." Arturo Barea recalled from his childhood in Madrid two illicit pedagogues. One was the Penny Teacher who lived in a hut made of petrol cans in the Barrio de las Injurias. "A horde of ragged pupils squatted round him in the open to learn the ABC at ten centimos a month." The other was the Saint with the Beard who gave classes in the Plaza Mayor in exchange for his pupils' collection of cigarette-ends. "The Penny Teacher was sent to prison as an anarchist and died there. The Saint with the Beard was warned off from his corner and disappeared. But he turned up again eventually and went on secretly lending tattered books to his pupils, for the love of reading."

Just as the philosophy of the detached youth worker has grown up in the social work field, so we may have to recreate the informal street teacher. During the late 1960s Vancouver had a Town Fool (with a grant from the Canada Council) who sat on the court house steps dispensing his folly and wisdom. Liverpool has a story-cart trundling round the by-ways of Toxteth, with its load of books, music, and things to do on the pavement. The Inner London Education Authority employs a street story-teller, Roberto Lagnado. "Once in the market place at Marrakesh, he watched an old Arab telling tales from the Koran, while dignified sheikhs, their veiled wives, servants and children sat around him in a circle, enthralled. He did not understand the Arabic words, but as he listened he decided that storytelling was the trade he wanted to follow . . ."

Apart from exploiting such "official" street people as may exist, the school which seeks to use instead of to ignore, the resources of the locality, will develop its network of contacts who can be visited on journeys of exploration or "street seminars". In every locality there are old and retired people who would be delighted to be interviewed by groups of children building up the *autobiography of a place* from the experiences of its inhabitants.

Aileen Boatman is an infant teacher who was involved in the North Islington Special Project, an attempt to give some additional impetus through the schools of a particularly deprived district. She was conscious of the isolation of the children in her classes, confined either to their homes or in the school. They seemed to know nothing of the district where they lived. She brought in an architect, Alan Strutt, from the Greater London Council, to talk to the children about buildings, and then took the class out into the neighbourhood to look at buildings and analyse what they liked, what they hated, and what they would prefer to see built. Their own pictures, drawings, models and written work were assembled into an exhibition in an old double-decker bus which toured the neighbourhood.

Finally they had a procession through the streets of the borough, with children dressed up as bits of the environment: houses, trees, vehicles, street crossings. They had a decorated lorry, a multi-racial steel band, and their parade through the streets caused great excitement—a man with his face covered in lather leapt out of the barber's chair to see them pass. The whole affair ended with a torchlight dance and barbecue in the school playground which was attended by all and sundry, including those parents who had never before made contact with the teachers. From the school's point of view the carnival can serve a variety of social and environmental purposes. For one thing, the experience of walking down the middle of a traffic-free street, enables children to *see* the street for a change. Mrs Boatman told me how she yearned for the carnival to be, not a special activity, but taken for granted as

The experience of shopping

Class Encounters

something the school did annually, closing the streets to vehicles and making a gesture of solidarity between the school and its heterogeneous surrounding population. It would certainly be a good idea to invent an ancient local tradition of Beating the Bounds of the Catchment Area.

In a junior school in an even more battered and ruthlessly reconstructed part of the inner city, Ken Mines of Princess May School, London, involved his nine and ten-year-olds in an exhibition and slide/tape presentation of the past and present of the surroundings of the school, which drew a rich harvest of recollections and old photographs from old residents who had thought themselves totally left behind by change in the city. What could this antiquarian delving mean to the black and brown children in his class? The answer turned out to be that however much these streets and this old school were some-one else's past, they were these children's present. The embittered old man who loathed his immigrant neighbours found himself patiently explaining to their children what the place used to be like when he was a child (sixth from the left in the old photograph) at the very school they now attended. The school's investigation of the neighbourhood proved to be a valuable social cement.

If the teacher's concern is with education for *mastery* of the environment, it soon becomes apparent that this is more than a matter of exhorting the class to "find out about the district where you live." Michael Storm, who is inspector for geography and environmental studies in London, notes that "despite a considerable experience of orthodox local study" of the descriptive, fact-accumulating kind, pupils "leave school ill-equipped to understand the *processes* at work in their society", and that instead of starting with the question "what should people know about the locality," we should ask "what issues are currently alive in the area." The child, like the adult, learns the art and the technique of citizenship, not through admonitions or through lectures on civics, but from involvement in real issues.

Teaching in an inner city district of Sheffield, Dot Dromgoole noticed that one house was different from the little terraces of housing all around.

Gambling Machine

The children knew it too, it was called the White House, but none of them had been inside. She arranged with the old lady who lived there for the class to visit her and to be shown the wooden panelling and the stone-flagged kitchen. A visit to the public library revealed that the house was over 200 years old and had been built by one of the pioneer industrialists of the city. But they also learned that it was due for demolition to make more parking space for the firm next door. This distressed the class, because they had become involved with the old lady and her husband and because they had come to see that it was valuable to have one building that was in some way special in their district. They sought the advice of the City Architect who explained to them the procedure for getting the house "listed" as of historic interest by the Department of the Environment. The DOE, after investigation declined to list the building, so the children thought up other ideas for saving the White House, which involved writing letters to everyone from the Queen to the chairman of Sheffield United Football Club, (as one of the boys thought the club might buy the house as a hostel for visiting teams). Then they turned their attention to running a local petition. As a result they were interviewed by the press, radio and television. In fact they saved the White House. The headmaster of the school, Chris Rosling, makes three points about the effect of this involvement: the children enjoyed it, they "discovered that amongst the dross of their environment there were some pearls of history" and they had a glimpse of the idea that democracy depends on "us" being prepared to tackle "them" about "our" heritage. He notes that in addition the children were motivated to use the basic skills of careful observation, letter-writing, group discussion and persuasion and learned how to handle and use the mass media. "But to my mind the most important thing is their realisation that they can actively play a part in shaping their surroundings, that what *they* say about where and how they live will be listened to and that the key to their future lies in their own awareness."

Town Child as Country Child

"Rousseau's Emile seems to have been taught in a well-furnished country house, surrounded by a well-cultivated garden with all variety of natural phenomena within easy reach. That may be the ideal environment for the unfolding sensibility of a child—personally I believe that it is."   HERBERT READ

Iona and Peter Opie tell the story of a young black boy from Notting Hill, taken for a week's holiday in a Wiltshire village, who, asked how he felt about the country, replied, "I like it—but you can't play in the road as you can in London." He might have added that you can't play in the fields either, though he probably took that for granted. Recollections of pastoral childhood in the English countryside usually look back in fact to the neglected pastures, choked ditches, overgrown coppices and broken fences of the long period of agricultural depression that ended in the second world war. Generations of urban children grew up whose vision of "the country" was one of picturesque decay. Generations grew up in the country for whom it was an environment to get away from.

It was assumed in antiquity, and has been ever since, that it is a good thing for the urban child to spend part of the year in the country, though the reasons behind the assumption have varied. They have been social, political, economic, educational, recreational, sanitary and compassionate. They have also been aesthetic, for rural life and rural sights and sounds have always been the raw material of literature, music and the graphic arts, with the urban scene, except in a perjorative sense, far behind as acceptable subject matter. Until the Impressionists, few painters celebrated the *feel* of urban civilisation as opposed to its topography, though it was a composer from rural England who wrote *Paris: Song of a Great City*. From that city came the greatest of urban poets, Baudelaire, whose biographer notes that "Where a child born in the country dreams of mountains, rivers, lakes and the sandy shore of the sea, he saw long meandering streets crammed with houses rising sheer and pointing their roofs and chimneys at the skyline, instead of fields and meadows. It was not the song of the birds which filled his waking hours, but the droning murmur of the crowds in the narrow thoroughfares below, which he heard at evening, leaning out of his window, when it often seemed to him that he was on a high mountain listening to the harmony which night made of the discordant sounds in the streets beneath him. It was not nymphs and shepherdesses who peopled his dreams, but typical Paris characters—the working people, gigolos and pimps, weary prostitutes, shop-girls coming from their work, beggars in the gutters. Ordinary city life was teeming with all the things which he needed for his art, the mystery and the beauty which others failed to find there."

But Baudelaire was a poet, not a social reformer, and to his contemporaries concerned with the welfare of the young, these were the very aspects of the city from which children should be shielded. Their image of childhood, permeated as it was by sentimental ruralism and notions of arcadian innocence, was affronted by the perils, contacts and contaminations of the street. The theme permeates the 19th-century discussion of city childhood, in spite of a cogent comment by J. M. Welding on the "City boy versus country boy" debate: "In looking up the biographies of the many great men who started in life as farmer-boys, we observe this one significant fact, that invariably they availed themselves of the very first opportunity of quitting rural surroundings and employment. They formed

Overleaf: *Ice cream in Tirana*

"This is a tough ball park to have to play in."

Willie Mays. Fresh Air Fund Board Member.

Willie Mays knows. That's why he joined the Fresh Air Fund team. To help get ghetto kids out of the city for a couple weeks this summer. To give them a chance to run and slide on dirt and grass instead of rubbish and glass.

You can help, too. A thirty-dollar donation gives a city kid two weeks in the country. But, any donation is an important one.

Please help. Join the Fresh Air Fund team. Show these kids why New York is the town with the big league heart.

Mail to: **Fresh Air Fund**
300 West 43rd Street New York, N.Y. 10036

Enclosed is my contribution of _____
Contributions are tax deductible. Cancelled check is your receipt. Please make checks payable to The Fresh Air Fund.

Name_____ Address_____
City_____ State_____ Zip_____

The child's need for the country is recognized by the Fresh Air Fund in New York the very cream, so to speak, of the country population, which seeking its natural position of affinity with kindred minds of the city, created the impression that the country is a very magazine of force and mental strength, whereas the simple truth is that it is but a mass of refuse that remains after the best element has been extracted . . . The general tendency is, whenever a country boy rises to eminence as a man, to add the fact of his country training to his fame. If one of equal eminence is known to have been city-bred, no comments are made as his success is considered as a matter of course. In cases where the early life of a distinguished man has been of a mixed town and country training, it is usual to attribute the entire credit to his rural experience . . ."

A mixed town and country training is precisely what parents who were conscientious enough, or wealthy enough, have sought for their children. It is one of the explanations for the mass exodus in the twentieth century to the suburbs. As one of the deprivations of urban childhood, Leila Berg notes that "the children on Council estates cannot keep animals, and cannot grow flowers. I am sure children need to be in touch with the earth, need to have their fingers in soil, and their eyes looking into an animal's or a bird's eyes."

The rich, in bringing up their children, have always been able to mingle urban and rural experiences. The need to include a town house as one of the amenities of a rural estate, whether we are thinking of imperial Rome, 18th-century England or 19th-century Russia, ensured that the children of the family gained the experience of both, as well as that of the drama of the transition between the two. It was expedient for the patricians that their children, or at least their sons, should gain the experience of negotiating with gamekeeper and forester as well as with gaminghouse keeper and tailor. It was expedient for their own sakes that they deserted their estates in wintertime, even if only for those little winter assembly towns where they built themselves houses for times when the country roads were impassable. The sons and daughters rehearsed their urban roles in these small towns. Jane Austen watched them. Least fortunate were those children of the rich who lived at home in the country, were sent off to a boarding school also in the country, and spent their holidays in someone else's country. The ordinary urban experience passed them by.

For families lower in the social hierarchy, the effort to provide a rural holiday for the children was aided for generations by the fact that so many had grandparents living in the country. There was always someone who would welcome them to a place where the flour came from the miller and the milk, butter and cheese from the farm next door. This was true for centuries for a large section of the city population, and even urbanites of several generations maintained these links. As late as the 1840s Copenhagen Fields in Islington brought country ways to the city: "A favourite outing-place for middle-class families, where especially at harvest time they would bring their children to toss the hay alongside little local boys. The steam engines raced into the cow-strewn meadows, pulling their yellow and black carriages and open trucks for the poor."

And as late as the 1940s the tradition prevailed of the boisterous annual pilgrimage of poor families from east and south London to the hop-gardens of Kent to pick hops for the brewing industry. It was a fortnight of open-air living (and sleeping in dark corrugated iron sheds) for children who would otherwise be imprisoned in the city for the summer. Mechanised picking has ended this annual event in London life, just as the mechanisation of agriculture as a whole prevents town children from having a part to play in the cycle of food production. The 19th-century discovery of "Nature", coinciding with the fantastic pace of growth in the cities of Britain and the United States, led to a variety of attempts to give some kind of rural experience to the urban child. The first of these was "nature study" as a school activity, usually conducted solely in the classroom with pussy-willows in jam jars. This was totally divorced from the actual experience of "nature" that city children accumulated from the remaining vacant lots in the city whose uses were celebrated in Herman Wouk's *City Boy*: "In Public School 50, teachers were always trying in vain to wake the love of nature in the boys by reading poetry to them. The compositions on the subject of nature were the dreariest and most banal of all the writing efforts wrung from the urchins, and the word 'lots' never appeared in them. But the moment the lads were free of the prison of school they scampered to the lots, chased butterflies, dissected weeds and flowers, built fires, and watched the melting colours of the sunset. It goes without saying that parents and teachers were strongly opposed to the practice of playing in the lots, and were always issuing orders against it."

Isolated teachers rebelled against the aridity of classroom nature study, and there have been continual attempts to set up simulations of the rural experience in town. Peter Schmitt remarks that "bringing the country into the school yard had reassuring precedents: Comenius had cultivated the school garden for its beauty, Pestalozzi for its training in industry, and Froebel for its system" and he describes Fannie Parsons' "Children's School Farm" started in 1902 in DeWitt Clinton Park, New York, and the "Garden City" developed in 1907 in Dead Cat Dump at Worcester, Massachusetts.

It was apparent quite early in the quest for arcadia that the most obvious way to give city children a rural experience was to take them to the country. *The New York Times* programme of one-day excursions for slum children began in 1872, the *New York Tribune*'s Fresh Air Fund in 1877. By 1897 seventeen American cities had organised "Fresh Air Relief", and in London the Children's Country Holiday Fund fulfilled the same function. The next stage was the Summer Camp, hardly known at the beginning of the century, which had become "the customary thing" in America by 1915, and involved a million children and seven thousand camps by 1929. Mr Schmitt traces the mingled motives and ideologies behind this movement, which though it has less institutionalised equivalents in the other industrial nations, is a pre-eminently North American institution, lampooned in literature, but a standard component, and an ultimately beneficial one, of growing up in the American city. As with so many other facilities for the city child, millions of inner city children, those for whom the summer camp was first conceived, don't benefit from it.

There were parallel developments in British cities. Leslie Paul recalls how, before the Scout movement was organised as such, the serial publication of Baden-Powell's *Scouting for Boys* met an urban audience ripe for its message. "With an astonishing perception they leapt at Scouting as at something for which they had long been waiting, divining that this was a movement which took the side of the natural, inquisitive, adventuring boy against the repressive schoolmaster, the moralizing parson and the coddling parent. Before the leaders knew what was happening groups were springing up spontaneously and everywhere bands of boys, with bare knees, and armed with broomsticks, began foraging through the countryside ... The Scout movement was the very breath of hope and love and encouragement to many a child." In Europe, the lengthening period of paid holidays and the growth of the travel and tourist industries have greatly increased the proportion of city families who take an annual holiday for granted. A city like Paris seems to empty out its own population every August, only to be filled by a new transient population of visitors from less glamorous cities; but there, as in the cities of Britain, the children of the inner city stay on the hot familiar pavements unless taken away by youth organisations, school camps, church groups, local charities and family service units. Those who have acquired the knack of using the facilities which the middle class child knows about, find that they can get themselves a holiday cheaply through camping, cycling, hitch-hiking, using the network of Youth Hostels, or attending a work camp. Most poor children do not.

City schools themselves have developed their own rural centres at an accelerating rate since the second world war. Every inner London school has access to one; many secondary schools have exclusive use of their own. But urban teachers at both primary and secondary levels readily confirm that the sights, sounds, smells and ways of the animals and plants of the countryside are "totally beyond the experience of city school children", and that there is "a general lack of knowledge about agriculture and its place in our economy."

Does this matter? Or is the feeling that it does matter merely a reflection of that sentimental ruralism that ignores the fact that our ancestors fled to the city to escape from that precious contact with nature? And that the rural poor of Asia, Latin America and Africa are today flocking to the cities in millions because they recognise that in the bursting city lie the best hopes for their children? What kind of rural activities should city children learn? In Britain the Countryside Commission and the Association for Agriculture organise very popular Farm Open Days for the urban visitor, and several education authorities have toyed with the idea of setting up demonstration farms for the primary purpose of urban school visits. The City of Birmingham actually has one. I remember a passionate debate in the Council for Environmental Education between those who wanted such enterprises to be run as old-fashioned mixed farms and those who regarded this as a proposal for deceiving the urban child who should be shown the reality of battery hens and prairie-style monoculture. I was on the first side, for if you want a child to understand printing or weaving you take him to a small workshop where he can handle type or work a loom, and if you want him to comprehend husbandry he must stroke and handle animals and see a variety of crops and vegetables, and pull some up to take home and cook.

The rural needs of the urban child are not just the sights of the farm or the pleasures of running untrammelled through the woods or exploring the country park. They include vital personal experiences and discoveries like silence, solitude and the sensation of utter darkness. In other respects there are signs that we are returning to an appreciation that some "rural" activities can be pursued in the city. There are two "farms" in inner London and others in other British cities, as well as plans for more. The City Farm in Kentish Town was started by Inter Action in 1972 on land rented from

Goats in the Surrey Docks

British Rail and the local council. It has a community workshop, riding school, stables and sheep, goats, pigs, rabbits, geese, chickens, ducks and a cow. There is a conscious aim of mixing age-groups, with children and young people looking after the animals while adults working on their own projects are constantly around. Other adults, including old people, are working on the allotments, community garden and picnic area. The Association for Neighbourhood Use of Buildings and Space (NUBS) which runs City Farm, claims, with justification in my view, that the cheapness of adapting buildings and improvising with local community labour, the intense use and the notable absence of vandalism, make their kind of enterprise in the densely populated district where they work infinitely more sensible and economical and more appealing to the whole community than comparable local authority playground provision. The second such venture, in the derelict Surrey Docks in South London, is the work of Hilary Peters who, with Ken Bushell keeps goats, hens, ducks, geese and bees. She remarks, "I find farming methods in the country very cruel and difficult to stomach. Farming in London is easier and freer." We have already seen that her guarantee of freedom from vandalism is to involve the local children. Many

local adults are now concerned with the adjoining allotment gardens. Here initiative has made people reflect that, with the different public authorities completely deadlocked in the discussion about the future of the vast area of the former docks in East and South East London, and with no likelihood of funds for the kind of comprehensive redevelopment that was fashionable until very recently, it would be more sensible to encourage interim redevelopment as an area of market-gardening, stock-raising and public open space.

The domestic back garden in the city is a family asset of incalculable value, not just for growing things, but because it is another room for the house: a workshop, a playpen and a playground. The uses are incompatible of course, and each household makes some compromise between garden as garden, garden as playspace and garden as wilderness. Each of these uses brings its own riches. Richard Mabey, finding the unofficial countryside in his own backyard, says, "I have counted over twenty different species of wild flower (excluding grasses) on my lawn, many of them just those plants through which, in children's games, we have our first physical intimacy with nature: dandelion seed-heads for telling the time; daisies for chaplets; buttercups under the chin; couch grass to wind into sister's hair as a Chinese Torture; ratstail plantains for guns; Lady's slippers and clovers to suck for nectar. These flowers are part of children's lives precisely because they are weeds, abundant and resilient plants that grow comfortingly and accessibly close to us. If we drive them out of their domestic refuges into ghettoes in the deep countryside they will be driven out of what remains of our folklore as well".

The rare urban parent for whom gardening is a passion, rather than an occasional burst of activity, and who, more rarely still, communicates this passion to his children, has offered them a priceless gift. George Gill, the father of the late Marjorie Allen of Hurtwood, was a rate collector for a water company and when this was merged into the Metropolitan Water Board, was paid off with a modest pension, enabling him to realise a long-cherished dream to buy a smallholding. This was the idyllic setting of his daughter's early life—"Jersey cows, pigs and chickens and a wonderful harvest of greengages, apples and gooseberries." It is not surprising that she trained as a gardener and from this grew the major interests of her life: campaigning for nursery schools, the de-institutionisation of residential children's homes, tree planting, play parks and adventure playgrounds. "When I worked among children condemned to live in barbaric and sub-human surroundings," she wrote, "my thoughts always returned to my early good fortune. The remembrance has made me more determined than ever to restore to these chidren some part of their lost childhood; gardens where they can keep their pets and enjoy their hobbies and perhaps watch their fathers working with real tools; secret places where they can create their own worlds; the shadow and mystery that lend enchantment to play."

John Raynor had an unusual city childhood. He was born at No 3 Little Dean's Yard in the shadow of Westminster Abbey. This house was unique among its neighbours in that it had a garden, long, narrow and bounded on three sides by high walls. Here Raynor's father "had years ago conceived the idea of turning the bank into a little wood of real country trees. And so every year, a wild sapling had been brought back from the summer holiday and planted on the bank. Father knew the history of every tree, the date of its planting and from where he had dug it." By the time John was five or six, many of the trees were twenty or thirty feet high: two oaks, an ash, two mountain ashes, a beech, an elm, a birch and other forest trees. It was "a place of great magic, and adored by each child in turn. It served a double purpose, for besides providing one of the great joys of our lives, it supplied also the provender for the caterpillars we brought back each September, and which needed feeding on birch, oak or beech leaves, a diet hard to come by in a great town."

Another of his recollections was of being entrusted with the task of lifting the bulbs for storage in the spring: ". . . by lunchtime it would be empty and smoothly raked, prepared for the summer bedding-out plants. And in the afternoon, under the hot spring sun, we would heel-in the bulbs we had removed in the rich mould of the little roofless potting-shed. Father would do the planting, and I would collect the bulbs from the edge of the lawn where we had piled them, in the little wheelbarrow. Then Father would stand in the open doorway of the little brick building, waiting with open arms and smiling face to receive the barrowloads of bulbs. Or perhaps, as I am now inclined to think, waiting to receive me."

This touching testimony to the city garden as a seed-bed of the domestic affections is reinforced in the context of the surroundings of the city school. Commenting on the opinions gathered from children in the UNESCO survey of *Growing Up in Cities*, Kevin Lynch says "the hunger for trees is outspoken and seemingly universal." In Britain, Manchester Polytechnic has a research project on Planning the School Site, and canvassed the opinions of children. "I do not think a school would really be a school without trees, flowers, etc" writes a 13-year-old, whose school evidently has them, and a veteran of 16 recalls, "In my experience, when I was a child the playgrounds I enjoyed were not necessarily spacious, but were hilly with trees, and most important, had lots of corners where groups could make their own hide outs . . . There should be places of darkness and light, of grass and of earth."

19

Four Exemplary Enterprises

"The empty church in Great George Street, blackened by time, came to be known as the Black Church. Now it is simply the Blackie. Make your way up to Liverpool Cathedral and ask around. Everyone up there knows it. Yes, but what is it? 'It's a disco; we play games there: it's just the Blackie: it's a door.' It is all things to all kids. Once inside, you begin to see that kid was right, it is a door. It is a door for kids and adults to walk through and find workshops, shows, card games, camera work, floor mopping, money lending, theatre, a bed for the night. And more. You begin to see that the Blackie has survived and grown strong because they have opened doors. They have not tried to change people, they have helped people to become themselves."

ALAN BREW

The Great George's Community Arts Project, known as The Blackie, has spent seven creative years trying to meet some of the needs of people of all ages in a deprived and neglected community in central Liverpool. Every conceivable activity from playgroups to community video goes on there. One of the slogans of this "sports centre of the arts" is "What you want is what you get" and it is complemented by the phrase "The problem is knowing what you want." The people working there have had plenty of spectacular success stories, of teenagers who rejected, and were rejected by school, and came in to bounce around on the giant balloons or play five-a-side football, or just to make trouble, and found themselves seduced into other activities, finally embarking on training in the arts. But in one sense these are not the important justifications of the place. The important thing is the sharing of skills. James Brown explains: "If the Blackie was run by car designers and car mechanics it would be the sort of garage where you could go and learn to repair a car; learn to build a car; talk about cars and transportation; join with the mechanics and designers at their work; or call in for a tea or coffee. As it is the Blackie is run by artists. It's the sort of artists' studio where you can come along to the programme of activities organised by artists and friends, join in (or watch) artists at their work, undertake your own creative activities, or call in for a drink and a talk. This openness to the community (with its pleasures and its discomforts) is a principle of Blackie's work. But when artists at the Blackie decide to buy a printing press, or video equipment, or sound equipment, they do so primarily because they want to play with it. They are prepared to share this equipment, and their skills, with people who come through the door." The staff at the Blackie come and go—as a matter of deliberate policy. The constant factor since 1968/9 has been Bill and Wendy Harpe who have held the enterprise together with incredible stamina and ingenuity, rewarded now by the finance to make structural alterations to the building so that it complies with the fire regulations for even more intensive use. "We are all generally agreed that we should take care of our family," says Wendy, "The real question is—where does our family end?"

A second exemplar for involving even the most deprived and rejected of inner city children has been Centreprise in the London Borough of Hackney. It is a grey, blighted district, and in educational terms it is one of those areas whose children show particularly low scores in tests in English, mathematics and verbal reasoning. Two hundred and eight thousand people live there, and there is not a single bookshop. At least there was not one until Centreprise came. Centreprise was dreamed up by an American, Glenn Thomson in 1970. It provides a bookshop, richly stocked, especially with

Great George's Project, Liverpool

the kind of paperbacks which don't usually find their way to the East End, and a coffee bar, as well as meeting rooms, offices and office equipment, made available to any group or individual in the borough who want to use them. The best-known initiatives of Centreprise are its publishing ventures. Ken Worpole, when he was a teacher at Hackney Downs School, was active in generating interest for the production of a teaching pack about the history of Hackney, sold at a very low price, and of an illustrated reading book for slow learners with its story built around local scenes and local footballers. After he joined the Centreprise team he inspired a continuous stream of Centreprise books: poetry by local children and their elders, autobiographies of local residents: people young and old, whose writings and experiences had never been thought worthy of the dignity of print. They have produced 24 books in four years, ranging from *The Gates*, the self-told story of two truant boys, who belong to another East End literary group, the Stepney Basement Writers, to a photographic history of the borough.

It was Ken Worpole who conceived the notion of a "people's autobiography of Hackney" and of the device of getting school children to interview old residents and record their reminiscences, a really creative educational technique now widely emulated elsewhere. When *The Municipal Journal* visited Centreprise, its reporter Jim Higgins found that, "Literally any community activity that can be encompassed within the walls of Centreprise receives active support and encouragement. If someone wants to start a tenants' group, a theatre group, a reading circle, to learn silk-screen printing or simply to pursue some private hobby-horse, the typewriters, duplicators and cheap duplicating paper are available, together with advice and help. The coffee bar is clean, well-lit and, even more important, warm. Old-age pensioners, housewives, children, social derelicts and students can, and do, sit as long as they like over a cup of coffee, reading newspapers and magazines, talking, or just sitting. The coffee, incidentally, is freshly made from coffee beans . . . There is a play-group for the under-fives, run by the mothers themselves. With the help of a £300 grant from Hackney Borough Council a playbus was bought and is joyfully used by local kids. Truant children can drift in, drink coffee or lemonade, talk to one another, and, unless they ask for help, not be bothered by anybody at all."

What struck Jim Higgins, and what strikes me, knowing its vulnerability, is the absence of vandalism and robbery at Centreprise (in spite of some spectacular instances of both). "The theory," he says, "that people with an interest in something they can themselves control, apply a self-discipline more effective than any set of arbitrary regulations seems to be true." Another aspect which I feel bound to record is that this kind of activity, which cannot possibly be self-supporting, has to spend an inordinate amount of time seeking financial support from the public authorities, the charitable trusts, concerned individuals and companies, while the function it performs for the whole district is enormous in comparison with the effect of the kind of provision people expect from local authorities.

My third exemplar of urban involvement is the Notting Dale Urban Studies Centre. In Britain we have a Council for Urban Studies Centres, which, extrapolating from the experience of field studies centres in the countryside, has urged the need for providing similar facilities in our cities. Its members saw a threefold function for such centres: firstly as an educational facility available to schoolchildren, both from the locality and from afar; secondly as visitor centres, the urban equivalent of the Interpretation Centres in the American National Parks; and thirdly as providing the Community Forum sought in the British government's Skeffington Report on public participation in planning, which saw the need for a patch of neutral ground on which community groups and official planners thrashed out their differences. The handful of such centres that exist, vary in their emphasis. Some are purely educational facilities, some are just visitor centres, but the one at Notting Dale triumphantly vindicates the expectations of its founders. (It is privately financed by Harrow School.)

Notting Dale always was a grim district. Dickens called it the plague spot of London, and in its present state it concentrates in a tiny area all the dreadful errors of postwar housing and planning policy: inhuman blocks of flats in a swathe of no-man's-land on either side of a motorway. The Centre itself is a Victorian vicarage, richly equipped with reprographic equipment and directed by Chris Webb, an impressive ex-teacher. It has simple sleeping accommodation for groups of children and access to the gym next door with a trampoline, table tennis and snooker. "The centre works in three ways," Chris Webb explains, "all of which overlap and sustain the others." Firstly it is a resource centre for the locality; the secretary is a community secretary. Secondly it is an educational experience, heavily used by school groups of all ages and by individual children. Thirdly it makes schoolchildren the researchers for the community. "Often we merely provide the hardware for a momentum already achieved but other times we involve ourselves with local groups in wholesale collaborative exercises. These can be the formulating, printing, delivery, collection and analysis of questionnaires on a particular estate, the results being used by the Tenants' Association to help remedy defects in their area and to put pressure on the council from a position of strength over tenants' management. Or it can be playing a part in a planning inquiry, acting as a witness and helping to produce materials for evidence and so on."

One of the things which amazes visitors to the centre (who invariably get drawn into whatever activity is going on) is the maturity and capacity of very young children there. Here is a typical "Day Package" for a class of eight-year-olds:

10.00–11.30 Urban Trail introducing them to the area and various things of interest to look at, draw, photograph, think about and tape
11.30–12.30 Small group discussion on the issues raised by the kids
12.30– 1.45 Lunch/recreation
1.45– 3.30 Problem solving tasks directed at the issues raised by the Trail. This would involve design tasks, limited architectural exercises, building up estates and playspaces with our wood-block game, lay-out exercises on the magnetic boards, mental-map making.

Chris Webb sees this as an extension of, or complement to, the children's school work, but even when this is not possible he aims in this limited day package to introduce children to their locality in an organised and purposeful way, "then to offer them ways of considering it, using ideas of space and design to suggest that the urban fabric is plastic and not God-given."

When a class of ten and eleven-year-olds from St Andrew's Primary

On the Pioneer
Railway, Budapest

School, Golborne, moved into the centre for a week, cooking and clearing up their own meals (Josie said "we had bigger portions and a better choice—especially the salad"), their teacher Sue Wagstaff reported that it was "without a doubt, the most successful venture we, as a class, have ever undertaken." She explained that "Hidden talents, obscured by the normal classroom situation and restrictions, suddenly came to light. Children who rarely contributed to class discussion established themselves with confidence. One very emotionally disturbed "remedial" boy became so adept at photographic skills that he was soon teaching a group of his fellow classmates and using a complex camera. The development of new and varied skills was something which the children valued highly. Amongst these were photographic developing, printing and enlarging; interview, questionnaire and survey techniques; understanding and application of primary historical data; and presentation techniques to display these skills."

In this most forlorn and foresaken district of the city, Chris Webb, Angus McLewin and their helpers know exactly what they are seeking. "We try," says Webb, "to allow things to happen which perhaps couldn't happen in schools. The aim is to make a much more potent population—people who can cope with local authorities, who can get over the feeling that they have no power."

One of the impressive things about these three exemplary enterprises is that they are not there to provide facilities for children, even though in practice they are all swarming with children. They are there to serve the whole community. Nor are they there to entertain. They are there to help people discover their own skills. They each have a focus. At Centreprise it is the power of the printed word, at the Blackie it is the power of the expressive arts, and at Notting Dale it is the power of environmental education as a lever for change.

My fourth exemplary enterprise is of a quite different character. Near the Hotel Budapest in the Hungarian capital you can take a railcar up the steep slopes of the Buda Hills to the terminus of the Pioneer Railway. This is a narrow-gauge railway 13 miles long which winds through wooded hills and meadows overlooking the Danube. It is staffed, with the exception of the engine-driver, by 10 to 15 year old members of the Young Pioneers. They come from local schools and take turns in performing the functions of station masters, ticket clerks, conductors, telegraphers and signalmen. The Pioneer Railway was set up in 1952, in imitation of the thirty such ventures in the Soviet Union, and has run ever since with no mishaps. It is one of the attractions of the city for visitors, both for the beautiful route and for the novelty of a child-run railway. It is also widely used by the children of the city and by school parties dropping off at the various stations for field trips. One Western visitor writes that the boys and girls have a certain comic dignity, another notes that they take the job very seriously "and it seems impossible for passengers to distract them from their duties." Others see the enterprise as a carefully contrived ideological device for inculcating in the young the virtues of industrial discipline and for ensuring a supply of labour for the railway system, or else they comment on how meticulously kept are the stations and trains. The comparison that occurs to me is with the state of the railways of London or New York. I would also reflect on the fact that vandalism costs British Rail £1 million a year and costs London Transport £200,000 annually.

20

In the Sandbox of the City

"A sandbox is a place where adults park their children in order to converse, play or work with a minimum of interference. The adults, having found a distraction for the children can get on with the serious things of life. There is some reward for the children in all this. The sandbox is given to them as their own turf. Occasionally, fresh sand or toys are put in the sandbox, along with an implicit admonition that these things are furnished to minimize the level of noise and nuisance. If the children do become noisy and distract their parents, fresh toys may be brought. If the occupants of the sandbox choose up sides and start bashing each other over the head, the adults will come running, smack the juniors more or less indiscriminately, calm things down and then, perhaps in an act of semicontrition, bring fresh sand and fresh toys, pat the occupants of the sandbox on the head, and disappear once again into their adult involvement and pursuits." GEORGE STERNLIEB

Nearly sixty years ago Berthold Brecht wrote a play *In the Jungle of the City*, set in the fantastically exotic dream-America which was his image of capitalist society. The metaphor gained currency and we have by now become over-familiar with phrases like the asphalt jungle or the concrete jungle as images of the city. Today they are deceptive. It would be closer to the truth to see the city as a wasteland. "Glasgow," declared *New Society*, "could well become the first city to be classified as industrial waste." The economic centre of gravity and the demographic focus has moved, permanently, from the inner city. George Sternlieb's mordant analogy of the city as sandbox gives a more illuminating picture of the place of the inner city in national preoccupations. Increasingly the inhabitants of the inner city are superfluous people, a drag on the national economy. This is more evident in the United States than in Britain, though there are British cities too, which grew at an enormous pace in the nineteenth century, whose whole economic *raison-d'être* has collapsed, and which can never recover either the industry or the population they sustained, after a fashion, in those days. Governmental programmes with a bewildering series of initials, follow each other in rapid succession, as fresh sops to, or fresh toys for, the inner city.

The citizens look on with a resigned cycnicism. For a besetting fault of the city administrations is that they have failed to take their electorate seriously. The cities, Murray Bookchin remarks, "are disintegrating administratively, institutionally, and logistically; they are increasingly unable to provide the minimal services for human habitation, personal safety, and the means of transporting people and goods." Even where they retain some semblance of formal democracy, "almost every civic problem is resolved not by action that goes to its social roots, but by legislation that further restricts the rights of the citizen as an autonomous being and enhances the power of super-individual agencies." It is ironical, since the whole burden of my argument is that we should give responsibilities to our city children, that city governments see their *adult* citizens as feckless juveniles, whose own aspirations and initiatives are not susceptible of incorporation into the official reality. Thus a disillusioned city planner, Mike Franks, writes of the dreadful plight of the city of Liverpool, "For the last hundred years the men of the corporation, both political and technical, have run a closed shop in local government. Liverpudlians have long been actively denied the knowledge and learning they would have needed to have stood up to the brave new world plans of their leaders. The city council has treated them like children whose needs must be administered to, and in doing so have created retarded adults uncertain whether to expect what they need or to go out and get it."

It is beyond the scope of this book to formulate policies for the rebirth of our dying cities. In fact it is not policies that are needed, but merely a willingness to elicit and facilitate people's own policies. Foremost in these facilitatory exercises would be the bursting of the bubble of urban land values. Roger Starr, the housing administrator for New York told me of his mystification at the way land retains its price long after it has lost its value. In Britain there is what can only be called a capitalist plot to which the government is a party, to keep up the price of urban land, simply because in the speculative paradise of the property boom in the 1960s, institutional investors, like the great insurance and pension funds, invested so heavily in property shares. What has this to do with the child in the city? Simply that it is only when the thousands of acres of derelict inner city land in every British city are valued as the derelict land that they really are, that ordinary people's aspirations for housing at human densities, for domestic and public open space, for low-rent premises for small businesses, and for all those activities which are the very essence of urban civilisation but show a low rate of return on capital invested, can be realised. "What the best and wisest parent wants for his own child," said John Dewey, "that must the community want for all its children." And that includes the space to grow up in.

Most of the environmental policies which would improve the lives of children in our cities would benefit adults too. In particular everything that would make the city a more tolerable place for the old, would make it more enjoyable for the young. The German writer Alexander Mitscherlich remarks that "The anthropologist cannot get over the fact that the commercially-oriented planning of our cities is clearly aimed at one age group only—working adults—and even then inadequately enough. How a child is to become a working adult seems to be a negligible factor. The world of the child is a sphere of the socially weak, and is ruthlessly manipulated." His comment points to an important distinction. Do we want to provide for the child as a special kind of person or as someone who is becoming an adult? There is a pendulum in the philosophy of child-rearing that swings between these two views. There are cities in the world with a terrifying absence of the reverence we feel we owe to the child, but there are also cities where we make it incredibly difficult for the child to enter a world of adult freedom and responsibility. In the cities of the West, we get in some ways the worst of both worlds. We no longer cow our children into submission, in fact we indulge them as consumers, with the powerful aid of the advertising industry, but we fail to induct them into a world of adult decision-making, perhaps just because as adults we have delegated to others the habit of deciding.

Watch the scrimmage at the bus stop when the city child comes out of school, interview tenants on a housing estate terrorised by its children, learn that the annual cost of vandalism in England, Scotland and Wales is, at a minimum estimate, well over £114 million, or read that one out of every eleven children in the city of Atlanta will be murdered if he or she stays there, and you will be in no doubt that the city has failed its children. It fails to awaken their loyalty and pride. It fails to offer legitimate adventures. Jane Addams, an astute urban reformer of seventy years ago observed the "inveterate demand of youth that life shall offer a large measure of excitement" and she asked whether we oughtn't to assume "that this love of excitement, this desire for adventure is basic and will be evinced by each generation of city boys as a challenge to their elders?" It is certainly a challenge in the form of the manufactured excitements to which they resort and which they themselves usually attribute to boredom. Paul Corrigan's study of "Doing Nothing" describes the evening activities of boys in a city in Northern England, hanging around and waiting for something to happen, and in the end creating some kind of incident, a fight, the breaking of milk bottles, just to make some kind of diversion from the tedium.

The modern city in Jane Addams' view, has failed to cater for "the insatiable desire for play, whereas the classical city had promoted play with careful solicitude and the mediaeval city held tourneys, pageants, dances and festivals." To advocate more circuses really is to recognise the city's function as a sandbox; but for the young, if the whole city is not their playground, what else is it? There is an urgent need for a modern equivalent of the rituals of a calendar of excitement provided in the cities of traditional society. The Christmas pageant at Las Rosas mentioned in Chapter One, played an important part in the lives of the children interviewed there; the carnival at Islington described in Chapter Seventeen made a social bond between the school and the locality. But the very fact that, looking for a means of providing excitement and adventure, we have to settle for notions of festivals and carnivals, is the measure of the extent to which we have drained both these characteristics out of ordinary urban life.

In the United States the playground enthusiasts, landscape architects and environmental psychologists with a concern for the needs of the child in the city, keep in touch with each other through a valuable newsletter called *Childhood City*, and it is tempting to use their title to draw together the threads of evidence and observation collected together in this book. But the very concept of a city for children suggest in our day a kind of Disney fantasy, and its built form would be Disneyland. The real world is somewhere else. If anyone in the Western world set up a Pioneer Railway of the kind described in the last chapter, it would be as a joke, with an amusingly antiquated locomotive. The children could expend all their "comic dignity" on playing trains, but not on providing a valued service to the community. It's all fine, so long as they don't impinge on the real world.

I don't want a Childhood City. I want a city where children live in the same world as I do. If we seek a shared city, rather than a city where unwanted patches are set aside to contain children and their activities, our priorities are not quite the same as those of the crusaders for the child. We have enormous expertise and a mountain of research on the appropriate provision of parks and play-spaces for use by children of different ages, but the ultimate truth is that children play anywhere and everywhere. Because some bit of the city is designated as a play space on a plan, there is no guarantee that it will be used as such, nor that other areas will not be. If the claim of children to share the city is admitted, the whole environment has to be designed and shaped with their needs in mind, just as we are beginning to accept that the needs of the disabled should be accepted as a design factor. I can think of no city that admits the claim of children, though I can think of many which seem deliberately designed to exclude them. How can a child *use*, for example, central Birmingham? Every step the city takes to reduce the dominance of motor traffic makes the city more accessible to the child. It

Shared city

also makes life more tolerable for every other citizen.

I have mentioned that my educational priority in the city is in pre-school and nursery education. I would combine this with the need to provide "relevant" educational experiences for older children. There is a time-honoured but grossly neglected educational adage: each one teach one. This implies firstly that children learn best from older children, and secondly that teaching other children is itself a learning experience. In the search for "relevant" experiences for reluctant learners in the secondary schools, several successful attempts have been made to give them tasks in nursery and infant schools. When Chris Webb was teaching at Sir William Collins School in central London, he sought out such a task for fifteen-year-old Bill. Bill rejected school and had been involved in a wide range of petty crimes. Under the banner of "community education", and with some misgivings, Webb sent him to work among the five-year-olds in a local infants school. When he went round to see how Bill was getting on, he found him engulfed by the infants. They and he were totally absorbed in the making of Easter bunnies from cotton wool and egg cartons. Bill, for the first time in his life was a socially-approved success. The primary school headmistress sought to find a formula to enable the boy who was due to leave school at the end of the term to be employed there. Nursery nurse, teaching auxiliary? But his school attainments were too meagre for him to be thought either employable or worthy of training. He just left and resumed his life in the criminal margin of society. Every city has thousands of boys and girls in the situation of Bill, hundreds of whom might find in themselves a talent for caring for the young.

The obstacle to matching the urgent community need with the bored and rejected teenagers is not fundamentally one of money, and is certainly not one of premises. It is one of unwieldy procedures, professional status-anxiety, and our belief that nothing worth doing can be improvised. In Philadelphia, Lore Rasmussen argued her way into getting the use of an old school building, set up a nursery school, staffed it with high school drop-outs, many of who had been pushed out of school because they were pregnant. She gave them a continuous course in child care and got them to bring in the putative fathers—often also high school drop-outs, and bullied them into starting a toy-making workshop.

My second priority in integrating the child into the city, is again a demand which the city fails to satisfy for many adult citizens: the chance to earn money and the opportunity to be useful. Much of our provision for children seems almost designed to exclude them from the *process* of providing, so that they are positively obliged to be the listless and ungrateful consumers of services supplied by others. There are education authorities in Britain who spend more per head on their primary school meal service than they do on the provision of books, paper, writing and drawing materials. A whole industry, with its own expertise, has grown up, of educational catering. Yet when the children from a London primary school spent a week catering for themselves at the Urban Studies Centre, "Budgeting was tight because we were minus our ILEA subsidy, but the children reckoned they had large portions and a better choice." There would still be an important educational and supervisory role for the "dinner lady", but wouldn't it be sensible for the children, by rota, to prepare their meals, and to pay them for doing so?

Why shouldn't they keep chickens and sell the eggs? Why shouldn't *they* be employed to maintain the parks and playgrounds? Consider the economics of the material recovery industry. Already scout and guide groups are involved in waste paper collection, and the fluctuations of the price of salvaged paper are not because of over-supply, but for lack of storage space. The best lesson about our prodigality with raw materials is to earn money by gathering them for recycling. I would like to see our refuse collectors with a horde of assistants in every street and every school. If it became a racket, that too would be a lesson on how the city functions. I would happily see the kids unionised in a junior branch of the National Union of Public Employees. In the parks of the city of Zurich, Betty Pinfold reports that "The Swiss have found that the children have a real need for contact with animals. The children look after them themselves, and it is only those who undertake to do this who are allowed to handle and play with them. The enthusiasm is such that at one park the children have organised a circus and go on tour." Animal husbandry is one of the very few areas of city life which have not been buttoned up by the adult world, and I am waiting for the day when every city school has its donkeys, goats and pigs. Northcliffe Community High School, like many another sixty-year-old school building, has two quadrangles surrounded by classrooms, but I have never yet seen another school where these have been turned into something between a menagerie and a farmyard. The fact that these points seem trivial and almost sentimental by comparison with the issues faced by our cities, is the measure of the way in which we have accepted the exclusion of children from real responsibilities and real functions in the life of the city. In the ideal city every school would be a productive workshop and every workshop an effective school.

Bottom Right: *Yenan primary school children help with the foundations of a new extension*

Delhi : preparing school lunches

The theme that runs all through this book is that we have to explore every way of making the city more accessible, more negotiable and more useful to the child. We have seen that some children develop the habit of exploiting everything their environment can provide. They unfold as individuals through creatively manipulating their surroundings. But there are many others who never get a foot on that ladder, who are isolated and alienated from their city. Often they take revenge on it. John Holt, in formulating, very delicately and reasonably, the right of the child to escape from childhood, says "City children do, of course, learn to get around, at least to certain places—many of them tend, for safety, to stick pretty close to home. But even when they explore farther, go downtown, there is too often a sense of doing it in defiance of adult authority. There is surely a big difference between how it feels to explore a city, or a country, as forbidden territory and how it feels to explore it as a larger neighbourhood in which you are welcome, your city, your country, your world."

Yet there is an ultimate paradox about the lives of city children. Readers must have had the experience of watching television documentaries exposing some social evil, and of contrasting the solemn words of the Social Problems Industry with the evidence of the cameraman. You hear about the inhuman living conditions of the slums of Naples, but you see wonderfully vivacious and happy people who never stop to worry about whether they or their children are well-adjusted or whether they are deficient in the capacity to form "meaningful social relationships." They are too busy living or keeping others alive. You hear about the wickedness of child labour, but you see children who are resentful that interfering reporters and officials are making it even harder to spend the long summer holiday earning their purchasing power instead of indulging in petty theft which is a statistical norm of juvenile urban life. Similarly, although throughout this book you read about the deprivations of the city child, you see through the eyes of the photographers how children colonise every last inch of left-over urban space for their own purposes, how ingeniously they seize every opportunity for pleasure. The words spell deprivation but the pictures spell joy.

In 1975 the National Portrait Gallery in London staged an exhibition consisting largely of thousands of photographic records of children admitted a century earlier into Dr Barnardo's homes. This "man of tender violence" as the exhibition described him, had by the time of his death in 1905 cared for over 62,000 children of the city streets. Their involuntary portraits revealed every kind of suffering and deformation. The visiting voyeurs read into these faces a multitude of preconceptions: a general impression of cowed indifference or bovine resignation, with every now and then, a face of outstanding beauty, or nobility, defiance or wildness.

The faces of contemporary city children don't have that haunted look which we read into those of the long-dead nineteenth century children. We are touched by the way in which they seize what fun they can from an environment which others have shaped without their needs in mind. "Alas, regardless of their doom, the little victims play" we think, following Thomas Gray's reflections on a distant prospect of, of all places, Eton College, as we ourselves reflect that the city is going to offer them much less joy in adult life. Alexander Herzen asked himself what childhood was for. "Is it simply the purpose of a child to grow up, simply because it does grow up? No, the purpose of a child is to play, to enjoy itself, to be a child, because

if we follow any other line of reasoning, then the purpose of all life is death."
But at what particular age do we cease to think of our city children as cute
and begin to think of them as a social menace? Most people's recollections of
childhood include some moment in some context when their pride and self-
esteem were lifted by the fact that they were being treated as though they
were not children. They rose to the occasion. Rather than throw in a few
playthings, shouldn't we help them climb out of the sandbox and into the
city?

NOTES AND SOURCES

Book
page

INTRODUCTION

vi Margaret Mead: remarks at the symposium on "Children, Nature and the Urban Environment" Washington March 1975

Frank Musgrove: *Youth and the Social Order* (London: Routledge and Kegan Paul 1964)

Philippe Ariès: *Centuries of Childhood* (London: Jonathan Cape 1962, Harmondsworth: Penguin 1973)

Peter Laslett: *The World We Have Lost* (London: Methuen 1965, 2nd edition 1971)

Lloyd deMause (ed) *The History of Childhood* (London: Souvenir Press 1976)

vii Paul Goodman: *Growing Up Absurd* (New York: Random House 1960, London: Gollancz 1961)

Leslie Lane: "Humber" *The Architects' Journal* 19 Jan 1966

C. A. Moser and W. Scott: *British Towns* (Edinburgh: Oliver and Boyd 1961)

viii Gaston Bachelard: *The Poetics of Space* (Boston: Beacon Press 1969)

Chapter 1 Paradise lost?

2 Edward Hyams: *From the Waste Land* (London: Turnstile Press 1950)

Ernest G. Schachtel: "On Memory and Childhood Amnesia" (*Psychiatry: The Journal of the Biology and Pathology of Interpersonal Relations* Vol 10 February 1947). Reprinted as No P-301 in the Bobbs-Merrill Reprint Series in the Social Sciences

4 Lionel Trilling: *The Opposing Self* (London: Secker and Warburg 1955)

George Orwell: *The Road to Wigan Pier* (London: Gollancz 1938)

Vladimir Dudintsev: *Not by Bread Alone* (London: Harvill Press 1957)

Thomas Burke: *Son of London* (London: Herbert Jenkins 1947)

Raymond Williams: *The Country and the City* (London: Chatto and Windus 1973)

5 Emerson's journal quoted by Morton and Lucia White: *The Intellectual versus the City* (New York: Mentor Books 1964)

Maurice Samuel: *In Praise of Yiddish* (Chicago: Cowles Book Company 1971)

Peter Laslett: *op cit*

7 Dolly Scannel: *Mother Knew Best* (London: Pan Books 1973)

Louis Heren: *Growing Up Poor in London* (London: Hamish Hamilton 1973)

Chris Searle (ed) *Stepney Words* and *Stepney Words II* (London: Reality Press 1970 and 1972)

John Clarke, Stuart Hall, Tony Jefferson, Brian Roberts: "Subcultures, Cultures and Class" in Stuart Hall and Tony Jefferson (eds) *Resistance Through Rituals* (London: Hutchinson 1976)

8 Robert Roberts: *A Ragged Schooling* (University of Manchester Press 1976)

Yuri Kapralov: *Once There Was a Village* (New York: St Martin's Press 1974)

9 A. M. Battro and E. J. Ellis: "International Study of the Impact of Economic Development on the Spatial Environment of Children: Salta, Argentina" Typescript in UNESCO Applied Social Science Division, Paris, 1972 This is summarised in Kevin Lynch: *Growing Up in Cities* (Studies of the Spatial Environment of Adolescence in Cracow, Melbourne, Mexico City, Salta, Toluca and Warsaw) (Cambridge, Mass: MIT Press 1978)

Chapter 2 Happy habitat revisited

10 Albert Eide Parr: "The Happy Habitat" *Journal of Aesthetic Education* July 1972

William Godwin: *The Enquirer* (London: G. and J. Robinson 1797)

Albert Eide Parr: "The Child in the City: Urbanity and the Urban Scene" (*Landscape* Spring 1967)

11 Bernard Rudofsky: *Streets for People* (Garden City, New York: Doubleday 1969)

Joseph P. Lyford: *The Airtight Cage* 1966, quoted by Rudofsky, *op cit*

Lynda Chalker MP in the House of Commons 1 August 1975

13 The old man's recollections are told in Paul Thompson: "Voices from Within" in H. J. Dyos and Michael Wolff (eds): *The Victorian City: Images and Realities* Vol 1 (London: Routledge and Kegan Paul 1973)

Geoffrey Moorhouse: *Calcutta* (London: Weidenfeld and Nicholson 1971, Penguin Books 1974)

John Betjeman: "Parliament Hill Fields" *Collected Poems* (London: John Murray 1962)

Simon Jenkins in the *Evening Standard* 1971

Jane Jacobs: *The Death and Life of Great American Cities* (New York: Random House 1961, Harmondsworth: Penguin Books 1965)

16 John Ezard: "Textbook City Fails to Make Happiness" *The Guardian* 17 April 1975

Michael Rutter: "Why are London Children so Disturbed?" *Proceedings of the Royal Society of Medicine* Vol 66, 1973

17 H. J. Dyos: "The Slums of Victorian London" *Victorian Studies* Vol XI, 1967–8

Alan Sillitoe: "Poor People" *Anarchy* 38, April 1964

18 Alasdair Maclean: "Slum Pickings" *Times Literary Supplement* 4 July 1975

Matt McGinn: "I've Packed Up My Bags" on RCA International record INTS 1368

Scottish Education Department: *The Raising of the School Leaving Age in Scotland* (Edinburgh: HMSO 1976)

19 Department of the Environment: *Planning in the UK*. Report prepared for the United Nations Conference on the Human Habitat, Vancouver 1976

Chapter 3 How the child sees the city

22 Frank Conroy: *Stop-time* (New York: Viking Press 1967)

Yi-Fu Tuan: *Topophilia, A Study of Environmental*

Book
page

Perception, Attitudes and Values (New Jersey: Prentice-Hall 1974)
A. K. Lukashok and Kevin Lynch: "Some Childhood Memories of the City" Journal of the American Institute of Planners Summer 1956
Child's Eye View exhibition, devised by Paul Ritter, at the Co-operative Education Centre, Nottingham May 1959
Yi-Fu Tuan: remarks at the symposium on "Children, Nature and the Urban Environment" Washington March 1975
23 Paul Shephard: "Play and Human Development", Address to the symposium on "Children, Nature and the Urban Environment" Washington, March 1975
Kevin Lynch: The Image of the City (MIT Press 1960)
24 Jean Piaget: The Child's Conception of the World (London: Routledge and Kegan Paul 1929)
J. Flavell: The Developmental Psychology of Jean Piaget (New York: Van Nostrand 1963)
Jeff Bishop: Environmental Education for Schoolchildren (Kingston Polytechnic, Architectural Psychology Research Unit Research Report No 5, 1975)
25 Brian Goodey, A. Duffett, J. R. Gold and D. Spencer: City Scene: An Exploration into the Image of Central Birmingham as seen by Area Residents Research Memo No 10 (Birmingham: Centre for Urban and Regional Studies, 1971)
David Spencer and John Lloyd: A Child's Eye View of Small Heath: Perception Studies for Environmental Education Research Memo No 34 (Birmingham: Centre for Urban and Regional Studies, 1974)
27 Robert Maurer and James C. Baxter: "Images of the Neighbourhood and City among Black, Anglo and Mexican American Children" Environment and Behaviour Vol 4 No 4 December 1972
See also David Uzzell: "Children's Perception and Understanding of their Environment" Bulletin of Environmental Education No 66 October 1976
Jeff Bishop and J. Foulsham: "Children's Images of Harwich" (Kingston Polytechnic, Architectural Psychology Research Unit, Environmental Education Research Report No 3, 1973)
28 J. Bruner: The Process of Education (New York: Vintage Books 1960)
Gary Moore: "The Development of Environmental Knowing" in David Canter (ed) Psychology and the Built Environment (London: Architectural Press 1974)
David Stea: Toy Geography: A Study of Environmental Modelling in Puerto Rican Children Ages Five Through Eight Place Perception Report No 5 (Worcester, Mass: Clark University, 1969)
Jeff Bishop and R. Booth: "People's Images of Chelsea Football Club and its Surroundings" (Kingston Polytechnic, Architectural Psychology Research Unit, Environmental Education Research Report No 10, 1974)
Trevor Higginbottom, Schools Council Geography for the Young School Leaver Project, Avery Hill College, London
29 John Brierley HMI, in Trends (Department of Education and Science, Spring 1975)
Erik Erikson: Childhood and Society (London: Imago 1951, Penguin 1965)
Kevin Lynch: Growing Up in Cities (Studies of the Spatial Environment of Adolescence in Cracow, Melbourne, Mexico City, Salta, Toluca and Warsaw) (Cambridge, Mass: MIT Press 1978)

Chapter 4 Antiquarians, explorers, neophiliacs

32 Michael Locke and Moira Constable: The Kids Don't Notice: a Shelter report on the effects of bad housing conditions on children (London: Shelter 1974)
Enid Gauldie: Cruel Habitations: A History of Working
James Boswell: Journal of a Tour to the Hebrides (1785, Oxford University Press 1965)
Class Housing in Britain (London: Allen and Unwin 1974)
Jack Common: The Freedom of the Streets (London: Secker and Warburg 1938)
John and Elizabeth Newson: Infant Care in an Urban Community (London: Allen and Unwin 1963, Penguin 1971) Four Years Old in an Urban Community (London: Allen and Unwin 1968, Penguin 1970) Seven Years Old in the Home Environment (London: Allen and Unwin 1976)
33 Charles Mercer: Living in Cities: Psychology and the Urban Environment (Harmondsworth: Penguin 1976)
34 John and Elizabeth Newson: Seven Years Old . . . op cit
35 Robert Roberts: The Classic Slum (Manchester University Press 1971, Penguin Books 1973)
38 Elizabeth Ring: Up the Cockneys (London: Elek 1975)
Jack Common: Kiddar's Luck (London: Turnstile Press 1951)
Arthur Newton: Years of Change (London: Centreprise 1974)
Molly Weir: Shoes Were For Sundays (London: Hutchinson 1970, Pan Books 1973)
A. S. Jasper: A Hoxton Childhood (London: Barrie and Rockcliffe 1969, Centreprise 1974)
40 Hazel Robbins in Images of Youth: Growing Up in Birmingham in the 1970s (City of Birmingham Education Committee 1974)
A. M. Battro and E. J. Ellis: "International Study of the Impact of Economic Development on the Spatial Environment of Children: Salta, Argentina" Typescript in UNESCO Applied Social Science Division, Paris. See also Kevin Lynch: Growing Up in Cities (Cambridge, Mass: MIT Press 1978)

Chapter 5 Privacy and isolation

42 David Canter: The Psychology of Space (London: Architectural Press 1977)
Wednesday's Children: a Report on Under-Five Provision in Handsworth (Birmingham: Lozells Social Development Centre 1975)
Sue Cameron in The Teacher 28 April 1973
George Dennison: The Lives of Children (Penguin 1971)
Vittorio de Seta: "Diary of a School Teacher", a RAI film, based on Un Anno a Pietralata by Alberto Bernardini
Kevin Lynch and Tridib Banerjee: "Growing up in Cities" New Society 5 August 1976
43 Aryeh Leissner: Street Club Work in Tel Aviv and New York (London: Longmans 1969)
J. F. Short and F. L. Strodtbeck: Group Process and Gang Delinquency (University of Chicago Press 1965)
James Patrick: A Glasgow Gang Observed (London: Eyre Methuen 1973)
46 Florence Ladd: "Black Youths View Their Environment" Journal of the American Institute of Planners Vol 38 1972

Book
page

Lee Rainwater: "Fear and the House-as-Haven" *Journal of the American Institute of Planners* Vol 32 1966
Claude Brown: *Manchild in the Promised Land* (New York: New American Library 1965)

47 Maxine Wolfe and Robert Laufer: "The Concept of Privacy in Childhood and Adolescence" in P. H. Carson (ed): *Man-Environment Interactions: Evaluations and Applications* Part II (Stroudsburg, Penn: Dowden Hutchinson & Ross 1974)

50 Martin Deutsch: "The Disadvantaged Child" in John Raynor and Jane Harden: *Cities, Communities and the Young* (London: Routledge and Kegan Paul 1973)
John and Elizabeth Newson: *Seven Years Old in the Home Environment* (London: Allen and Unwin 1976)

51 The distinction between 'slums of hope' and 'slums of despair' originates from C. J. Stokes: "A Theory of Slums" *Land Economics* Vol 38, 1962
Oscar Lewis: "The Culture of Poverty" *Scientific American* Oct 1966

Chapter 6 Adrift in the city

52 George Konrad: *The Case Worker* (London: Hutchinson 1975)
Theodore Dreiser, quoted by Morton and Lucia White: *The Intellectual versus the City* (New York: Mentor Books 1964)
Eric Sevareid: "You Can Go Home Again" *Colliers Magazine* 11 May 1956
Page Smith: *As a City Upon a Hill: The Town in American History* (New York: Alfred A. Knopf 1966)

54 George Godwin: *Town Swamps and Social Bridges* (1859, Leicester University Press 1972)
Guy de Maupassant: "In the Country" *Short Stories* (London: Everyman's Library 1934)

55 Kenneth Allsop: *Hard Travellin'* (London: Hodder and Stoughton 1967)
Thomas Minehan: *Boy and Girl Tramps of America* (New York: Farrar and Rinehart 1934)

56 John Holt: *Escape from Childhood* (New York: E. P. Dutton 1974, Harmondsworth: Penguin Books 1975)
"Twin Boys Evade Social Services Department Help for More than a Year" *Community Care* 23 October 1974

57 Joseph M. Hawes: *Children in Urban Society: Juvenile Delinquency in Nineteenth Century America* (New York: Oxford University Press 1971)
Ivy Pinchbeck and Margaret Hewitt: *Children in English Society* Vol 1 (London: Routledge and Kegan Paul 1969)

58 Albert Smith: *Gavarni in London* (1849) quoted in Irina Stickland: *The Voices of Children 1700–1914* (Oxford: Basil Blackwell 1973)
Andie Clerk: *I Have Been Young and Now Am Old* (Liverpool: James E. James 1973)

60 Sarita Kendall: "Street Kids of Bogota" *New Society* 16 January 1975
Jailakshmi, reported by Sevanti De: "Slum Children are Free Birds" *Teachers World* 24 January 1975
Henry Mayhew: *London Labour and the London Poor* (1851) Selections ed. by Peter Quennell (London: Spring Books)

61 Tony Gibson: "Copping in Ecuador" *Anarchy* 79, September 1967

Richard Holloway: "Street Boys in Addis Ababa" *Community Service Journal* Vol 5 No 3 July 1970

62 Kellow Chesney: *The Victorian Underworld* (London: Maurice Temple Smith 1970)
John Willis, Director and Michael Deakin, Producer: *Johnny Go Home* Yorkshire Television 21 July 1975
Di Burgess in *TV Times* 17 July 1975

64 John Willis and Michael Deakin: *Johnny Go Home* (London: Futura 1976)

65 Don Busby in *The Examiner* No 7, September 1975

Chapter 7 A suburban afternoon

66 J. M. Richards: *The Castles on the Ground* (Architectural Press 1946)
Roderick McKenzie: "Ecological Process and the Internal Structure of Community" *American Journal of Sociology*, November 1924, reprinted in Lambert and Weir (eds): *Cities in Modern Britain* (Fontana 1974)
H. J. Dyos: *Victorian Suburb* (Leicester University Press 1961)

67 Louis H. Masotti and Jeffreyk Hadden (eds) *Suburbia in Transition* (New York: New Viewpoints 1974)
David Thorns: *Suburbia* (London: Palladin Books 1974)
Keith Waterhouse: *There is a Happy Land* (London: Michael Joseph 1957)
Enid Gauldie: *Cruel Habitations* (London: Allen and Unwin 1974)

71 Nicholas Taylor: *The Village in the City* (London: Maurice Temple Smith 1973)

72 John Holloway: *A London Childhood* (London: Routledge and Kegan Paul 1966)
James Kenward: *The Suburban Child* (Cambridge University Press 1955)
Anne Kelly: "For the Sake of the Children" in Masotti and Hadden (eds) *op cit*

73 Ebenezer Howard: *Garden Cities of Tomorrow* (1899) (London: Faber and Faber 1946)
Michael Hughes (ed) *The Letters of Lewis Mumford and Frederic J. Osborn* (Bath: Adams and Dart 1971)
Peter Self: *Cities in Flood* (London: Faber and Faber 1959)

Chapter 8 Adapting the imposed environment

86 Patrick Geddes: *Cities in Evolution* (London: Williams and Norgate 1915)
Arvid Bengtsson: *Environmental Planning for Children's Play* (London: Crosby Lockwood 1970)
Joe Benjamin: *Grounds for Play* (London: Bedford Square Press of the National Council for Social Service 1974)
Lady Allen of Hurtwood: *Planning for Play* (London: Thames and Hudson 1968)
Department of the Environment: *Children at Play* (London: HMSO 1973)
Paul Friedburg in *Landscape Architecture* October 1970

87 Dennis Woods: "Free the Children! Down with Playgrounds" (unpublished paper)

Prof. Hermann Mattern, University of Berlin at the Congress of the International Federation of Landscape Architects, June 1968

Iona and Peter Opie: *Children's Games in Street and Playground* (Oxford University Press 1969)

Alice Gomme: *The Traditional Games of England, Scotland and Wales* (1892–6) reprinted by Dover Books 1964)

Alice Gomme: *Children's Singing Games* (London: David Nutt 1894)

Norman Douglas: Introduction to 1931 reprint of *London Street Games* (London: Dolphin Books 1931)

Alan Milberg: *Street Games* (New York: McGraw Hill 1976)

Arnold Arnold: *World Book of Children's Games* (London: Macmillan 1975)

Iona and Peter Opie: *op cit*

89 Jeff Bishop: "The Memo I Stole from the Ministry" (*Bulletin of Environmental Education* No 48, April 1975)

Cecil Beaton: *Cecil Beaton's New York* (London: Constable 1939)

91 Richard Dattner: *Design for Play* (New York: Reinhold Book Corporation 1969, MIT paperbacks 1974)

94 Lawrence Halprin: Annual Discourse at the Royal Institute of British Architects (*RIBA Journal* July 1971)

Newcastle Evening Chronicle 3 June 1971

Norman Schreiber in *The Village Voice* 2 June 1975

95 John Millar: "How Europe's Biggest Paddling Pool Came to Manchester (*Bulletin of Environmental Education* No 12, April 1972)

Chapter 9 Play as protest and exploration

96 Iona and Peter Opie: *op cit*

Paul Thompson: "The War with Adults" *Oral History*, Journal of the Oral History Society Vol 3 No 2 Autumn 1975

Steen Eiler Rasmussen: *Experiencing Architecture* (London: Chapman and Hall 1959, Cambridge, Mass: MIT Press 1964)

97 Joe Benjamin: *Grounds for Play* (Bedford Square Press of the National Council for Social Service 1974)

Interviews kindly made available by Jenny Mills

102 Steen Eiler Rasmussen: *op cit*

104 "Council decides to ban children on new estate to stop vandalism" *South London Press* 24 February 1976

Charles Fourier: *Le Nouveau Monde Industriel* (Paris: 2 Vols., 1829)

Oslo – see Colin Ward: *Tenants Take Over* (Architectural Press 1975)

105 Vandalism – see Colin Ward (ed) *Vandalism* (Architectural Press 1973), *Protection Against Vandalism* (Home Office Standing Committee on Crime Prevention 1975)

Chapter 10 The specialist city

108 Linda Whitney in *Out of Our Minds* (London: Parliament Hill School 1975)

110 Paul Neuburg: *The Heroes' Children: The Post-War Generation in Eastern Europe* (London: Constable 1972)

111 Frank Dawes: *A Cry From the Street* (Wayland Publishers 1975)

Louis Heren: *Growing Up Poor in London* (London: Hamish Hamilton 1973)

Leslie Paul: *The Republic of Children* (London: Allen and Unwin 1938)

113 John Alexander: *Boy Scouts* (c. 1911) quoted in Peter J. Schmitt: *Back to Nature: The Arcadian Myth in Urban America* (New York: Oxford University Press 1969)

Waldo Eager and Peter Green quoted in Dawes *op cit*

114 John Ewen: Introduction to *Developmental Work with Young People* (Leicester: National Youth Bureau 1974)

John Eggleston: *Adolescence and Community* (London: Edward Arnold 1976)

Cyril Smith, M. R. Farrant and H. J. Marchant: *The Wincroft Youth Project* (Tavistock Publications 1972)

Saul Alinsky: *Reveille for Radicals* (New York: Vintage Books 1969)

Richard Bryant in Gulbenkian Foundation: *Current Issues In Community Work* (London: Routledge and Kegan Paul 1973)

Chapter 11 Traffic and the child

116 Mayer Hillman, Irwin Henderson and Anne Whalley: "Unfreedom Road" *New Society* 3 May 1973 and *Bulletin of Environmental Education* July 1973

Arthur Newton: *Years of Change* (London: Centreprise 1974)

Russell Miller: "Suburban Depression" *Sunday Times* 21 March 1976

Jack Common: *Kiddar's Luck* (London: Turnstile Press 1951)

E. M. Forster: *A Room With a View* (London: Arnold 1908)

118 Peter Cole: "Parents blamed for child road deaths" *The Guardian* 3 April 1974

Lucy and Michael Mulcay: "The Motorist and the Child: Where does the Responsibility Lie?" *The Guardian* 9 April 1974

John and Elizabeth Newson: *Seven Years Old in the Home Environment* (London: Allen and Unwin 1976)

121 Mayer Hillman, with Irwin Henderson and Anne Whalley: *Personal Mobility and Transport Policy* (London: Political and Economic Planning 1973)

Mayer Hillman: "Problems Before Needs" *Municipal Journal* 28 March 1975

122 Mayer Hillman and Anne Whalley: "Is the Car Cheating Your Child?" *Where* No 103, April 1975

Richard Hoggart: *The Uses of Literacy* (Harmondsworth: Penguin 1958)

Robert Roberts: *The Classic Slum* (Manchester University Press 1971, Penguin 1973)

123 Geoffrey Penny "Child Deaths on West German Roads" *Evening Standard* 3 July 1974

Siegfried Buschschluter: "Child Accidents" *New Society* 12 June 1975

Stina Sandels: *Children in Traffic* (London: Paul Elek 1975)

Colin Ward: "The Road to Children's Safety?" *Municipal Review* October 1975

124 Pauline Pratt: "Too young to die" *Drive Magazine* March–April 1976

Chapter 12 Wheels in the street

126 Paul Goodman: *Five Years* (New York: Brussel and Brussel 1966, Vintage Books 1969)
Hillman, Henderson and Whalley: *op cit*
128 P. J. Downton: "Children's Perception of Space Project: Melbourne Study" Typescript in UNESCO Applied Social Sciences Division, Paris 1973
Alan Brien: "Sunderland Echoes" *Sunday Times* 18 April 1976
"Awa' for a hurl on the midden cairt" = away for a ride on the refuse truck
Sonia Keppel: *Edwardian Daughter*, quoted in Irina Stickland: *The Voices of Children 1700–1914* (Oxford: Basil Blackwell 1973)
132 Sean Jennett: *Paris* (London: B. T. Batsford 1973)
John Gale: *Travels with a Son* (London: Hodder and Stoughton 1972)
133 Eleanor Laycock: "At Play in African Villages" in Jerome S. Bruner, Alison Jolly and Kathy Sylva (eds): *Play – Its Role in Development and Evolution* (Harmondsworth: Penguin Books 1976)
Norman Douglas: *An Almanac* (London: Chatto and Windus 1945)
James Kenward: *The Suburban Child* (Cambridge University Press 1955)
134 Ian Taylor and Paul Walton: "Hey, Mister, this is what we really do" in C. Ward (ed) *Vandalism* (Architectural Press 1973)
Eleanor Laycock: *op cit*
James Kenward: *op cit*
136 "Child thieves put up statistics" *The Guardian* 11 March 1976
Howard J. Parker: "The Joys of Joyriding" *New Society* 3 January 1974
137 Howard J. Parker: *View from the Boys* (Newton Abbott: David and Charles 1974)
Joseph M. Hawes: *Children in Urban Society : Juvenile Delinquency in Nineteenth Century America* New York: Oxford University Press 1971
"Scrumping in a meter orchard" *The Guardian* 22 March 1973

Chapter 13 Filling the shelves in the supermarket

138 Farrukh Dhondy: "What is a Child?" *Teachers World* 1 August 1975
141 *The Story of W. H. Smith and Sons* (London: W. H. Smith and Sons 1936)
142 Henry Mayhew: *London Labour and the London Poor* 1851) Selections ed. by Peter Quennell (London: Spring Books)
145 Jonathan Power and Anna Hardman: *Western Europe's Migrant Workers* (London: Minority Rights Group 1976)

Anne Garvey and Brian Jackson: *Chinese Children* (Cambridge: National Educational Development Trust, 1974)
147 Nottinghamshire Branch, National Union of Teachers: *Discussion Document on Behavioural and Disciplinary Problems in Secondary Schools*, 1976
148 W. Emrys Davies: *Work Out of School* (London: Councils and Education Press 1972)
Samir Shah: *Immigrants and Employment in the Clothing Trade* (London: Runnymede Trust 1975)
149 Barbara Fletcher: "Children with Part-Time Jobs" *Where* No 118 July 1976
Arthur Young: "Earning and Learning Your Way Through School – the Possibilities" *Bulletin of Environmental Education* No 43 November 1974

Chapter 14 The girl in the background

152 Elena Gianini Belotti: *Little Girls* (London: Writers and Readers Publishing Cooperative 1975)
Lucy H. Montague: "The Girl in the background" in E. J. Urwick (ed) *Studies of Boy Life in Our Cities* (London 1904). Other books of this period giving attention solely to the city boy are Charles E. B. Russell: *Manchester Boys, Sketches of Manchester Lads at Work and Play* (Manchester 1905), Reginald Bray: *The Town Child* (London 1907), Reginald Bray: *Boy Labour and Apprenticeship* (London 1911), J. H. Whitehouse (ed) *Problems of Boy Life* (London 1912), and Arnold Freeman: *Boy Life and Labour* (London 1914). Their American equivalents include such works as William Byron Forbush: *The Boy Problem : A Study in Social Pathology* (Philadelphia 1902). There is a total absence of any such literature devoted to the lives of city girls. The whole genre ends abruptly with the first World War.
Peter Laslett: *The World We Have Lost* (London: Methuen 1965, second edition 1971)
Geoff Mungham and Geoff Pearson (eds) *Working Class Youth Culture* (London: Routledge and Kegan Paul 1976)
Angela McRobbie and Jenny Garber: "Girls and Subcultures: an Exploration" in Hall and Jefferson (eds) *Resistance Through Rituals* (London: Hutchinson 1976)
154 Eileen Byrne, education officer of the Equal Opportunities Commission, interviewed in *The Guardian* 20 April 1976
Norman Douglas: *London Street Games* (1916, new edition, London: Dolphin Books 1931)
Mary Lynch's study reported by Alex Finer: "Girls will be Girls" *Sunday Times* 27 July 1975
156 Mollie Weir: *Best Foot Forward* (London: Hutchinson 1972, Pan Books 1974)
Gwenda Linda Blair: "Street Hassles" *Peace News* 19 March 1976
Anna Coote: "Girls on Scouts Honour" *The Guardian* 26 March 1976
Eleanor Emmons Maccoby and Carol Nagy Jacklin: *The Psychology of Sex Differences* (Stanford University Press 1976)
157 Dottoressa Moor: *An Impossible Woman*, ed by Graham Greene (London: Bodley Head 1975)
Barbara Wootton: *Social Science and Social Pathology* (London: Allen and Unwin 1959)
158 Joseph Sorrentino: *The Concrete Cradle* (New York 1975)

Book
page

Peter Watson: "Crime and Femininity" *Sunday Times* 22 July 1973

Carol Smart: *Women, Crime and Criminology: A Feminist Critique* (London: Routledge and Kegan Paul 1976)

159 Urie Bronfenbrenner: *Two Worlds of Childhood* (New York: Russell Sage Foundation 1970, London: Allen and Unwin 1971)

162 Peter Kropotkin: *Mutual Aid: A Factor in Evolution* (1903, London: Allen Lane 1972)

163 Tom Davies: "Bar-L Estate – the violent world of Mary C." *The Observer* 23 September 1973. Rosemary Collins: "The Children of Violence" *The Guardian* 13 October 1973

George Mackie of British Rail, quoted in *The Guardian* 11 April 1973

Chapter 15 At school in the alien city

164 Paul Goodman: *Growing Up Absurd* (New York: Random House 1960, London: Gollancz 1960)

Philippe Ariès: *Centuries of Childhood* (London: Jonathan Cape 1962, Penguin 1973)

Kenneth Little: *Urbanisation as a Social Process: Movement and Change in Contemporary Africa* (Routledge and Kegan Paul 1974)

Douglas Butterworth: "A Study of the Urbanisation Process Among Mixtec Migrants from Tilatongo in Mexico City" in William Mangin (ed) *Peasants in Cities* (Boston: Houghton Mifflin 1970)

166 Sir Ashley Bramall, leader of the Inner London Education Authority, in *Education* 3 December 1976

167 Puerto Rican girl's story told by Alma Bagu in Jeffrey Kobrick: "The Compelling Case for Bilingual Education" in Marvin Leiner (ed) *Children of the Cities* (New York: New American Library 1975)

168 A. M. Kallarackai and Martin Herbert: "The Happiness of Indian Immigrant Children" *New Society* 26 February 1976

169 "The Home Problems of Black Teenagers" *South London Press* 27 September 1974

Farrukh Dhondy in *Race Today* June 1976

Bernard Coard: *How the West Indian Child is Made Educationally Sub-Normal in the British School System* (London: New Beacon Books 1971)

David Milner: *Children and Race* (Harmondsworth: Penguin Books 1975)

170 Claude Brown: *Manchild in the Promised Land* (New York: New American Library 1965)

Charles Silberman: *Crisis in the Classroom* (New York: Vintage Books 1971)

Ernesto Galarza: *Barrio Boy* (University of Notre Dame Press 1972)

Boston Task Force, see Jeffrey Kobrick *op cit*

Graham Lomas: *The Inner City* (London Council of Social Service 1975)

Community Relations Commission: *Unemployment and Homelessness – A Report* (London: Home Office 1974)

171 Joe Benjamin: *Grounds for Play* (London: Bedford Square Press of the National Council for Social Service 1974)

Colin MacGlashan: "England's Teenage Apartheid" *The Observer* 20 August 1972

Amrit Wilson: "Loaded Coaches" *The Guardian* 14 October 1975

John Gretton: "Bussing: the Wrong Route for Britain" *Times Educational Supplement* 19 September 1975

172 Terence Lee "Unwittingly to School" *Psychology Today* May 1975

Roger Hart: "The Child's Landscape in a New England Town" PhD Thesis, Worcester, Mass: Dept of Geography, Clark University.

Everett Reimer: *School is Dead* (Harmondsworth: Penguin Books 1971)

P. Townsend and N. Bosanquet (eds) *Labour and Inequality* (Fabian Society 1972)

174 John Bird, Chairman of Wolverhampton Education Committee in *Education* 3 December 1976

Department of Education and Science: *Education, A Framework for Expansion* (London HMSO 1972)

A Right to be Children: Designing for the Education of the Under-Fives (London: RIBA Publications 1976)

Chapter 16 The city as resource

176 Albert Hunt: *Hopes for Great Happenings* (London: Eyre Methuen 1976)

Mario D. Fantini and Gerald Weinstein: *The Disadvantaged: Challenge in Education* (New York: Harper and Row 1968)

Edgar Gumpert: "The City as Educator: How to be Radical Without Even Trying" in John Raynor and June Harden (eds) *Equality and City Schools* (London: Routledge and Kegan Paul 1973)

Paul Goodman: *The Grand Piano* (San Francisco: Colt Press 1942) reprinted as part of *The Empire City* (Indianapolis: Bobs-Merrill 1959)

177 Paul Goodman: *Compulsory Miseducation* (New York: Horizon Press 1964, Penguin 1971)

John Bremer and Michael von Moschzisker: *The School Without Walls* (New York: Holt, Rinehart and Winston 1971)

Keith Kennedy: "Two Portraits from School Life" *Radical Education* No 6, Summer 1976

180 Gerald Haigh: *The Reluctant Adolescent* (London: Maurice Temple Smith 1976)

Peter Mackenzie: *Reminiscences of Glasgow and the West of Scotland* (Glasgow 1868)

181 Arturo Barea: *The Forging of a Rebel* (London: Davis-Poynter 1972)

Michael Storm: "School and the Community – An Issue-Based Approach" *Bulletin of Environmental Education* No 1, May 1971

184 Dot Dromgoole: "The White House" *Bulletin of Environmental Education* No 28/29 Aug-Sept 1973

Chapter 17 Town child as country child

188 Herbert Read: *Education Through Art* (London: Faber and Faber 1943)

Iona and Peter Opie: *Children's Games in Street and Playground* (Oxford University Press 1969)

Book
page

Enid Starkie: *Baudelaire* (London: Faber and Faber 1967)

J. M. Welding: "City Boy versus Country Boy" 1892, reprinted in Anselm L. Strauss (ed) *The American City: A Sourcebook of Urban Imagery* (London: Allen Lane 1968)

190 Leila Berg: *Look at Kids* (Harmondsworth: Penguin Books 1972)

Charles Harris: *Islington* (London: Hamish Hamilton 1974)

191 Herman Wouk: *The City Boy* (London: Jonathan Cape 1956)

Peter Schmitt: *Back to Nature: The Arcadian Myth in Urban America* (New York: Oxford University Press 1969)

Leslie Paul: *Angry Young Man* (London: Faber and Faber 1950)

192 "Town Boys and the Countryside" *New Society* 10 September 1964)

City Farms: Inter-Action Advisory Service Ltd, 14 Talacre Road, London NW5 3PE

196 Richard Mabey: *The Unofficial Countryside* (London: Collins 1975)

Marjorie Allen and Mary Nicholson: *Memoirs of an Uneducated Lady* (London: Thames and Hudson 1975)

John Raynor: *A Westminster Childhood* (London: Cassell 1972)

Kevin Lynch: *Growing Up in Cities* (Cambridge, Mass: MIT Press 1978)

Ask the Kids, report of the Planning the School Site Research Project, Institute of Advanced Studies, Manchester Polytechnic (London: Councils and Education Press 1976)

Chapter 18 Four exemplary enterprises

198 Alan Brew: *Liverpool Daily Echo*

Great George's Community Arts Project, Great George Street, Liverpool 1

James Brown: "Join the Professionals 'Get on Up, Get Involved, Get Into It'" in *7-Up* (Liverpool: Great George's Project 1976)

Centreprise Trust Ltd, 136/138 Kingsland High Street, London E8

199 Jim Higgins: "Community Centreprise" *Municipal Journal* 11 April 1975

Anthony Fyson: *Council for Urban Studies Centres Reports* (London: Town and Country Planning Association 1974, 1976)

200 Notting Dale Urban Studies Centre, 189 Freston Road, London W10

201 Vandalism: figures cited by Tim Rathbone MP in the House of Commons 20 December 1976

Chapter 19 In the sandbox of the city

202 George Sternlieb and James W. Hughes (eds) *Post-Industrial America: Metropolitan Decline and Inter-Regional Job Shifts* (New Brunswick: Centre for Urban Policy Research 1975)

Murray Bookchin: *The Limits of the City* (New York: Harper and Row 1974)

Mike Franks: "Liverpool: Resuscitation or Decline?" *Built Environment* March 1975

203 Alexander Mitscherlich: "Was soll aus unseren Städten werden?" *Bauen und Wohnen* March 1968

Vandalism: figure cited by Tim Rathbone MP in the House of Commons 20 December 1976

Atlanta: figure cited from MIT study reported by Jeremy Campbell, *Evening Standard* 5 January 1977

204 Jane Addams: *The Spirit of Youth and the City Streets* (New York: Macmillan 1930)

Paul Corrigan: "Doing Nothing" in Hall and Jefferson (eds) *Resistance through Rituals* (London 1976). See also Paul Corrigan: *The Smash Street Kids* (London: Palladin 1977)

Childhood City – newsletter distributed by the Environmental Psychology Program, Graduate School of the City University of New York, 33 West 42, New York City 10036, USA

206 Sue Wagstaff: "City Life" *ILEA Contact* 24 September 1976

Betty Pinfold: "Urban Parks for Youngsters" (*Royal Institute of British Architects Journal* March 1973)

210 John Holt: *Escape from Childhood* (New York: E. P. Dutton 1974, Harmondsworth: Penguin Books 1975)

Alexander Herzen: *From the Other Shore* (London: Weidenfeld and Nicholson 1956)

INDEX